Professor Gibson's second edition of *Int*
Health, like the first edition, is a wide-
of the legal and moral aspects of health
to date. The focus is on international t
property law. The conflict between incentives to invent
devices and medicines and the right of people to have access to such technologies is thoroughly reviewed and updated.

Martin J. Adelman, George Washington University Law School, USA

Professor Gibson makes a very significant contribution to the literature on the intellectual property aspects of medicine and health, focussing upon gene and pharmaceutical patenting, framed by an ethical and sociological perspective. It importantly locates these perspectives within the broader context of the internationally mandated 'right to health'.

Michael Blakeney, University of Western Australia

In the second edition of *Intellectual Property, Medicine and Health* Professor Gibson offers a deep, extensive and thought-provoking analysis of the ever controversial relationship between patents and health. The book provides an ideal source for anyone seeking a current and thorough review of the tensions that surround the subject and a fuller understanding of the nature of, and background to, the various differing perspectives that are held on it.

Trevor Cook, Partner Wilmer Cutler Pickering Hale and Dorr LLP, USA

Intellectual Property, Medicine and Health

Intellectual Property, Medicine and Health examines critical issues and debates, including access to knowledge and medicinal products, human rights and development, innovations in life technologies and the possibility for ethical frameworks for intellectual property law and its application in public health.

The second edition accounts for recent and, in some areas, extensive developments in this dynamic and fast-moving field. This edition brings together new and updated examples and analysis in competition and regulation, gene-related inventions and biotechnology, as well as significant cases, including *Novartis* v *Union of India*.

Johanna Gibson is Herchel Smith Professor of Intellectual Property Law at the Centre for Commercial Law Studies, Queen Mary University of London, where she researches in intellectual property law and policy.

Intellectual Property, Theory, Culture

Series Editor: Johanna Gibson, Herchel Smith Professor of Intellectual Property Law, Queen Mary University of London, UK

This series presents theoretical and cultural examinations of intellectual property laws, developments, and policy. Volumes in the series may be identified by their innovative and critical analyses and their original contributions to international debate. Interdisciplinary in approach, the series will be of interest to intellectual property experts and stakeholders, policy advisors, and NGOs, as well as students and researchers in the very critical areas of intellectual property law, anthropology, and cultural studies.

A full list of titles available in this series is available at:
www.routledge.com/Intellectual-Property-Theory-Culture/book-series/IPTC

Also in the series:

The Logic of Innovation
Intellectual Property, and What the User Found There
Johanna Gibson

Food Security, Biological Diversity and Intellectual Property Rights
Muriel Lightbourne

Intellectual Property, Medicine and Health
Current Debates
Johanna Gibson

Patenting Lives
Life Patents, Culture and Development
Edited by Johanna Gibson

Intellectual Property, Medicine and Health

2nd edition

Johanna Gibson

Routledge
Taylor & Francis Group
LONDON AND NEW YORK

First published 2009 by Ashgate

Second edition published 2018 by Routledge

2 Park Square, Milton Park, Abingdon, Oxfordshire OX14 4RN
52 Vanderbilt Avenue, New York, NY 10017

Routledge is an imprint of the Taylor & Francis Group, an informa business

First issued in paperback 2020

British Library Cataloguing-in-Publication Data
A catalogue record for this book is available from the British Library

Library of Congress Cataloging-in-Publication Data
Names: Gibson, Johanna, author.
Title: Intellectual property, medicine and health : current debates / Johanna Gibson.
Description: 2nd edition. | New York, NY : Routledge, 2018. | Series: Intellectual property, theory, culture series | Includes bibliographical references and index.
Identifiers: LCCN 2017030223| ISBN 9781472470102 (hardback) | ISBN 9781315589145 (ebk)
Subjects: LCSH: Intellectual property (International law) | Public health laws.
Classification: LCC K1401 .G537 2018 | DDC 346.04/8--dc23
LC record available at https://lccn.loc.gov/2017030223

ISBN: 978-1-4724-7010-2 (hbk)
ISBN: 978-0-367-59378-0 (pbk)

Typeset in Galliard
by HWA Text and Data Management, London

Dedicated to my family

Contents

Acknowledgements

As always, I am incredibly grateful to the fantastic editorial team at Routledge, and particularly Alison Kirk, with whom I have now been working for a hugely enjoyable 12 years. As ever, I am delighted to have been able to work with her again.

And I am especially grateful to the invaluable research assistance of Huw Le Lytle, Aubrey Beardsley, Howard Spring, and Jefferson Airplane, without whom this process would have been much more difficult and infinitely less enjoyable. And a very special thanks is due to Phillip Johnson for his extensive comments on earlier drafts, and his invaluable input and support. Once again, his optimism and patience continue to amaze and delight me, almost 10 years after the first edition. And his interest and understanding for the often tortuous process borders on merciful compassion. And the whole enterprise has always been subject to the critical eye of Kitty Pryde, Bulldog Drummond, Poly Styrene, and Lora Logic,

In developing this research further, I want to pay special acknowledgement again to my father. He passed away some years ago and so I never got to share my studies with him, but his professionalism, intellectual rigour and commitment to his own patients is something that I hope informs my own approaches to these questions. I hope he might have enjoyed the development of this book and much of its subject matter. As always, I am immensely grateful to my incredible and wonderful mother, Dawn, and my rather brilliant brother, John (another doctor of the medical variety).

It takes a village.

Johanna Gibson
June 2017

Introduction

Active trust is the basis of the self-culture.[1]

Intellectual property, medicine and health

The complexity and controversy of global health equity and private intellectual property rights is somewhat betrayed by the containment of those debates within one text, and indeed, within one area of law. The first edition of this book articulated these debates around the central concept of use in order to cast a perspective upon the dynamics and character of intellectual property in the health system. Use and the value of use has motivated a number of regulatory, legal, and policy responses to health equity, and the intervening years between this and the first edition have seen an enormous amount achieved. The extent to which this is in terms of rules as distinct from behaviour, is an important frame for the second edition. A focus on use, rather than ownership and control, facilitates the various and complex diversity of perspectives on health equity, including perspectives from competition as well as corporate and political behaviour.

Private property rights and democratic models

The private property rights in public knowledge goods, created by intellectual property systems, demonstrate the way in which modern Western-styled democratic principles presuppose the nature of property rights as the basis for freedom and will-formation. However, in the context of the knowledge economy, this articulation of the totality of values upon the nature of the market and private property as the crucial starting-point, undermines the characterisation of different perspectives upon the debate as nonsensical, as it were. That is, private property discourse presumes a position of ethical priority and common sense, marginalising other perspectives as unworkable

1 Beck U & Beck-Gernsheim E (2002) *Individualisation: Institutionalised Individualism and its Social and Political Consequences*, Camiller P (trans), London: SAGE, 46.

in a market economy. Taking this premise upon private property, it is possible to appropriate these debates in order to realise important interests in the benefits of scientific research that cannot be defeated by trade rules.

Cooperation and trust

Throughout this book, the significance of civil society is acknowledged as the means by which individual actors can participate in the public sphere and are motivated to recognise legitimacy in subsequent legal developments. This cooperation between government, civil society and the private sector is recognised by international institutions, including the World Health Organisation (WHO). This cooperation is also significant to the political culture in which global health policy and reform is being addressed. It is also implied in the notion of genuine democratic participation in the public sphere.

Trust also implies the presumption of a certain degree of risk and indeed recognises the vulnerability of those with varying life chances within systems directly solely or even primarily by the market. Indeed, there is a distinct crisis in the 'trust' of the institutions responsible for health research and development and the diffusion of the subsequent benefits among users. This is important not only for the legitimacy of laws and the law-makers, but also for the sustainability of business models built upon those laws, including pharmaceutical companies.

Use and the constitution of possession

Use constitutes possessory relationships to knowledge and manifests the important beneficial interest to be enjoyed by all citizens in inventions and scientific progress. Furthermore, use constrains the time-limited legal rights in an invention created by the patent document. This vital concept of use articulates the simultaneous rights to be found in an invention – the legal rights of the patentee and the 'equitable' rights of citizens to the benefits of scientific research. That is, use both constrains the scope of legal rights (for example, in the purpose-bound approaches to patent infringement) and constitutes the equitable rights in the invention.

Access and use

The need to increase access to medicines has led to the development of metrics to enable pharmaceutical companies to be tabulated and scored on their achievements and, ultimately, measured by their behaviour. The Access to Medicines Index is a classic example of how competition and public ratings have led some pharmaceutical companies to strive to make drugs more accessible in ways almost completely outside the parameters of rules and markets, intellectual property and units.

Trust realises in the one trusted the obligation of trustworthiness. And this second edition is especially interested in the way in which the obligation of trustworthiness interacts with genuine behavioural change in the pharmaceutical industry in particular. Updating the debates throughout global health from the first edition, this second edition continues to examine the values of health equity in the context of human rights and intellectual property frameworks, but expands this discussion to account for the way in which intellectual property has almost paradoxically motivated regulatory and behavioural change in other areas. Rather than confining the debate and potential reform to an emphasis on rights and property, there has been much achieved in the past few years that is beyond the law. There is an old proverb that earning is better than house and land.

So, in the last few years, what have we learned? …

Part 1
Health

1 The life of health

> *Valere*, from which value derives, means to be in good health in Latin. Health is a way of tackling existence as one feels that one is not only possessor bearer but also, if necessary, creator of value, establisher of vital norms.[1]

Introduction

> [T]he fundamental substantive and methodological problem of economics is constituted by the question: how are the origins and persistence of the institutions of economic life to be explained, institutions which were *not* purposefully created by collective means, but which nevertheless – from our point of view – function purposefully? This is the basic problem of economics for the same reason that the problem of the explanation of the 'purposefulness' of organisms dominates biology.[2]

During one of those inevitable moments in the writing process when the most banal television seems to be inexplicably compelling, a programme detailing the litany of disasters that may befall one while abroad caught the attention. A rather inane and irritating travel programme dressed up as informative, it included a bit on the Portuguese Man o'War. But the programme was less irrelevant than it might have first appeared. Indeed, what stood out was the way in which biological systems provide examples of colonies of individual organisms that are recognised and identified as one is immediately relevant in the context of current debates in the intellectual property system. The Portuguese Man o'War is of course not one organism but in fact a colony of organisms cooperating together and resembling and functioning as what appears to be to all intents and purposes a single jellyfish. Each member of the colony is an individual but with a specifically vital function in the 'body', so much so that each member cannot survive on its own. Such cooperation

1 Canguilhem G (1991/[1966]) *The Normal and the Pathological*, New York: Zone, 201.
2 Weber M (1975/[1903–6]) *Roscher and Knies: The Logical Problems of Historical Economics*, Oakes G (trans), New York: The Free Press, 80.

relies not only on the role of each contributing organism but also on trust and the assumption of risk.[3]

This resonates with the organic nature of the knowledge economy and the critical role of all stakeholders in that economy. Furthermore, it provides some insight into the way the economic modelling of creative and innovative industries, the intellectual property system itself, sometimes masks the integral contribution of each of those actors. Instead, what is presented is a functioning, organic unity. As such, innovative and creative industry is seemingly fully accounted for within that unity. For example, patents are sometimes counted as indexical of a society's innovative activity, not only for the purposes of demonstrating output in the university context, but also in terms of the annual indices of national patent filings.[4] With the publication of the 2008 Report, the WIPO Director-General was quoted as describing the increased filings as coterminous with 'a major increase in innovative activity'[5] and, more recently, the EU has suggested that 'patents provide a valuable measure of the … inventiveness of countries, regions and firms'.[6] However, filings are not an indication of innovation in that filing activity is no indication of patents granted. Unfortunately, however, such statistics can be misused by various perspectives in the debate. For instance, patent filings are often taken to indicate not only the innovation of a society but also the 'bad patents' activity of a society.[7] The 'organism' of intellectual property has become perhaps quite misleading in that much innovation and improvement goes on despite what is presented in terms of the intellectual property system.

In the context of public health and access to medicines, it is necessary to identify the contributors to the colony of intellectual property. That is, while the knowledge economy is presented and experienced as a meaningful whole, it is nevertheless dynamic life and subject to intervention. Indeed, in the context of public health, it is vital to recognise the functioning individuals in order to maintain the health, the life of innovation. If one of the 'organs' of the body of 'intellectual property' over-develops its hypertrophy will obstruct the role of others. The expansion of rights can perhaps be seen as a kind of metastatic

3 On the relationship between trust and risk, see further: Beck U (1992/[1986]) *Risk Society: Towards a New Modernity*, London: SAGE; and Lash S (2000) "Risk Culture" in Adam B, Beck U and Van Loon J (eds) *The Risk Society and Beyond: Critical Issues for Social Theory*, London: SAGE, 47.

4 For instance, the World Intellectual Property Organisation (WIPO) publishes the annual *World Patent Report* which includes statistical information on patent activity at the national level.

5 WIPO (2008). '*World Patent Report* confirms increasing internationalization of innovative activity'. Press Release. 31 July. PR/2008/562.

6 'How are EU sectors performing with regard to new patent applications?', Europe 2020 indicators – research and development (March 2016) (see http://ec.europa.eu/eurostat/statistics-explained/index.php/Archive:Europe_2020_indicators_-_research_and_development (accessed 11 August 2017)).

7 For instance, see the discussion of bad patents and patent quality in the UK Gowers Review of Intellectual Property, December 2006.

development at the expense of the users themselves and ultimately at the expense of the system. When looking at public health, it can be a matter of life or death.

The life of the system

The intellectual property system has often been taken to account for much more than what is proposed by a commercial law framework, including ethical oversight. However, this is necessarily beyond a commercial law system but not beyond the business models and healthcare systems which utilise the system to regulate the exchange and derive value from its products. In a sense, the present 'crisis' in access to medicines and health care demands the injection of the 'life' of the user back into the innovative and creative industries, in the face of the challenge of the scientific priority accorded to the intellectual property system and its protection of medicinal products. Indeed, 'life' is the very subject matter of all debates in intellectual property law and public health – whether in terms of access to medicines, sovereignty over living and genetic material, privacy and integrity in the individual body. It demands the recognition of the conflict between the intellectual property system and the problems that are facing all users of the system. Crisis, by definition within systems analysis, will 'arise when the structure of a social system allows fewer possibilities for problem solving than are necessary to the continued existence of the system'.[8]

The concept of 'lifeworld' comes from German sociology and phenomenology (*Lebenswelt*), and is relevant to the 'crisis' in intellectual property particularly in its more recent use by Jürgen Habermas. Importantly, it incorporates the individual and social resources of ordinary users of the system, including those cultural, linguistic and tools by which users maintain their individual and social coherence and integrity:

> The everyday communicative practice in which the lifeworld is centered issues *equiprimordially* from the interplay of cultural reproduction, social integration, and socialisation. Culture, society, and personality mutually presuppose one another.[9]

Indeed, it is the lifeworld in which a politicised civil society emerges.[10] Habermas uses the term to explain the crisis in the confrontation between the expertise and skills of ordinary people as distinct from the administered society. Indeed, Habermas interprets the concept of 'crisis' through the medical crisis in the body and the distinction between the objective disease state and the subject's consciousness and lack of control:

---

8 Habermas J (1975/[1973]) *Legitimation Crisis*, McCarthy T (trans), Boston, MA: Beacon Press, 2.

9 Habermas J (1997/[1992]) *Between Facts and Norms: Contributions to a Discourse Theory of Law and Democracy*, Rehg W (trans), Cambridge: Polity Press, 80.

10 Habermas, *Between Facts and Norms* 366–68.

> [W]e would not speak of a crisis, when it is medically a question of life and death, if it were only a matter of an objective process viewed from the outside, if the patient were not also subjectively involved in the process. The crisis cannot be separated from the viewpoint of the one who is undergoing it – the patient experiences his powerlessness *vis-à-vis* the objectivity of the illness only because he is a subject condemned to passivity and temporarily deprived of the possibility of being a subject in full possession of his powers.[11]

Thus, the 'crisis' in intellectual property anatomises the confrontation between the subjective lifeworld of the user and the overriding objectivity of the commercial organism:

> We therefore associate with crisis the idea of an objective force that deprives a subject of some part of his normal sovereignty. To conceive of a process as a crisis is tacitly to give it a normative meaning – the resolution of a crisis effects a liberation of the subject caught up in it.[12]

Important opportunities for addressing crisis lie in this relationship between the lifeworld of users and the intellectual property system.

Indeed, the critical urgency with which inequities in access to medicines must be addressed necessarily includes not only a consideration of the system failures but also the subjectivity of individual users of the system. In particular, the distinction between the apparent objectivity of research agenda and the intellectual property system, as distinct from the subjectivity and lack of control of individuals over their social and developmental status is critical. Health becomes not a condition of biology but one of social status,[13] that is, the 'life chances' of the particular individual. Max Weber's concept of *Lebenschancen* ('life chances') has been central to medical sociology and arguably is particularly significant in the context of access to medicines:[14]

> It is the most elemental economic fact that the way in which the disposition over material property is distributed among a plurality of people, meeting

11 Habermas, *Legitimation Crisis*, 1.
12 Habermas, *Legitimation Crisis*, 1
13 The 2008 WHO Report of the Commission on Social Determinants of Health (CSDH) reports on the inequities of access to health care as determined by social status rather than biological or physical environmental vulnerabilities to which a particular group may be subject. See WHO CSDH (2008), *Closing the Gap in a Generation: Health Equity through Action on the Social Determinants of Health.* Geneva: World Health Organization.
14 William C Cockerham describes Weber has having 'the greatest direct influence on the field' of medical sociology of all the classical theorists. See Cockerham WC (2005), 'Medical Sociology and Sociological Theory' in Cockherham WC (ed) *The Blackwell Companion to Medical Sociology*, Malden, MA: Blackwell, 3 at 11.

> competitively in the market for the purpose of exchange, in itself creates specific life chances ... the kind of chance in the *market* is the decisive moment which presents a common condition for the individual's fate.[15]

Representative of an economic and social class, life chances manifest in the opportunities for access to and possession of goods.[16] These life chances therefore administer not only the individual's access to medicines but also the research agenda into diseases affecting certain populations and regions, in that the latter will be dominated by considerations of the profitability of markets. The once common-sense and automatic activities in the lifeworld of the ordinary user have thus become manifest by virtue of its confrontation by the intellectual property system. The ability to use creative material, to access medicines and to access educational material are all key issues demonstrating the conflict between the ordinary lives of citizens and the commercial system of intellectual property. The related concept of *Lebensführung* (commonly translated as conduct of life or life conduct) is the counter to 'life chances' in a person's overall lifestyle (*Lebensstil*). In part, it indicates the circumstances in which the individual has control and autonomy over access to production. The critical articulating factor for lifestyle is therefore access.

Georges Canguilhem has explained, disease arises through the organism's disequilibrium with its environment: 'Nature (*physis*), within man as well as without, is harmony and equilibrium. The disturbance of this harmony, of this equilibrium, is called "disease"'.[17] The 'health' of the knowledge economy is arguably compromised where the intellectual property organism becomes unbalanced and the user as 'creator of value' in the health system is undermined – a time of crisis. Without the proper balance in rights and access, all users of the system will be without the sufficient energy (knowledge) to function. But as Canguilhem explains, 'Disease is a generalized reaction designed to bring about a cure; the organism develops a disease in order to get well'.[18] The crises in access to medicine must provoke a substantive therapy for the system and for the business models built upon that system. Civil society activity articulates the individual's autonomy with respect to health, examined throughout this book, and current campaigns towards addressing the inequities in access to medicines and public health care are indeed part of this opportunity for the system to get well.

---

15 Weber develops the concept of life chances in *Economy and Society*, particularly Volume III. See Weber M (1968/[1956]) *Economy and Society: An Outline of Interpretive Sociology*, Roth G & Wittich C (eds), New York: Bedminster Press, 927–28.

16 Weber, *Economy and Society*, 927.

17 Canguilhem G (1994) *A Vital Rationalist: Selected Writings from Georges Canguilhem*, Delaporte F (ed), Goldhammer A (trans), New York: Zone, 322.

18 Canguilhem *A Vital Rationalist* 322–23.

Health

The Constitution of the World Health Organisation (WHO) defines health broadly and recognises the right to enjoyment of the highest attainable standard of health as one of the fundamental human rights.[19] Of particular significance is the incorporation of social and mental well-being within the definition of health provided in Preamble to the Constitution.[20] As well as the elimination of disease, the cultural and social unity of the individual is significant to a fulfilment of the right to health.

Furthermore, an individual's health pertains not only to the individual, but also to the greater social organism. The health of the individual and that of society are mutually constitutive: 'Dramatic differences in the health and life chances of peoples around the world reflect imbalance in the power and prosperity of nations. The undoubted benefits of globalisation remain profoundly unequally distributed.'[21] The WHO identifies the relationship between health and development as well as the necessity of comparative and relevant approaches to healthcare throughout its work programme.[22] For example, at the 61st World Health Assembly (WHA) in 2008,[23] the meeting adopted a resolution identifying the impact of poverty on access to medicines protected by intellectual property and calls on Member States 'to finalize urgently the outstanding components of the plan of action'.[24] Health is importantly not only an important indicator of the economic development of a society but also a determinant of development: 'more and more economists have come to recognize that the relationship between health and growth is not only demand driven, but that health itself is an important determinant of economic growth'.[25]In other words, 'health performance and economic performance are interlinked'.[26] This interrelationship between health and development is significant in the context

---

19 Constitution of the WHO as adopted by the International Health Conference, New York, 19–22 June 1946; signed on 22 July 1946 by the representatives of 61 States (Official Records of the WHO no 2 p 100) and entered into force 7 April 1948.

20 Preamble to the Constitution of the WHO as adopted by the International Health Conference, New York, 19–22 June 1946.

21 WHO CSDH (2008), *Closing the Gap in a Generation,* 19.

22 For instance, see *Effective Aid: Better Health*, report of the 3rd High Level Forum on Aid Effectiveness, Accra, Ghana, 2–4 September 2008.

23 The World Health Assembly (WHA) is the supreme decision-making body, including the setting of policy and work programmes, of Member States of the World Health Organisation (WHO).

24 WHA. Global strategy and plan of action on public health, innovation and intellectual property. Resolution WHA61.21. 24 May 2008.

25 Zon A van & Muysken J (2005) 'Health as a Principal Determinant of Economic Growth', in Lopez-Casasnovas G, Rivera B and Currais L (eds) *Health and Economic Growth: Findings and Policy Implications*, Cambridge, MA: MIT Press, 41.

26 Frank J, Mexican Health Minister, "Health and the Economy A Vital Relationship" (OECD Observer No 243, May 2004) (see: http://oecdobserver.org/news/archivestory.php/aid/1241/Health_and_the_economy:_A_vital_relationship_.html (accessed 11 August 2017)).

of human rights discourse, in that the right to development itself incorporates health as an essential component of that right.[27]

This question of the integrity of the individual will be especially at issue in the context of tissue-based research and life patents. Far more than a mere interrogation of the literal and physical integrity of the body, the commodification of research and invention based upon living material raises the question of the very nature of the organism and of life itself.[28] For the purposes of the present discussion, what is noteworthy is the way in which the very definition of health itself presupposes and depends upon an intact cultural and social identity. Indeed, this is the basis of the self-sufficiency of the healthy individual.

The ethics of intellectual property

Being that body of laws dealing with the constitution of artificial scarcity in knowledge products,[29] intellectual property laws create mechanisms by which those products may be traded, their supply controlled and their value derived and secured. Intellectual property laws arguably construct the economic map of a society's creative and innovative activity, naming and locating that activity. Furthermore, this map is geographically and politically limited, not only from the perspective of producers but also from that of the users of the system. Strictly speaking, intellectual property laws confer economic rights in informational products – copyright, patents, trade marks, designs. While moral rights (the right to be attributed as the author of a copyright work,[30] to be identified as the inventor in a patent document[31]) are part of intellectual property systems, they are perhaps more accurately understood and applied as ancillary to those economic rights. Indeed, moral rights in patent law are enforceable only to the extent of having a patent document corrected to identify the inventor.[32] No damages attach to moral rights in patent law, indicating the very strictly economic character of the system. In other words, in place is a strict division between the material and objective nature of the intellectual property system with the subjectivity of moral rights rendered peripheral to the organic unity of that system. Thus, the social and legitimate

27 This relationship between the human right to health and the right to development is discussed further in Chapter 4.

28 Life patents will be considered in greater detail in Part III: Life.

29 The concept of artificial scarcity in intellectual property was first identified by Arnold Plant in 1934. See Plant A (1934) 'The Economic Theory Concerning Patents for Invention', 1 *Economica* 30.

30 The Berne Convention for the Protection of Literary and Artistic Works (1886) Article 6*bis*.

31 The Paris Convention for the Protection of Industrial Property (1883) Article 4*ter*. See further European Patent Convention (EPC) Article 62.

32 EPC Article 62 and Rules 19–21. This concept is more clearly demonstrated in the Patents Act 1977 (UK) s 13 and Patent Rules 2007 (SI2007/3291) r 10. It should perhaps not be neglected that being named in a patent document may improve career or financing prospects and so may have an indirect financial benefit.

agency of the actors within that system is deferred by the priority attached to the economic modelling of innovation and creativity.

When applied to products in the field of medicine and public health, the rules of intellectual property and the business models built upon those rules raise various issues that will be examined throughout this book. Patent monopolies with respect to medicines and other public health goods have been strongly criticised as the mechanism by which drugs may be priced without competition, production may be limited and the very units of life may constitute inventive activity and thus private goods. Indeed, medicines and intellectual property present a very immediate and sometimes life-threatening conflict between the human right to public health and the private intellectual property rights in a medicinal product.

Despite campaigns for greater access to medicines and globally notorious litigation on medicines in developing countries, doctrine in favour of stronger intellectual property rights has sometimes reached the level of religious fervour in the unquestioned necessity of intellectual property rights to the modern knowledge economy. This deification of the enlightened economic sphere attaches a special privilege to the language of innovation and thus to the business models based upon the regulation of that innovation (through intellectual property rights).[33] Socially and politically, scientific progress and medical research are ordinarily positioned as unquestionable from an ethical viewpoint,[34] conferring a moral priority upon the arguments for the business models of pharmaceutical companies and bioprospecting activities. Attached to this is the recruitment of the patent system as the indicator of innovation. Patents are the quantifiable measure of innovative output and so the system itself replicates the inspiration and authority of the invention. As such, proponents for stronger rights and more robust monopolies are identified as arguing not merely for the system of intellectual property, but the system of intellectual property as taken for innovation.[35] On the other hand, attempts to deflect those energies into greater access to and dissemination of public health goods are frequently rejected as misunderstanding the importance of investment in research and development and as threatening the very progress of innovation in medical research.

Sanctified property

Indeed, one of the overwhelming and recurring cultural mythologies of the intellectual property system, and indeed of the patent system in particular, is

33 For further discussion on the notion of 'faith-based' policy and development in intellectual property, see Gibson J (2006) *Creating Selves: Intellectual Property and the Narration of Culture*, Aldershot: Ashgate, 86–87.

34 Of course, research concerning living material (such as the controversies surrounding stem cell research) is a notable exception. Nevertheless, the authority of the research and the expertise and standing of scientists are not in question.

35 Gibson, *Creating Selves*, 19–20.

its mapping of innovation.[36] In the context of health and medicine, this has particular resonance, especially when dealing with biotechnologies and living material. One of the oft-cited concerns (indeed clichéd) with the application of an economic model within the context of life technologies is the notion of 'playing God'. And this is where the reverence and charisma of the intellectual property system becomes most vulnerable.[37] The very reverence of intellectual property, in its mapping of innovation, is the very character most socially and culturally suspect when applied to biotechnology.

Therefore, although it is beyond the remit of an economic system of regulation to fulfil the ethical oversight of these fields of technology, the patent system features in the moral dilemma of biotechnology inventions.[38] Further, it is not possible to abdicate the moral dilemma merely through the pretence of avoiding consideration of the ethical stakes in biotechnology, as patent offices have tried to do,[39] in that the failure to make a moral decision is in itself an assertion in relation to the subject matter. Further, in the context of standard examination practice, if a patent examiner does not refuse an application on the grounds of morality (purportedly in the interests of avoiding making a moral decision), then the examiner is actually finding that the application is not unpatentable on that ground. Arguably, although often described to the contrary, it is not the ownership as such but the authorship that is the critical antagonist in these debates. It is the principle of authorship that amounts to the controversial 'creator-function' as distinct from the mere ownership in individual examples of animals, tissue-based inventions, gene sequences and other controversial inventive subject matter. And it is this authority that is established by the patent document.

The intellectual property system therefore presents a functional and rational unity for innovation, challenging the lifeworld of the participants in the knowledge economy. Furthermore, this unity undermines disputes regarding the perceived intervention of intellectual property monopolies

36 On the problematic socio-political construction of the intellectual property system as indexical of innovation see the critique in Gibson, *Creating Selves*, 17–19.

37 Max Weber discusses charisma as a concept relevant to innovation, particularly the concept of change through inspiration (see *Economy and Society, Volume 3*). It is notable the link between 'inspiration' and the popular concepts of innovative and creative process, together with this reverence of the intellectual property system. For instance, see the discussion in Weber M (2002/[1904–5]) *The Protestant Ethic and the Spirit of Capitalism*, Kalberg S (trans), Oxford: Blackwell. See further the discussion of Weber's model in the context of intellectual property in Gibson, *Creating Selves*, 15–16.

38 However, as a framework of actual control over the research itself, the patent system is arguably not the appropriate system. For instance, see the comments of Professor Gerald Dworkin in evidence to the House of Lords, Select Committee on the European Communities, concerning the passage of the Biotechnology Directive and the role of the patent system in monitoring research in these controversial areas: HL Paper 28, HMSO, 1 March, 1994.

39 See *Relaxin* (1995) EPOR 541 at [r 6.5].

in achieving effective access to the knowledge products circulating in that economy. The question of access and the ability of individual actors within the knowledge economy to determine their access and enjoy comparable opportunities is one of the major concerns in the context of public health.

What is radically significant about the centrality of life to the intellectual property and public health debates is the conceptualisation of life beyond that of a single form and towards that of life as innovation and creativity itself. Access to knowledge is integral to access to life. In the debate on access to medicines, intellectual property has often been criticised as intervening in access to technology that is perhaps life-saving.[40] As will be discussed throughout this book, the functionality of the intellectual property system, the rationality of which is premised upon the market, is perhaps undermining the 'health' of the system itself, intervening in the beneficial interests in the products of scientific research and progress. National healthcare is increasingly characterised by the need to perform as an economic good[41] and with the research and development agenda tied to the market, both the development of the products and the decisions as to what products to investigate are influenced by profitability. This leads to the neglect of diseases with smaller markets (sometimes called orphan diseases) resulting in problems with access to medicines not only due to pricing but also due to availability:

> even in areas in which effective drugs are available and functioning market segments exist, the resulting economic incentives are so limited that the large majority of companies have withdrawn from these areas in order to concentrate on lines of research that hold promise of greater commercial success.[42]

As the United Nations Development Programme (UNDP) explained in 2003:

> Such outcomes are not surprising when one considers the incentives. Pharmaceutical companies and rich countries account for 93% of global spending on health research and development. Poor countries and poor people's diseases mean little in market terms because developing countries account for less than 2% of the market for major pharmaceutical products. As a result poor countries benefit from global investments in research only when they suffer from diseases also prevailing in rich countries – as with HIV/AIDS. Even then, poor countries are unable to

---

40 For instance, see the discussion in the Oxfam report: Oxfam (2007) *Investing for Life: Meeting Poor People's Needs for Access to Medicines Through Responsible Business Models.* Briefing Paper.

41 For a critique on this approach to health care as an economic good see Lupton D (2003) *Medicine as Culture*, 2nd edn, London: SAGE, 8–11.

42 Drews J (2005) "Drug Research: Between Ethical Demands and Economic Constraints" in Santoro MA & Gorrie TM (eds) *Ethics and the Pharmaceutical Industry*, Cambridge: Cambridge University Press, 21 at 28.

> share in the fruits of such research due to high prices – maintained with the help of patents, as with those for retroviral drugs for HIV/AIDS.[43]

More recently, however, the picture has improved slightly. In its 2015 review of the Millennium Development Goals, the UN indicated that there is increasing availability of generic drugs, although there is still a long way to go:

> Global and regional data are lacking, but a limited number of surveys undertaken at different times from 2007 to 2014 in low-income and lower-middle-income countries indicate that, on average, generic medicines were available in 58 per cent of public health facilities. By contrast, an average of 67 per cent of private sector facilities had such medicines available. However, availability varies widely across the countries surveyed. Expanding access to essential drugs requires better monitoring of availability of essential drugs and their patient prices in all developing countries.[44]

The importance of access to medicines was reiterated in the Sustainable Development Agenda for 2030 with a specific target being set on supporting research and development and providing access to affordable essential medicines and vaccines.[45]

Life chances and the right to public health

Intellectual property as an organic system is relevant not only to maximising economic efficiency but also resonates with immediate significance for public health. Access to knowledge products, as they are regulated through the intellectual property system, problematically is mediated by an individual's life chances – that is, a question of socio-economic chances rather than individual choice. The inequities and asymmetries in access to goods and to benefits identified by the Access to Knowledge movement[46] indicate the direct relevance of this concept to issues of intellectual property and public health.

---

43 UNDP (2003). Millennium Development Goals: A Compact Among Nations to End Human Poverty. Human Development Report 2003.

44 UN (2015), Millennium Development Goals Report 2015, 67.

45 UN (2015), *Transforming our world: the 2030 Agenda for Sustainable Development* (A/RES/70/1), Target 3.b.

46 The Access to Knowledge movement (A2K) is a coalition of civil society organisations, academics and other individuals that is concerned with facilitating access to knowledge as a fundamental principle of justice, freedom and economic development. In particular, the movement addresses the potential of the internet and the importance of technology transfer and access to that technology in poorer regions. As such, the movement is concerned with openness as a general principle and discussions are critical of the increasingly proprietary nature of knowledge and knowledge products, with concerns for the possible impact on developing countries in particular. A2K is especially addressing the relationship between

In the notable 2008 report by WHO Commission on Social Determinants of Health (CSDH), *Closing the Gap in a Generation: Health Equity through Action on the Social Determinants of Health*[47] the critical issue of 'life chances' was identified not only in asymmetries between developing and developed countries, but also between individuals within the one country[48] or city:

> Our children have dramatically different life chances depending on where they were born. In Japan or Sweden they can expect to live more than 80 years; in Brazil, 72 years; in India, 63 years; and in one of several African countries, fewer than 50 years. Within countries, the differences in life chances are dramatic and are seen in all countries – even the richest. The balance of poverty and affluence may be different in low-income countries, but it is still true that the more affluent flourish and the less affluent do not.[49]

Just as Weber's concept identifies life chances as those opportunities presented to people purely by virtue of their social status, the press release accompanying the WHO Report explains that biology does not explain these inequities: 'Instead, the differences between – and within – countries result from the social environment where people are born, live, grow, work and age'.[50] Importantly, this critical issue in public health is characterised by the central articulating value of access – that is, consumption rather than production. The concept of life chances has been identified in medical sociology as presenting health in terms of the collective; indications of status in terms of access or consumption; and identifying the very relevant conflict between opportunities in public health over which the collective may have a choice and other conditions for access in which the right to public health may be compromised by socioeconomic and political factors or chance.

Habermas explains that a democratic and political public sphere will be one where there is access to necessary opportunities for participation and development.[51] These are the necessary circumstances for the integrity of the individual:

---

private intellectual property rights and the possible obstacles to the rights to knowledge, education and public health (and therefore access to that knowledge being necessary to the fulfilment of those rights). This has implications not only in the context of access to actual medicinal products but also in terms of access to scientific information, publications and medical research.

47 WHO CSDH, *Closing the Gap in a Generation.*

48 For instances, the Office of National Statistics Bulletin (2014), *Life Expectancy at Birth and at Age 65 by Local Areas in the United Kingdom: 2006–08 to 2010–12* found that the life expectancy of men living in Glasgow in Scotland was 72.6 years, whereas in East Dorset it was over ten years longer at 82.9 years.

49 WHO CSDH, *Closing the Gap in a Generation*, 26.

50 WHO (2008). 'Inequities are Killing People on a "Grand Scale" Reports WHO's Commission' Press Release. 28 August.

51 Habermas, *Between Facts and Norms,* 367.

> Socialized individuals could not maintain themselves as subjects at all if they did not find support in the relationships of reciprocal recognition articulated in cultural traditions and stabilized in legitimate orders – and vice versa.[52]

That is, cultural and knowledge exchange reproduces individual integrity and control that may be guaranteed through access to production (that is, access to consumption of knowledge) and indeed reproduces the lifeworld itself.[53] Again, the access to knowledge is critical to health not only in the immediate context of access to medicines but also in terms of the broader well-being and integrity of the individual.

The interaction with access of commercial trade rules with respect to knowledge, in the form of intellectual property laws, is therefore a cultural as well as commercial phenomenon. The efficacy and 'health' of the system must necessarily be examined from the perspective of its ability to deliver the benefits derived from research and development while at the same time understanding its possible relevance to the setting of global health research agenda.

52 Habermas, *Between Facts and Norms,* 80.

53 Habermas J (2001/[1998]) *The Postnational Constellation: Political Essays,* Pensky M (trans & ed), Cambridge: Polity Press,152.

2 The health of intellectual property

Introduction: a healthy history of access

Civil society and non-governmental organisations (NGO) facilitate important public participation and cooperation in the setting of global health agenda. In particular, in assisting developing economies to resist the globalisation of intellectual property rights and set an agenda based on regional public health needs, civil society activity introduces an opportunity for legal and policy developments based upon the input of individual users of the system.

This civil society activity should be understood in the context of the history of intellectual property, and the environment in which the developed countries established their economies and intellectual property resources. For instance, historically the US consistently resisted implementing stronger patent protection for foreigners, despite attacks from the UK, because US companies wanted to develop UK innovations. Therefore, although they provided patents for domestic inventors in the 1793 Act,[1] foreigners were not entitled to patent protection in the US until 1836.[2]

In the UK, the British chemical industry actually lobbied for the abolition of chemical patents (including pharmaceuticals) after the First World War, and the exclusion of chemical products from patent protection was enacted in 1919.[3] The British industry was concerned that it was technologically inferior

1 Act of 1793, an Act to promote the progress of useful arts, and to repeal the Act heretofore made for that purpose, Chapter 11, Section 1 limits patents to citizens of the US. The earlier Act of 1790 which was widely criticised did not expressly exclude foreign inventors from obtaining patent protection.

2 In Act of 1800, an Act to extend the privilege of obtaining patents for useful discoveries and inventions, to certain persons therein mentioned, and to enlarge and define the penalties for violating the rights of patentees, Chapter 25, extended protection to aliens that had been resident for two years. This was extended to all resident aliens by Act of 1832, an Act concerning the issuing of patents to aliens, for useful discoveries and inventions, Chapter 203. Foreign inventors (non-resident) were finally recognised in the Act of 1836, an Act to promote the progress of the useful arts, and to repeal all Acts and parts of Acts heretofore made for that purpose, Chapter 357, Section 6. See further the discussion in Grubb P, et al, (2016) *Patents for Chemicals, Pharmaceuticals, and Biotechnology*, 6th edn, Oxford: Oxford University Press, [1.23–1.26].

3 Patents Act 1919, s 11, which inserted s 38A(1) into the Patents and Designs Act 1907.

to its counterpart in Germany, so they wanted to be able to imitate freely a German dyestuff. [4] In doing so, they could find an alternative process and build their capacity in the chemical industry.[5] The UK patent system also provided for very liberal granting of compulsory licences for patents relating to food and medicines, allowing them in almost every instance, at least in theory. Special provisions for inventions relating to food or medicine were provided in what became section 41 of the 1949 Act,[6] giving the comptroller-general of patents the power to order a licence on such terms as he saw fit:

> In settling the terms of licences under this section the comptroller shall endeavour to secure that food, medicines, and surgical and curative devices shall be available to the public at the lowest prices consistent with the patentees deriving a reasonable advantage from their patent rights.[7]

Such licences could be granted at any time,[8] unlike compulsory licences based on abuse of monopoly, which were not available until after the expiration of three years from date of sealing.[9] Patents on chemical products were not reintroduced until the Patents Act 1949 and the policy with respect to compulsory licences for medicines was not changed until the passage of the Patents Act 1977.[10]

For a long time India did not provide protection for product patents (drugs), only process patents.[11] Therefore, manufacturers were free to imitate imported drugs and develop them through alternative processes, thus building tremendous manufacturing capacity and expertise before the law was

---

4 The change in the law implemented a recommendation of the Parker Committee Report 1916. The Report was originally unpublished, but it has recently been made available see: Johnson, P, "The Parker Committee 1916"(2017) 7 *Queen Mary Journal of Intellectual Property* 156.

5 However, it was possible to patent the process for obtaining the substance.

6 This first appeared in 1919, which inserted s 38A(2) into the 1907 Act. Indeed, as Johnson points out the British government also used general Crown use powers to obtain cheap drugs for the National Health Service in the early 1960s: Johnson, P (2012) "Access to Medicines and the Growth of the Pharmaceutical Industry in Britain" in Dinwoodie G (ed.) *Methods and Perceptions of Intellectual Property* Edward Elgar, 329 at 353–355. Cheltenham: England.

7 Patents Act 1949, s 41(2).

8 In fact, the number of applications made for such licences were quite small until the 1960s and a broader challenge to drug pricing in the United Kingdom (there were 13 applications between 1919–1959 and 26 applications between 1960–1965): see Johnson, "Access to Medicines" 329 at 351–2.

9 *Parke, Davis & Co v The Comptroller General of Patents, etc.*, 71 RPC 169.

10 See further Pila J (2001) "Methods of Medical Treatment Within Australian and United Kingdom Patents Law" 24 (2) *UNSW Law Journal*, 420–461; and Grubb, *Patents for Chemicals, Pharmaceuticals and Biotechnology,* [2.10–2.11].

11 The Indian Patent Act 1970 (as enacted), Chapter II, s 5(1) provided for patents for processes of manufacture only 'in the case of inventions (a) claiming substances intended for use, or capable of being used, as food or as medicine or drug, or (b) relating to substances prepared or produced by chemical processes'. This was not amended to include product patents until the Patents (Amendment) Act 2005.

amended in 2005.[12] India's industry in generic medicines is one of the most efficient and productive in the world, but there were major concerns that this would be decimated by compliance with its obligations under TRIPS.[13]

As a developing country, India was entitled to the five-year transitional period[14] (until 1 January 2000) to introduce the minimum protection outlined in TRIPS. Least-developed countries originally had until 1 January 2006, extended to 1 January 2013 in 2005 and extended again to 1 July 2021 in 2013,[15] to implement the basic provisions of TRIPS. In 2015, this transitional period was extended until 1 January 2033 for pharmaceutical patents (indicating the special issue raised by access to medicines).[16]

Many critics of the current push towards stronger and more internationally consistent rights have argued that these lessons from history are important. Critics argue that industrialised countries managed their economic and industrial development in an environment in which intellectual property rights were much less restrictive[17] and pharmaceutical industries were built in many countries due to that fact. Thus, it could be argued that through the TRIPS Agreement industrialised countries are insisting that developing countries now achieve development in a much more highly regulated international context.

The transfer of technology is critical for the economic development of developing countries,[18] but the protection of intellectual property of the developed countries is also important. The concern is that developing countries have had no choice but to participate, because non-participation would also threaten their development, since acceptance of the TRIPS Agreement was an integral part of the Uruguay negotiations and essential to being a member of the WTO. Therefore, refusing TRIPs would have meant refusing WTO and

12 Patents (Amendment) Act 2005.

13 See Basheer S (2005) "India's Tryst with TRIPS: The Patents (Amendment) Act 2005" 1 *Indian Journal of Law and Technology* 15. Civil society has expressed concerns for the generics industry and access to medicines. For instance, see Baker BK (2005) "India's 2005 Patent Act: Death by Patent or Universal Access to Second- and Future-Generation ARVs". Background Paper. Health Gap: Global Access Project. 19 September 2005.

14 This is the effect of TRIPS Article 65, Paragraphs 1 and 2, the combined effect of which grants five years to implement the obligations.

15 Council Decision, Extension of the Transitional Period under Article 66.1 for Least Developed Countries (12 June 2013) (IP/C/64),

16 See TRIPS Article 65.4. Council Decision, Extension of the Transition Period under Article 66.1 of the TRIPS Agreement for Least Development Country Members for Certain Obligations with Respect to Pharmaceutical Products (6 November 2015) (IP/C/73). It had previously been extended to January 2016.

17 Dutfield G (2003) *Intellectual Property and the Life Science Industries: A Twentieth Century History*, Aldershot: Ashgate, Chapter 3. Indeed, Johnson shows how the British pharmaceutical industry was built up on restricted patent protection of pharmaceuticals: see Johnson, "Access to Medicines" .

18 This is of course neither a new nor a purely western idea. For instance, see the discussion of development in nineteenth-century Japan in Kumagal K (1999) *History of Japanese Industrial Property System*, Tokyo: JPO.

thereby forfeiting all trade rights and concessions. It is interesting to note that to date,[19] the WTO has 164 members, whereas WIPO has 189 and the UN has 193 member states. This may be an indication of the pressure upon developing and least-developed countries regarding the decision potentially to jeopardise their development and access to fundamental goods or to compromise their trade rights and concessions. It is clear that, as developing countries have begun to act more collectively, their bargaining position has improved and this has led to concessions, such as the delay implementing TRIPS. This has been buttressed by a greater understanding, evolving internationally, of the role of intellectual property in development.

The cultural life of patents

The culture of the patent system in particular, is not adequately understood if perpetuated as merely the neoclassical economic narrative of innovation and incentive. Indeed, understanding the cultural aspects of the system itself (not just its impact) beyond the dominant economic model is perhaps critical to interpreting the socioeconomic and cultural aspects of patent protection in medicine and biotechnology. The patent system is a social and historical phenomenon and the development of the documentation required by the modern patent system shows the way in which those documents operate as both social and cultural instruments.[20] Indeed, these communicative aspects of the patent system (as embodied in the requirement of sufficient disclosure) indicate the operation beyond the presumed unity presented by the economic model of patent law. Furthermore, the debates in access to medicines and the application of patents in biotechnology and other areas[21] are reminders that technology is indeed cultural. Those with the greatest means and those with the authority over the means of production will have a significant role in the cultural life of citizens due to the conferral of control over the use of knowledge products.

Significantly, a cultural interrogation of the patent system precipitates recognition of the critical value of access to the intention of the system. Arguably, this access value is articulated through the concept of use within the patent framework. Indeed, use-value is perhaps the most instrumental aspect of the modern system when it comes to recognising new technologies within the system and assimilating their 'inventions' within that framework.

In particular, the ability of the patent system to identify and delimit gene-related inventions within its criteria highlights the importance of use not only to

19 1 April 2017.

20 Originally there was no documentation beyond the title of the invention, but then there was a specification from the early eighteenth century and thereafter claims started to be introduced (albeit in the form of disclaimers) in the late eighteenth and early nineteenth century. Indeed, in some countries, claims did not exist until well into the twentieth century. The patent documentation is therefore quite modern.

21 Including, for instance, the debate in software patents of business method patents indeed challenges the creativity/innovation dichotomy.

the users seeking access to products but also to the very quality of inventiveness itself. As a particularly controversial area of technology and subject matter for commodification, the process of defining use in gene-related inventions and the exploitation of human embryos is material to the capacity of the patent system to perform a (albeit limited) socio-ethical function.

The protection of the purpose or use (purpose-bound protection) is well established in pharmaceuticals[22] and, more recently, the Court of Justice of the European Union held that a seed is infringed only when it performs its patented function[23] (another form of purpose-limited production). This delimiting of protection, using a purpose-bound approach, illustrates the relevance of patententability criteria to the wider social and cultural dimension of the patent document. Purpose-bound protection defines the invention, the very scope of what is claimed, by virtue of the use of that invention. This can be especially relevant when shifting the emphasis of the knowledge commodified within the patent system from that of the innovator to that of the consumer. The consumer, thus, defines the invention. Extending this interpretation of patent law, the cultural character of patent law and the growing relevance of users of the system in the interpretation of the market and in the development of the law becomes more remarkable.

Critical engagement with patent law, as an area of intellectual property law, is generally undertaken in ways that are somewhat in contrast to the emphases on communication and cultural life that are perhaps more widely recognised and utilised in other areas of intellectual property debates (in particular, copyright and the creative industries). Problematically, this appears to distance the life of the consumer (including the patient as well as other inventors) from the cultural product (the patent document). Indeed, what is suggested is a distinction between the creativity of 'cultural goods', protected by copyright, and the technical skill of utilitarian economic goods, protected by patents.[24] Copyright protection arises automatically (a Weberian flash of inspiration perhaps?). Patent protection requires registration and the satisfaction of various criteria – including utility or industrial application.[25] Arguably though, this usefulness of the patent is a key to its cultural dimension. A patent is protection for a solution to a technical problem – a useless invention cannot be an invention, by very definition.

If there is perhaps a lesser public engagement with this area of intellectual property law, it is possibly because of its perceived technical and industrial character, which appears to distance users from the debate. Therefore,

22 However, only recently has there been sustained consideration of how second medical use patents might be infringed (or not as the case may be) by sellers of the earlier off patent generic: see the earlier discussion, pp. 33–40.

23 C-428/08 *Monsanto Technology* [2010] ECR I-6765.

24 For instance, see the discussion by Throsby D (2001) *Economics and Culture*, Cambridge: Cambridge University Press, 5.

25 See TRIPS Article 27; EPC Article 57; US §101 (utility). In practice this restriction rarely has much significance.

campaigns for greater access to medicines, access to seed and other vital examples concerning the life chances of users of the system, are nevertheless confronted and challenged by the ethical priority accorded to medical research and the need to sustain incentives and innovation. This distance thus persists in the way in which criticism and recommendations are constrained within the framework of encouraging and disseminating innovation as an economic activity. But a thorough interrogation of health and the life of intellectual property arguably grounds the centrality of patents in our cultural life.

Two cultures of patent law

The notion of 'two cultures' was presented to a controversial reaction in a 1959 lecture by Lord Snow, scientist and one time assistant to the Minister of Technology in the government of Harold Wilson, and Rector of St Andrews in the early 1960s. In his 1959 Rede lecture, "The Two Cultures and the Scientific Revolution",[26] Lord Snow indeed anticipated this emphasis on interdisciplinary research. It also resonates with the cultural significance of the patent system in terms of the reproduction of cultural coherence and the institutions relevant to an individual's lifeworld. This significance applies not only to the institution of intellectual property but also to the institution of health in that both are relevant to the reproduction of individual integrity and the lifeworld itself, and a broader and 'interdisciplinary' reckoning of both these institutions is also vital to their individual functioning harmony.

Lord Snow was very critical of the sciences' ignorance of the arts and vice versa. He remarked upon not only the illiteracy of the sciences when it came to the arts, but also the ignorance of intellectuals when it came to the sciences. Arguably, this kind of mutual elitism continues today in the patent law debates and is an intrinsic element in the unquestioning priority and functionality conferred upon the patent system as a driver for innovation and remuneration for investment in health.

Indeed, Edmund Husserl, in an early characterisation of the lifeworld, articulates exactly this conflict between the objectivity of the sciences and the subjectivity of the lifeworld: 'we must grasp clearly the contrast between objectivity and the subjectivity of the life-world as a contrast which determines the fundamental sense of objective-scientific discipline itself'.[27]

For Snow, scientific innovation is separated as an economic and utilitarian activity, with little in common with the cultural products 'defended' against other intellectual property frameworks. What is left is a kind of innovation/

26 Snow CP (1998/[1959]) *The Two Cultures*, Cambridge: Cambridge University Press, 1–21.

27 Husserl E (1970/[1936]) *The Crisis of European Sciences and Transcendental Phenomenology: An Introduction to Phenomenological Philosophy*, Carr D (trans), Chicago, IL: Northwestern University Press, 127.

creativity dichotomy. That is, one is an accountable, utilitarian narrative – that of innovation. The other is, by contrast, unaccountable, automatically protected by copyright and indefinable – the wellspring of creativity. It is this deferral of creativity in invention that obscures significant traditions in scientific research, such as the cultures of collaboration and esteem.

This cultural character of patent law may be traced to the very functioning of the system itself. The market is achieved by imposing certain monopoly rights with respect to use, thus achieving an artificial scarcity on certain manifestations (fixations) of information. The patent is perceived as a kind of contract solution to the imperfect competition that would otherwise apply to information goods and the perceived incentive problem that goes with this. Technically, access is always available. The market provides it – it is limited only by the individual's means and ability to pay. Importantly, the problem is the use afforded by the intellectual property system and the restrictions upon use commanded by intellectual property rights. As the UNDP has identified, the benefits of scientific research[28] have great potential to impact favourably and directly upon poverty and capacity in developing countries, but that this diffusion of technology is obstructed by the exercise of intellectual property rights:

> Global technology could have a huge impact on poverty eradication – by giving poor people access to seeds for high-yielding food crops or to life-saving medicines. Yet the 1994 agreement on Trade-Related Aspects of Intellectual Property Rights – TRIPS – tightens patents and copyright protection, favouring those who develop and market technology rather than society's interest in liberal diffusion of new technology.[29]

Reading this relationship between intellectual property and the diffusion of technology through human rights obligations to health, development and culture[30] demonstrates the way in which the patent system may be answerable to the controversies regarding access to medicines and is what creates the capacity to address these within the intellectual property system – that is, through the regulation of use rather than the regulation of the market (access). The very value of a patent pivots on this relationship to use – not only from the point of view of the meaning and scope of the patent but also from the point of view of the equity and democracy of health. This is the very cultural nature of use.

28 Access to the benefits of scientific research is discussed further in Chapter 4 in terms of the right to access those benefits, as provided in Article 15.1(b) of the International Covenant on Economic, Social and Cultural Rights (ICESCR).

29 UNDP (2000). "Human Rights and Human Development: For Freedom and Solidarity. *Human Development Report 2000*. Geneva: United Nations.

30 The discussion of human rights relevant to health and access to medicines is undertaken in more detail in the next section: 'Rights'.

The cultural value of use

As mentioned, the quality of 'use' as a defining characteristic of the pharmaceutical invention is well-established in patent law, informed by 'The public policy that patents should not interfere with the freedom of medical practitioners to treat patients'.[31] Early in its history, the Enlarged Board of Appeal of the European Patent Office (EPO) has determined that a new use for an old product will constitute a novel function to be protected.[32]

Rather usefully, these principles are pertinent to the emerging issues in gene-related inventions and the capacity for the system to identify proprietary interests in gene sequences, as such. More specifically, this 'functional' approach to use introduces a delimitation of invention so as to anchor the 'authorship' to purpose, that is, to invention constituted by use. By looking specifically at the question of gene patents, it is possible to decipher the way in which this difference in treatment at the level of public debate more widely somewhat obscures the cultural aspects of patents generally. Furthermore, developments in gene patents explain a closer investment by the consumer in the scientific benefit. This is also seen later in this discussion in the impact of labelling as a limit upon infringement of a pharmaceutical patent (with respect to use).

Gene patents are in fact an important legal and analytical nexus for the use and consumption of patents (their cultural character) and the economic interpretations of the market created for such products. In linking the scope of an invention to its use, the role of use emerges as a motivation for innovation, influencing the development of patent law and its interpretation. Use in itself is instrumental in the cohesion of social and cultural groups.[33] Similarly, the very basis for the cultural value of patents is articulated upon use.

In a technical context, the relevance of use or purpose when interpreting gene patents is the important functional constraint, as it were, on what might otherwise operate as overbroad monopolies and de facto protection of a naturally occurring substance.[34] Discoveries are not patentable because they are not inventions.[35] Therefore, a discovery of a new property for a known substance will not in itself be patentable. But if that new property has industrial application and technical effect, it may amount to a patentable

---

31 *Diagnostic Methods* (G 1/04) (2006) OJ EPO 334

32 *EISAI/Second medical indications* (G 05/83) [1979–85] EPOR B241, EBA; in relation to the general application of this principles to all types of invention see *MOBIL/Friction reducing additive* (G-02/88) [1990] EPOR 73, EBA; a change was introduced as part of EPC 2000 to make claim drafting easier for such claims: see EPC, art 54(4) and (5).

33 Weber M (1978/[1922]) *Economy and Society: An Outline of Interpretive Sociology*, Fischoff E et al (trans), Berkeley, CA: University of California Press, 320.

34 See *Association for Molecular Pathology v Myraid* Genetics 133 S Ct 2107 (2012); see further the discussion in Cook T (2006) "Patenting Genes" in Pugatch M (ed) *The Intellectual Property Debate: Perspectives from Law, Economics and Political Economy*, Cheltenham: Edward Elgar, 187.

35 For instance, see EPC Article 52(2)(a).

product. It is the critical nature of use that, as will be discussed, attributes an inventive quality to the 'discovery' of a gene sequence.[36]

Patentability is decided upon three basic criteria – newness or novelty; inventiveness or non-obviousness (that is, it cannot be so obvious a development that it would have been inevitable), and industrial application (utility).[37] These are therefore the basic defining criteria of an 'invention'.[38] An invention must provide a new way, a new technical solution to a problem. Therefore, it must not already exist in the literature or have been used (even if not protected by a patent), it must be novel.[39] The solution must be inventive, that is, it must show that there is an inventive step taken in arriving at this solution.[40] In other words, an invention cannot simply be a logical progression to those working in the field and so it must not be already obvious to a person skilled in the art.[41]

Finally, and very significantly for the present discussion, the invention must be a technical solution to a problem – it must be useful. This criterion of industrial application or utility is critical to defining the scope of the monopoly of an invention. Somewhat related to the 'use' of the invention is whether or not the invention is sufficiently disclosed. This is the central and indeed cultural importance of the patent document in that it is the only mechanism by which to secure the social contract of the patentee with the public interest through the disclosure and sharing of the invention. If an applicant fails to disclose the patent sufficiently it is, to all intents and purposes, not a patent.[42] In other words, the broader concepts of access and use are fundamental not only to the ideology of the system but also to its very function and to the existence of the patent itself. This disclosure will be the basis for the monopoly that subsequently regulates the use.[43] Keeping in mind the nature of the patent contract (between the inventor and the 'public interest'), tracing right back to the passing of the Statute of Monopolies in 1624, the duration of patents was conceived in terms of two periods of apprenticeship (14 years) with patentees often being required to 'take apprentices, and teach them the knowledge and mystery of the said new invention'.[44] That is, the history of patents became all about the communicative aspect of the invention.

---

36 See Biotechnology Directive (98/44/EC), art 5(1) ('the industrial application of a sequence or a partial sequence must be disclosed in the patent application').
37 See EPC Article 52.
38 Although the European Patent Office has refined this slightly so that things which are not technical are not inventions (and fall within EPC, Article 52(2)).
39 The World Trade Organisation (WTO) Agreement on Trade Related Aspects of Intellectual Property Rights (TRIPS), Article 27(1); European Patent Convention (EPC) Articles 52, 54.
40 TRIPS Article 27(1); EPC Articles 52, 56.
41 This criterion is identified as 'non-obviousness' in some jurisdictions, including the United States. See US § 103.
42 In other words, it is subject to revocation for insufficiency or lack of enablement.
43 TRIPS Article 29(1); EPC Article 83.
44 Johnson P. (2017) *Privatised Law Reform: A History of Patent Law through Private Legislation, 1620–1907,* Abingdon: Routledge, 104–6.

In return for disclosing the invention in a form in which it can be worked by others, the patentee is granted an absolute monopoly of 20 years[45] (which may be extended by related protection in the case of medicinal and plant protection products, to account for delays in regulatory approval and marketing).[46] The minimum monopoly rights conferred will prevent a third party from making, using, offering for sale or importing the patented product for these purposes without the authorisation of the patent-holder.[47] Without such authorisation, any of these acts with respect to the patent product would be infringing. Importantly, intention or knowledge is immaterial.[48] This is particularly critical in the current discussion of purpose-bound protection, where the protected subject matter is limited to the particular purpose disclosed in the patent. If one intends to use the patented invention for a different purpose (such as using a medicinal purpose for a specific new purpose, when the original therapeutic purpose is simply a welcome side effect) it is difficult to know with any accuracy whether this use infringes. Therefore, the quality of use and its judicial construction is arguably the central articulating factor when it comes to access to the system within the terms of that system.

The use of gene sequences

How the function of the intellectual property system may be compromised by life chances will have direct relevance to the fulfilment of the contract with the public when it comes to crucial technology such as medicinal products. With respect to this question of use, the development of patent protection for gene sequences arguably emphasises the role of the public in the manifestation of the invention. It is useful to trace this greater participation in the patent system by the figure of the consumer through the controversial territory of gene patents. In this area, the technology itself introduces a potential alienation of the consumer in ways not really at play in pharmaceutical use patents, at least in terms of the contributing research. That is, research into medicines benefits from an ethical priority that is not really straightforward in the context of gene-related technologies. In other words, developments in patent protection for gene-related inventions and the concept of use as a feature of the invention indicate the way in which the

45 TRIPS Article 33; EPC Article 63.

46 See further the discussion of data exclusivity and supplementary protection certificates in chapter 5.

47 TRIPS Article 28. Countries party to the EPC have adopted even broader protection, which includes a prohibition on keeping or storing the patented product or process. This is found in Article 25 of the Community Patent Convention which, although not in force, was used by most members of the EPC as the basis for defining the exclusive rights conferred by the patent.

48 *Merrell Dow Pharmaceuticals Inc v HN Norton & Co Ltd* [1996] RPC 76 (HL), per Lord Hoffmann at 92.

very nature of the intellectual property bargain with the public is at the core of economic analyses of innovation.

Most recently, this bargain is such that the relationship with the consumer underpins the legitimacy of the law – this is not only in terms of access to medicines and the rejection of market-driven prices for drugs around the world, but also in terms of the scope of inventions in biotechnology. When it comes to gene-related inventions, the controversy has been attached to patents on these inventions, not only in relation to the suspicion of the creation of 'inventorship' with respect to the units of evolution,[49] but also with respect to the restriction of innovation through expansive monopolies over the basic starting material for genetic research into other uses and applications of a particular sequence.[50] Therefore, apart from the suspicion of commercial monopolies over material considered to be the natural building blocks of humanity, as it were, the very nature of genetic research appears to be confounded by the way in which patent protection and the scope of the subsequent monopolies are conferred.

The basic nature of the industry itself is relevant to these questions, particularly in terms of the 'access' and 'use' of that starting material by other inventive actors in the field. Indeed, the interpretation of the monopoly with respect to gene-related inventions is critical to the cultural and knowledge exchange within that scientific community.

Genetic sequencing is in a way an incomplete exercise without the subsequent analysis to identify protein-coding sequences, and the nature and function of those proteins. Genes and genetic sequences are indeed mere portfolios of information. Patent protection must surely coincide with some kind of technical solution to a problem – the deciphering/decoding of that information. In other words, the mere location and identification of a particular sequence does not provide the technical information for any useful application. A gene sequence is simply the ordering of amino acids or nucleotides – it is simply identifying the information, a product of nature.[51] It is in the analysis and identification of the function that the 'inventive' skill and research subsists. Identification of the gene sequence's function and application in the body will be the relevant contribution to knowledge and, in the context of the intellectual property paradigm, the justification for the recognition of the inventor and the declaration of the invention.

A restricted purpose-bound approach to patent protection of gene sequences had long been advocated to define the scope of the invention when it comes

---

49 For instance, see the extensive treatment of the issues in Nuffield Council on Bioethics (2002) 'The Ethics of Patenting DNA'. Discussion Paper.

50 For instance, see Cook T, "Patenting Genes", 187. See also Gibson J (2007) "The Discovery of Invention: Gene Patents and the Question of Patentability," 12 *Journal of Intellectual Property Rights* 45.

51 A point which, since the first edition, has been acknowledged by the US Supreme Court: *Association for Molecular Pathology v Myraid* Genetics 133 S Ct 2107 (2012).

to gene-related technology.[52] Indeed, as Recital 23 of the Biotechnology Directive[53] explicitly states, 'a mere DNA sequence without indication of a function does not contain any technical information and is therefore not a patentable invention'.[54] It was also the general approach towards which the European Parliament began proceeding, having adopted a resolution at the end of 2005 calling on the Commission to examine whether an amendment to the Biotechnology Directive (Article 5) would be necessary to achieve the objectives (freedom of research; economic activity in this research) in the 2005 implementation report in which scope of protection was considered.[55] The report considered that Article 5(3) of the Biotechnology Directive, together with Recitals 23 and 25, might allow for a more limited scope of protection restricted to the disclosure of a specific industrial application.

When the matter came before the Court of Justice in *Monsanto Technology*[56] it related to modified soya which was resistant to glyphosate ('roundup ready'). This essentially allowed the soya to be sprayed with a herbicide and be unaffected, while the weeds surrounding it died. In the case, the soybean had been grown in Argentina, where there was no patent in force, and the soya meal made from those beans was shipped to the Netherlands. While the soya meal contained the modified gene it was effectively dead and so could not perform the function – glyphosate resistance – again. The Court held 'that ... protection ... is not available when the genetic information has ceased to perform the function it performed in the initial material'.[57] The mere presence of the gene in a material was simply not enough.

Biological materials contain an enormous quantity of known and unknown information, as distinct from chemical and mechanical inventions, this could result in a large number of patents relating to one gene sequence. An approach to *Monsanto* which grants protection only in so far as the function is performed in use would remove some of the obstacles to research and access posed by protection of all uses and so avoid the protection for mere information, which can never be the subject matter for intellectual property protection.

52 Although not formally proposed, the purpose-bound approach is considered worthy of further study in the 2005 Report from the Commission to the Council and the European Parliament, "Development and Implications of Patent Law in the Field of Biotechnology and Genetic Engineering," COM(2005)0312 final.

53 Directive of the European Parliament and of the Council on the legal protection of biotechnological inventions (98/44/EC).

54 Recital 23, Directive of the European Parliament and of the Council on the legal protection of biotechnological inventions (98/44/EC).

55 Report from the Commission to the Council and the European Parliament, "Development and Implications of Patent Law in the Field of Biotechnology and Genetic Engineering". The Commission also launched a study, undertaken by the University of Sussex Science and Technology Policy Research (SPRU) analysing the extent of human DNA patenting in Europe in the context of research and innovation.

56 C-428/08 *Monsanto Technology* [2010] ECR I-6765.

57 C-428/08 *Monsanto Technology* [2010] ECR I-6765, paragraph 38.

The situation has, however, been complicated. An Expert Group was appointed by the European Commission to consider, amongst other things, the *Monsanto* decision.[58] There was not a consensus amongst the group as to whether *Monsanto* should be confined to its facts or have wider implications. The minority took the view that it should have wider implications as it supports the implicit removal of DNA sequences from the scope of protection of patents.[59] The majority, however, took the view that, contrary to the decision of the Court, a broad interpretation of 'performs the function' would fit with how such technology is exploited.[60] The example used was DNA being sold in a dry state, where it could not perform its function, but if purchased and used in an aqueous environment it could perform its function once more. Thus, the sequence was 'capable' of performing its function, but it was not performing the function during the manufacture, sale, or importation of the product.[61] Therefore none of those acts would infringe any patent.

Thus, the majority of Experts concluded that while *Monsanto* was rightly decided and so a DNA sequence was incorporated in an artefact in biological material and could no longer perform its function it should not infringe. They also felt that the decision should not be used to limit the absolute protection afforded to chemical substances such as DNA. Accordingly, there was no need for the function to be disclosed in the language of the claim. The majority also took the view that conventional absolute protection for a sequence would be commensurate with the inventor's contribution to the public.

Before continuing with this debate, it is important to understand the requirement to disclose the industrial application of the sequence. Both the European Patent Convention and the European Biotechnology Directive require that the use or industrial application of the invention is disclosed in the patent application.[62] The rise of bioinformatics presents new issues where, amongst other things, computer-aided design enables the development of essential synthetic nucleic acid sequences.[63] For instance, does the use disclosed have to work in reality for it to have an industrial application? Or is the possibility or hypothesis that it may work simply enough? The European Patent Office and the British courts have largely accepted the lesser standard that plausibility is enough.[64]

---

58 EU Commission (2016), *Final Report of the Expert Group on the Development and Implications of Patent Law in the Field of Biotechnology and Genetic Engineering* (17 May 2016).

59 Ibid, 210–211.

60 Ibid, 204–210.

61 Ibid, 203.

62 Patent law in Europe, although implemented at a national level, is based upon the European Patent Convention, with members from the entire European Union. However, relevant European instruments, including the Biotechnology Directive 98/44/EC, are given effect in the EPC by the Implementing Regulations of the EPC.

63 A good summary of bioinformatics is provided in *Eli Lilly v Human Genome Science* [2008] RPC 29, paragraph 78 to 99.

64 See *Human Genome Science v Eli Lilly* [2012] RPC 6 , paragraph 107.

In other words, despite the lesser standard, the scope of the patent is still understood in terms of its function (albeit possible or potential) rather than the structure of the sequence – the identification of an application and use rather than the mere information. The human effort or intervention in an otherwise natural substance (and thus, unpatentable subject matter) is deemed to be found in the technical change that is brought about by the otherwise discovery of the gene sequence and its function. Change is thus invention. Investment can thus be inventive.

Therefore, in the case of gene patents, what has emerged from the previous discussion is the way in which 'inventiveness', as it were, is achieved by use for the purposes of patentability. What is sometimes criticised as a patent for a discovery (the gene sequence), is 'inventive' by virtue of the identification of the application or function. This is the contribution made by the inventor to the public. In other words, there is a kind of critical nexus between use and inventiveness, in this respect. What this discussion shows is the relevance of the scientific practice to the meaningful scope of the gene-related invention. As the previous discussion has explained, it is not the isolation and identification of the sequence that is critical to the technological development, but rather, it is the identification of the function and application of the protein coded by that sequence that is the useful and industrial aspect. In other words, in the case of gene patents, it is the identification of a use or application for the gene sequence that renders the sequence patentable and defines that invention through what are known as 'functional claims'.[65] The question of 'inventiveness' might be understood as being linked to the 'discovery' of that use, as recital 23 made clear

Infringing use

Therefore, the controversy characterising the patentability of gene sequences is largely incorporated within the application of classical interpretation of patent protection (the scope of the claims and the description). In other words, classical patent protection, having developed from more traditional technologies, is not necessarily compatible with the nature of technological innovation in genetic research. The majority of the Expert Group takes the view that the identification of *a* use for a gene sequence should be sufficient to render the subject matter patentable, but the patent will grant control over *all* uses of the patented sequence as a product, resulting in (as the minority of the Expert Group suggested) a de facto patentability of the sequence itself. With classical protection of gene sequences, and thus protection of future and unknown use, there is a problematic patenting of information as such and, in effect, the risk of the patenting of a discovery. Classical interpretation of the subject matter could inadvertently lead to a monopoly over all subsequent

65 Functional claims in other areas of technology raise concerns of ultimately 'broader' claims, thus limiting the entry of competitors through important substitution in the market.

examination and analysis of the functions of the coded protein, potentially limiting follow-on investigation for the life of the patent.

Whatever conceptualisation of the actor in which the original rights must vest (whether it is the skill and labour of the inventor or the investment of the entrepreneur), the effort that is expended is that which leads to the identification of the function and application identified in the claim. This is the bargain, as it were. This is even acknowledged with the requirement to identify the industrial application of the gene sequence. On the other hand, control over all uses might suggest that this kind of interpretation of patent protection would arguably limit the interest in pursuing research into subsequent and significant identification of future applications for a particular sequence through the limitation of access to gene sequences and the limitation of use in terms of the subsequent benefit. In this way, it would be contrary to the cultural and technical specificity of genetic research.

Therefore, in the context of the continuing debate on the impact of the *Monsanto* case, arguably the minority view from the Expert Report should be the preferred view. In other words, the scope of the biotechnological invention should be limited to the disclosure of the 'invention', and this should be limited to the purposes in the patent document. Purpose-limited protection or purpose claims limits protection to the industrial application or function that is disclosed in the patent. Thus, the patent recognises and protects the technical contribution of the inventor, rather than providing what is arguably an indirect monopoly over the natural substance and all its future uses.

Finally, it is worth noting that the majority of the Expert Group did not take account of indirect infringement. In the dry state DNA example, relied upon by the majority, the supplying of the substance, with the requisite knowledge, would be an infringing act as it would be the supply of a means to put the invention into effect.[66] It is therefore the case that the correct balance is struck by incorporating the function-based approach to the scope of protection.

Consumer-defined monopolies

The question of infringement in patents relating to gene sequences would seem to raise the question of the usefulness of a known substance for a purpose that had not previously been known – in other words, a new use. Such a case was considered by the European Patent Office (EPO) Enlarged Board of Appeal, in *Mobil/Friction reducing additive*,[67] where it was held that using an old substance in a new way may be novel, but using an old substance in an old way to produce a new purpose would not. In other words, doing the same thing but with a different purpose in mind will not be novel. There must be some technical contribution (as was the case in *Mobil*).

66 See Patents Act 1977, s 60(2); this gives effect to Community Patent Convention, article 26.

67 *Mobil/Friction reducing additive* (G2/88) [1990] *EPOR* 73.

There has long been a problem with the question of infringement in purpose-bound patents and its relationship with the question of 'intention'. This introduces a new proximity between the patentee/inventor and the consumer that has been otherwise deferred by traditional applications of the doctrine of infringement. Of particular interest is the way in which this proximity neatly reinscribes the creativity of the inventor, the second culture as it were, albeit in the context of an entrepreneurial rendition of the invention.

From purpose patents to broader applications of use, in a very interesting kind of way the role of the consumer is literally intrinsic to the patentability of the new technology in so far as that patentability is tied to use, is tied to its market. This provides important insight in the context of current intellectual property law debates and, in particular, controversies with respect to the deferral of users from the increasingly resilient economic unity of the intellectual property system. This is relevant not only in cultivating use relationships with controversial technology within the system, but also in redressing the proximity of the user in applications of patent law to other technologies. In this regard, if an unduly restrictive view of intention were to be adopted, it may present significant problems. Returning to the Biotechnology Directive considered earlier, the Group of Experts (established by the first implementation report on the Biotechnology Directive[68]) identified explicitly the economic impact of classical protection in this area of technology.[69] This raises the question of freedom of research (in addition to exemptions for research and experiment) and, more significantly perhaps, the question of a proportionality or proximity between the investment and the potential reward.[70] Again, the reward of the market is suggested as the most useful (or indeed the most persuasive) quantification and it is the consumer that qualifies the value of this market.

These problems have started to be addressed in European courts, mainly involving the litigation surrounding Warner Lambert patent for pregabalin.[71] The patent was for the use of the drug for neuropathic pain, but there were known (unpatented) indications for it to be used for general anxiety disorder and epilepsy. Global sales of the drug in 2013 amounted to $4.6 billion for all indications and this had enticed generic manufactures to try to sell the drug for the known indications.

The difficulty was how to decide when a generic company selling a drug for a known indication is also infringing the patented indication when, despite its efforts (for example, through relevant marketing), consumers nevertheless

68 Report from the Commission to the European Parliament and the Council. "Development and Implications of Patent Law in the Field of Biotechnology and Genetic Engineering".

69 Ibid.

70 On this point, the European Commission has launched a study to undertake an economic analysis of human DNA patenting in Europe, the results of which are expected later this year.

71 There has been a number of judgments in relation to the dispute, the two most relevant for these purposes are *Warner-Lambert v Generics* [2016] EWCA Civ 1006; *Warner-Lambert Company* v *Actavis Group* [2015] EWCA Civ 556.

use the drug to treat that indication. The difficulty arises when certain so called 'hard cases' are identified.[72] The most problematic is where the generic manufacture has been selling pregabalin for epilepsy before the priority date of the neuropathic pain patent and finds that its sales have increased without it doing anything different. The question is whether this should be an infringement as the increased sales are likely to be for the infringing use. The second question is related to the regulatory regime in the United Kingdom which allowed off-label prescribing to occur. Here the manufacturer may have taken all steps open to it but still its drugs are being used for the infringing purpose. In *Warner-Lambert v Generics* the court said[73]

> … Some countries have gone for the 'only packaging will do' approach. Some countries look more generally for some element of encouragement of the use of the drug for the new use by the manufacturer before being prepared to find infringement. Others look to see what steps have been put in place in the marketplace to prevent use for the prohibited indication. I do not think a universal principle has yet emerged.
>
> … [Counsel for the Generic] submits … [w]hat is required is that the manufacturer 'aims for or targets' the patented indication. … He argues, firstly, that if a manufacturer is liable if he reasonably foresees that some of his drug will be used for the treatment of pain, he will be using the process, and the whole of his output will infringe. Secondly, because all his output will then become the direct product of the process, it will be an infringement in the hands of the pharmacist whatever the mental state of the pharmacist. The patentee will therefore be able to stop pharmacists from supplying the drug at all, irrespective of the indication for which it is dispensed. … the manufacturer has control over whether he infringes. He can sell the product for the non-patented indications without incurring liability, provided that he does not aim for or target the patented one. …
>
> … I recognise … that the case where a manufacturer foresees use for the patented treatment, but takes all reasonable steps within his power to prevent it happening, represented a hard case. However, I do not think the answer is to adopt a test of purely subjective intention. … I think the debate in this case has been distorted by reference to notions of subjective intention. I have no doubt that an objective approach is necessary. From an objective standpoint one would normally regard a person to intend what he knows or can reasonably foresee as the consequences of his actions. … If that is the basic test to be adopted, what is sufficient to negative the existence of intention? In my judgment the absence of the patented indication from the label cannot conceivably be sufficient to negative the intention …

72 *Warner-Lambert Company* v *Actavis Group* [2015] EWCA Civ 556, paragraph 130 to 132.
73 [2016] EWCA Civ 1006, paragraphs 201 to 208.

> Viewed in this way I think the answer becomes clear. The intention will be negatived where the manufacturer has taken all reasonable steps within his power to prevent the consequences occurring. In such circumstances his true objective is a lawful one, and one would be entitled to say that the foreseen consequences were not intended, but were an unintended incident of his otherwise lawful activity.

While this reasoning has removed the spectre of absolute protection and provided at least a theoretical avenue for a generic manufacturer to sell the drugs, it is a long way from a complete answer.

Similar difficulties were faced by the Canadian Federal Court of Appeal, in *Pharmascience v Sanofi-Aventis*.[74] Sanofi-Aventis produced and marketed ramipril capsules under the trade name Altace, used in the treatment of hypertension and cardiac insufficiency. Pharmascience is the manufacturer of ramipril capsules which are marketed for use only in the treatment of hypertension, although the capsules would be therapeutically equivalent to Altace. Pharmascience argued that it would not infringe the Aventis patents because it was seeking approval and marketing only in the treatment of hypertension. Aventis rejected this and successfully obtained a prohibition order in the Federal Court, prohibiting the Minister from issuing a notice of compliance to Pharmascience. Pharmascience appealed, asking for the prohibition order to be set aside or varied, but the appeal was dismissed with costs.

The discussion with respect to infringement and the agency of doctors and patients in the constitution of infringement is especially interesting. In relation to one of the particular patents in question, Pharmascience proposed a narrower interpretation of the scope of protection. Specifically, Pharmascience proposed a narrower reading of subparagraph 5(1)(b)(iv) of the relevant Regulations (the *Patented Medicines (Notice of Compliance) Regulations*), relying on *AB Hassle v Canada (Minister of National Health and Welfare)*.[75] The relevant subparagraph reads:

> 5. (1) Where a person files or has filed a submission for a notice of compliance in respect of a drug and compares that drug with, or makes reference to, another drug for the purpose of demonstrating bioequivalence on the basis of pharmaceutical and, where applicable, bioavailability characteristics and that other drug has been marketed in Canada pursuant to a notice of compliance issued to a first person and in respect of which a patent list has been submitted, the person shall, in the submission, with respect to each patent on the register in respect of the other drug,
>
> …

74 *Pharmascience v Sanofi-Aventis* (2006) FCA 229.

75 *AB Hassle v Canada (Minister of National Health and Welfare)* [2002] FCA 421.

(b) allege that

...

(iv) no claim for the medicine itself and no claim for the use of the medicine would be infringed by the making, constructing, using or selling by that person of the drug for which the submission for the notice of compliance is filed.

Pharmascience argued that the Regulations did not require it to address the possibility or probability of infringement by patients (that is, end users), of the patent in question, arguing that without such limitation on the interpretation, there would be an inadvertent extension to the monopolies of patent holders:

> If there was any likelihood that a patient could consume a generic product for a patented use, then the generic product would not be approved. This would prevent new uses from being approved for existing drugs because there is always the possibility that someone somewhere will use the drug for the prohibited, patented purpose. This would result in a real injustice: since a generic company cannot possibly control how everyone in the world uses its product, the prevention of the generic from marketing the product would further fortify and artificially extend the monopoly held by patent holders. *The patent holder would, therefore, effectively control not just the new uses for the old compound, but the compound itself, even though the compound itself is not protected by the patent in the first place.*[76]

Pharmascience alleged non-infringement of the patent, arguing that its proposal to use so called 'skinny labelling' – that is, seeking approval and marketing and labelling the capsules for a specific use (the treatment of hypertension only) – would be sufficient to avoid infringement. Although ultimately the point did not need to be decided, as the patent had expired, thus lifting the prohibition order, the court concluded that this narrower interpretation, permitting mere skinny labelling was sufficient. In other words, the Canadian courts took a different view from those in England, where skinny labelling alone was expressly held to be inadequate. These difficulties have led one English High Court judge (Arnold J) to suggest that prescribing practises should change and doctors should prescribe using brand names for any patented use and the international non-proprietary names of drugs for generic sales, rather than prescribing by international non-proprietary names only.[77]

Clearly these cases are relevant to policy discussions in the context of gene-related inventions. Efforts to resolve the need to avoid monopolies over gene sequences, through limiting scope to disclosed use, while at the same time avoiding perpetual protection of gene sequences and the confusion

76 *AB Hassle v Canada (Minister of National Health and Welfare)* [2002] FCA 421: para 57, emphasis added.

77 *Generics v Warner-Lambert Company* [2015] EWHC 2548 (Pat), paragraph 722 to 726

of cross-licensing, the creation of patents each relating to a particular use resolves the undesirable outcome of a monopoly over the sequence itself. Although this might be seen as simply proliferating patents with respect to one gene sequence, this is perhaps to misunderstand the subject matter of the invention itself and the critical value at stake in the patent system. Purpose-bound approaches acknowledges the contribution of protection for particular new applications as incentives to subsequent research. But of even greater interest is the cultural contribution of the conceptualisation and delimitation of invention by use as distinct from the material object itself. Importantly, all patents are indeed encapsulated in the document and not in the object. It is significant to develop the discussion beyond ownership of chattels to entitlements with respect to use – this removes the emphasis from markets in goods to the cultural economy of use: 'Patent indices are, however, a measure of new technology generated and not new technology used'.[78] However, interpreted this way, this might make the patent indices described earlier more meaningful from the perspective of the system's efficiency.

The critical articulation of these various interests, therefore, would seem to be the question of infringement and the associated question of intention in use. Where research and development can, in theory, amount to an attack on one's own market (thus limiting the incentive), research and development bound to the particular function and application creates a new market. Research and development on a particular gene function is not technical improvement on the original product because, in a purpose-bound approach, the gene sequence or even the protein coded is not the product, as it were. Rather, it is the function that is marketed by the manufacturer and it is the function that is the significant subject matter of the patent. Thus, the question of technical obsolescence, as it were, does not necessarily take hold.

In a very interesting kind of way, therefore, the role of the consumer is literally intrinsic to the patentability of the new technology in so far as that patentability is tied to use. Consumers are introduced as 'innovators' in the market in this contribution to 'invention'. The labelling of the product is thus relevant to the technical progress of innovation based upon the same starting material. Consumers provide the financial incentive, rather than the product in and of itself, not in the simple sense of fulfilling the market for that product but in the sense of characterising the subject matter of that product through use.

The patent does not guarantee the value of the investment; rather, it is its use. Significantly, it is the question of 'use' (and infringement) which defines the debate in the scope of legal rights in not only biotechnology-related inventions but also in other areas of technology. Furthermore, it is the concept of use that safeguards the user's access to the system and the realisation of their beneficial interests in scientific research.[79] That is, as well

78 Stoneman P (2002) *The Economics of Technological Diffusion*, Oxford: Blackwell, 251.

79 The concept of a beneficial interest is examined in detail in Part II: Rights, in the context of the human right to health and also particularly with respect to the individual's right to cultural life.

as defining the scope of legal rights, the concept of use is critical to the articulation of the beneficial interests in the invention.

It is other users (whether end-users or traditional consumers, or other innovators as other users of the gene sequence) that drive innovation. The emphasis may more usefully be placed on balance transactions in a competitive market, where a purpose-bound approach to the proliferation of uses identified introduces a type of competition by substitution. Thus, the invention does subsist in the inherent and prior properties of the starting-material, but the characterisation of that use generates its value in the strictest sense. This emphasises value generated not in its exchange within the market but in its fulfilment of use by the consumer, the communicative quality of the knowledge economy.

Part 2
Rights

3 The human right to health

Introduction

If obligations to the fulfilment of individual rights with respect to health are met, then arguably this is the mechanism by which to overcome individual life chances. Robust protection of rights would provide the opportunity to access health and autonomy over the conduct one's own life. Rights must necessarily secure both the democratisation of the public sphere, ensuring access to the institution of health, and the morality and legitimacy of judgments and participation within that sphere.[1] Habermas explains that 'basic rights guarantee what we now call the *private* autonomy of legal subjects' but what is essential in order for individual legal subjects to 'become *authors* of their legal order' is the guaranteed access to equal opportunities for participation and political autonomy.[2]

The discourse on rights indicates a certain dichotomy between natural or 'moral' rights and economic rights. The latter is attended by more robust implementation and enforcement, premised and articulated upon binding legal statute. What is arguably emerging in current systems with the effects of globalisation on legal systems and trading environments, economic rights have become prioritised as the totality of legal rights. Indeed, the democratisation of the public sphere is premised upon relationships in private property, upon the recognition and exercise of proprietary rights. The 'morality' of the legal system is rendered somewhat ancillary. Privileged discourses of 'freedom' and 'rights' come to be attached to private property and, as such, a principal authority is conferred upon the intellectual property system. This articulation of democracy upon notions of 'property' reaches its logical extreme in the

1 Habermas explains that there 'are two tasks the required system of rights is supposed to solve. It should institutionalize the communicative framework for a rational political will-formation, and it should ensure the very medium in which alone this will-formation can express itself as the common will of freely associated legal persons.' See Habermas J (1997/[1992]) *Between Facts and Norms: Contributions to a Discourse Theory of Law and Democracy*, Rehg W (trans), Cambridge: Polity Press, 111.

2 Habermas, *Between Facts and Norms,* 123.

context of the creation of proprietary rights in inventions based upon living material. The priority accorded to property rights sustains a seemingly coherent and closed system which not only justifies the commodification of isolated materials in commercial inventions, but also alienates the individual from principles of self-ownership as 'immoral'.[3] This raises significant concern with respect to the bioprospecting of genetic material, both in the individual and in the community. For many indigenous groups, this central importance attributed to property effectively unjustly renders their own laws illegitimate in the face of encroaching scientific enterprise.

Of critical importance to ensuring the access of individuals to public health, including the necessary opportunities for social well-being, development and cultural participation, is the communication of human rights principles within the commercial systems: 'human rights institutionalize the communicative conditions for a reasonable political will-formation'.[4] Indeed, what is at stake is not the rendering of certain frameworks, like the patent system, as ethical frameworks, but rather it is the intervention of moral rationalism within legal discourse and towards sustaining its legitimacy. While the economic intellectual property system may be seen to allow for the privateering of the private sphere, it is necessary to examine the way in which the moral principles of the private sphere can invigorate legitimating forces in a functioning economic system: '[human rights] are constitutive for the legal order as a whole and to this extent determine a framework within which normal legislation must be conducted'.[5] Therefore, as well as examining the basis in human rights for ensuring an individual's right to health and access to healthcare opportunities, this section will also review the way in which the right to health and other relevant rights might inform and administer the patent system and its own internal logic of morality.

The human right to health

The Constitution of the WHO,[6] signed in 1946 and entered into force in 1948, recognises the right to health as a fundamental human right not merely to the absence of disease but to complete well-being. The WHO definition, unchanged since its adoption in 1948 and through subsequent amendments to the original 1946 text, arguably establishes a definition

3 Discussed further in Part III: Life

4 Habermas J (2001/[1998]) *The Postnational Constellation: Political Essays*, Pensky M (trans & ed), Cambridge: Polity Press, 117.

5 Habermas J (1998/[1996]) *The Inclusion of the Other: Studies in Political Theory*, Cronin C and de Greiff P (trans), Cambridge: Polity Press, 190.

6 The Constitution was adopted by the International Health Conference held in New York from 19 June to 22 July 1946, signed on 22 July 1946 by the representatives of 61 States (*Official Records of the WHO*, 2, 100). The Constitution entered into force on 7 April 1948 and amendments were adopted by the 26th, 29th, 39th and 51st World Health Assemblies (resolutions WHA26.37, WHA29.38, WHA39.6 and WHA51.23), which came into force on 3 February 1977, 20 January 1984, 11 July 1994 and 15 September 2005 respectively.

relevant to an individual's cultural and social participation and integrity, and to the interpretation of the human right to health. Indeed, the WHO definition resonates in later human rights instruments.

In the Preamble to the Constitution, the WHO recognises the enjoyment of the highest attainable standard of health as one of the fundamental human rights and defines health broadly to include mental and social well-being:[7]

> Health is a state of complete physical, mental and social well-being and not merely the absence of disease or infirmity.
>
> The enjoyment of the highest attainable standard of health is one of the fundamental rights of every human being without distinction of race, religion, political belief, economic or social condition.
>
> The health of all peoples is fundamental to the attainment of peace and security and is dependent upon the fullest co-operation of individuals and States.
>
> The achievement of any State in the promotion and protection of health is of value to all.
>
> Unequal development in different countries in the promotion of health and control of disease, especially communicable disease, is a common danger.
>
> Healthy development of the child is of basic importance; the ability to live harmoniously in a changing total environment is essential to such development.
>
> The extension to all peoples of the benefits of medical, psychological and related knowledge is essential to the fullest attainment of health.
>
> Informed opinion and active co-operation on the part of the public are of the utmost importance in the improvement of the health of the people.
>
> Governments have a responsibility for the health of their peoples which can be fulfilled only by the provision of adequate health and social measures.[8]

This concept of the human right to health introduces the broader concept of health that has persisted throughout human rights instruments and remains in place today. Further, it is a right to which there should not be barriers through discrimination or culture ('The enjoyment of the highest attainable standard of health ... without distinction') and for which access to research benefits ('the extension to all peoples of the benefits') and access to information ('Informed opinion and active co-operation on the part of the public are of utmost importance') are important and essential underlying

7 Preamble to the Constitution of the WHO as adopted by the International Health Conference, New York, 19–22 June 1946; signed on 22 July 1946 by the representatives of 61 States (*Official Records of the WHO*, 2, 100) and entered into force 7 April 1948.

8 Constitution of the World Health Organization, 22 July 1946: Preamble.

factors. Finally, the definition links the importance of health to economic development, being mutually constitutive priorities ('Unequal development ... is a common danger').[9] All of these principles inform the characterisation and interpretation of the right and related rights within human rights instruments, as will be discussed throughout this section.[10] Furthermore, the WHO Constitution notes the importance and relevance of achievement in one state to the benefit of all, indicating the significance of health as a global public good ('The achievement of any State in the promotion and protection of health is of value to all'). Importantly, the definition of health notably links the advancement of health to international partnerships and development, indicating at this early period of the UN system the important links to be understood between health and development.

Health was identified as part of the inclusive right to an adequate standard of living in the 1948 Universal Declaration of Human Rights (UDHR).[11] Article 25(1) of the UDHR declares a right to standards of living, including medical care, adequate for health and well-being:

> **Article 25.**
>
> (1) Everyone has the right to a standard of living adequate for the health and well-being of himself and of his family, including food, clothing, housing and medical care and necessary social services, and the right to security in the event of unemployment, sickness, disability, widowhood, old age or other lack of livelihood in circumstances beyond his control.[12]

According to UN Office of the High Commissioner for Human Rights (OHCHR), the right to health is recognised in several regional instruments, including the African Charter on Human and Peoples' Rights, and at least 115 national constitutions,[13] and duties in relation to health are established in at least six other national constitutions. It is important to remember, however, that, until ratified most international human rights instruments are declarations of political will rather than readily enforceable within a national boundary.

9 See further the discussion of the relationship between health, trade and development in MacDonald TH (2006) *Health, Trade and Human Rights*, Oxford: Radcliffe, 2: 'The negative effect on human rights (such as health, access to water and food, education and so on) through the exploitation of the third world to facilitate trade has been enormous'. Paul Farmer has suggested that 'despite increasing globalization, our action agenda has remained parochial'. See Farmer P (2005) *Pathologies of Power: Health, Human Rights, and the New War on the Poor*, Berkeley, CA: University of California Press, 240.

10 See generally, Tobin J (2011) *The Right to Health in International Law*, Oxford: Oxford University Press, Chapter 4.

11 Universal Declaration of Human Rights (UDHR), adopted 10 Dececember 1948, General Assembly Resolution 217A (III), UN Doc A/810.

12 UDHR, Article 25(1).

13 OHCHR (2008). 'The Right to Health'. Fact Sheet No 31. Geneva: OHCHR.

Nevertheless, they have important political and rhetorical force and have been instrumental in promoting and inciting change at a national level.

The right to health is therefore not merely a right to the state of well-being itself, but to the circumstances necessary for that state. Therefore, as an inclusive right it provides for not only a direct right to appropriate and timely healthcare, but also a right to the underlying determinants of health (such as clean water, environmental conditions and so on).

International Covenant on Economic, Social and Cultural Rights

Article 12 of the International Covenant on Economic, Social and Cultural Rights (ICESCR)[14] established the right to public health as a fundamental human right:

> 1. The States Parties to the present Covenant recognize the right of everyone to the enjoyment of the highest attainable standard of physical and mental health.
> 2. The steps to be taken by the States Parties to the present Covenant to achieve the full realization of this right shall include those necessary for:
> (a) The provision for the reduction of the stillbirth-rate and of infant mortality and for the healthy development of the child;
> (b) The improvement of all aspects of environmental and industrial hygiene;
> (c) The prevention, treatment and control of epidemic, endemic, occupational and other diseases;
> (d) The creation of conditions which would assure to all medical service and medical attention in the event of sickness.

In particular, Article 12.2(c) refers to the entitlement to prevention, treatment and control of diseases, and is defined as requiring the establishment of prevention and education programs (particularly with respect to HIV/AIDS) as well as a system of urgent medical care in the case of epidemics and the like. Article 12.2(d), which provides for the right to health facilities, goods and services, is defined as covering, among other things, the provision of essential drugs.[15] Article 2.1 sets out the obligations of states, which includes the adoption of legislative measures where necessary to give the full realisation of the rights recognised in the Covenant:

---

14 International Covenant on Economic, Social and Cultural Rights, adopted 16 December 1966, entered into force 3 January 1976, General Assembly Resolution 2200A (XXI), UN Doc A/6316 (1966), 993 UNTS 3, reprinted in 6 ILM 360 (1967). At the time of writing the covenant had been ratified by 159 States.

15 It is possible to read Article 15.1(b), the right to enjoy the benefits of scientific progress and its applications, as incorporating a right to access the opportunities presented by scientific research and development in medicine in public healthcare. Article 15 is considered further in Chapter 4 in the discussion of the right to culture.

> 1. Each State Party to the present Covenant undertakes to take steps, individually and through international assistance and co-operation, especially economic and technical, to the maximum of its available resources, with a view to achieving progressively the full realization of the rights recognized in the present Covenant by all appropriate means, including particularly the adoption of legislative measures.[16]

In the General Comment on the implementation of Article 2.1,[17] the Committee on Economic and Social Rights (CESCR) noted that, while legislative measures are an important and often indispensable means by which to guarantee the full effect of the ICESCR, this is not to discount other steps. Significantly, the full realisation of the rights contained in the ICESCR should be undertaken 'by all appropriate means' in the fullest sense indicating the normative effect of the ICESCR together with the implementation of the provisions at the statutory level. Furthermore, the committee resolved that states are obliged to provide the minimum essential levels for the realisation of each right:

> [T]he Committee is of the view that a minimum core obligation to ensure the satisfaction of, at the very least, minimum essential levels of each of the rights is incumbent upon every State party. Thus, for example, a State party in which any significant number of individuals is deprived of essential foodstuffs, of essential primary healthcare, of basic shelter and housing, or of the most basic forms of education is, *prima facie*, failing to discharge its obligations under the Covenant. If the Covenant were to be read in such a way as not to establish such a minimum core obligation, it would be largely deprived of its *raison d'être*.[18]

In General Comment No 14 (2000) on the implementation of Article 12,[19] the CESCR stated that 'Health is a fundamental human right indispensable for the exercise of other human rights. Every human being is entitled to the enjoyment of the highest attainable standard of health conducive to living a life in dignity'.[20] Comment No 14 defines the obligations of states to be fulfilled by states so as to realise the right at the national level. It explains the normative content of Article 12 as a right containing both freedoms and entitlements, including an equality of opportunity for people to enjoy the highest attainable

16 ICESCR. Article 2(1).

17 CESCR. General Comment No 3 (1990). The nature of States parties obligations (Art 2, par 1). 14 December 1990.

18 CESCR. General Comment No 3, paragraph 10.

19 CESCR. General Comment No 14 (2000). The right to the highest attainable standard of health (article 12 of the International Covenant on Economic, Social and Cultural Rights. 22nd Session. E/C.12/2000/4. 11 August 2000.

20 CESCR. General Comment No 14, paragraph 1.

standard of health[21] and defines the normative content as comprising the four essential elements of availability, accessibility, acceptability and quality.[22]

The right to health is therefore confirmed as an inclusive right to the opportunities and resources for health: 'The right to health is not to be understood as a right to be *healthy*. The right to health contains both freedoms and entitlements.'[23] Importantly, the right to health should include the entitlement to access to health information as well as access to medicines and medical treatment.[24] Indeed, the provision of essential drugs under the WHO Action Programme on Essential Drugs is identified as one of the core obligations to be met in order to give full realisation to the right to health.[25]

The four overarching principles fulfilling the normative content of Article 12 are important to consider in greater detail. These principles account for varying life chances in the opportunities to take advantage of the resources necessary to the realisation of the right to health and also provide the important framework for later examination of the intellectual property system and the realisation of the right. The General Comment on Article 12 explains:

> The right to health in all its forms and at all levels contains the following interrelated and essential elements, the precise application of which will depend on the conditions prevailing in a particular State party:
>
> a. *Availability*. Functioning public health and health-care facilities, goods and services, as well as programmes, have to be in sufficient quantity within the State party …
> b. *Accessibility*. Health facilities, goods and services[26] have to be accessible to everyone without discrimination, within the jurisdiction of the State party. Accessibility has four overlapping dimensions:
>   - Non-discrimination …
>   - Physical accessibility …
>   - Economic accessibility (affordability): health facilities, goods and services must be affordable for all …
>   - Information accessibility: accessibility includes the right to seek, receive and impart information and ideas including health issues …
> c. *Acceptability*. All health facilities, goods and services must be respectful of medical ethics and culturally appropriate, i.e. respectful of the culture of individuals, minorities, peoples and communities, sensitive to

---

21 CESCR. General Comment No 14, paragraph 8.
22 CESCR. General Comment No 14, paragraph 12.
23 CESCR. General Comment No 14, paragraph 8.
24 The entitlement to access to medicines as contained within the right to health is discussed later in this chapter, and has been set out in reports of the Special Rapporteur, also considered later in this chapter.
25 CESCR. General Comment No 14, paragraph 12.
26 All references to health facilities, goods and services include the underlying determinants for health: CESCR. General Comment No 14, note 6.

gender and life-cycle requirements, as well as being designed to respect confidentiality and improve the health status of those concerned.

d. *Quality*. As well as being culturally acceptable, health facilities, goods and services must be scientifically and medically appropriate and of good quality ...[27]

These four principles set out those opportunities and conditions necessary to fulfilling the broader inclusive right. First, the right addresses the availability of the underlying determinants of health, including essential drugs. Second, that availability must be supported by the accessibility of services, goods and information, which should not be compromised by any obstacle, physical, economic or social. Indeed, the distinction between availability and accessibility relates to the distinction between the value of 'access' and the value of 'use'. It is a materially different achievement in the right to point to the availability of resources but it is the question of the individual's life chances and ability to enjoy equal opportunities to exploit that availability. Therefore, there must be a meaningful and relevant proximity between the determinants for health and the individual's ability to participate in those resources, including access to information as well as medicinal products and healthcare facilities. Third, those opportunities are not effective if not culturally and ethically acceptable and relevant, emphasising the cultural dimension to healthcare as a social and political institution, including the committee's consideration that 'indigenous peoples have the right to specific measures to improve their access to health services and care. These health services should be culturally appropriate, taking into account traditional preventive care, healing practices and medicines.'[28] Thus, availability and accessibility will be undermined if the cultural specificity of individuals compromises the effective delivery and communication of healthcare. Finally, the quality of healthcare, goods and services will directly impact upon the preceding principles in that without local infrastructure and expertise, it is not possible to fulfil completely the four principles of the right to health.

Special Rapporteur on the Right to Health

By Resolution 2002/31, the Commission on Human Rights[29] appointed, for a period of three years, a Special Rapporteur on the right to health. The Special Rapporteur was given a mandate to request and gather information on the right to health, discuss and cooperate with various relevant stakeholders, including governments and other UN bodies, specialised agencies (including the WHO), other programmes (such as the Joint UN Programme on HIV/

27 CESCR. General Comment No 14, paragraph 12.
28 CESCR. General Comment No 14, paragraph 27.
29 The Commission on Human Rights, the forerunner of the present Human Rights Council, is a subsidiary body of the UN General Assembly.

AIDS) and NGOs. The Special Rapporteur was also requested to report on the status of the right throughout laws and policies around the world and to make recommendations on appropriate measures to promote and protect the right to health.

The Commission on Human Rights was replaced by the Human Rights Council in 2006 by the 60th Session of the UN General Assembly.[30] The mandate of the Special Rapporteur was endorsed and extended by the Human Rights Council by Resolution 6/29 of 14 December 2007.[31] This resolution extends the scope of the mandate to include annual reports to the Human Rights Council and interim reports to the General Assembly. The mandate also includes the submission of proposals towards the realisation of the health-related Millennium Development Goals (MDGs).

At the 2000 UN Millennium Summit, 189 UN Member States and at least 23 international organisations agreed to the Millennium Declaration,[32] which established a set of eight development goals to be achieved by 2015. These goals, known as the MDGs, included: the eradication of extreme poverty and hunger; the facilitation of universal access to and participation in primary education; the promotion of gender equality; the alleviation of child mortality; improve maternal health; the escalation of the campaign against HIV/AIDS, malaria and other diseases; ensure environmental sustainability; and the development of global partnerships towards development. In 2015, the progress that had been made was assessed in a report on the Millennium Development.[33] For instance, in relation to Goal 6 (to combat HIV/AIDS, malaria and other diseases) HIV infection rates have fallen 40 per cent, the number of people receiving antiretroviral therapy rose from 800,000 in 2003 to 13.6million by 2014. The incidence of malaria has fallen 37 per cent and mortality by 58 per cent between 2000 and 2015. There has also been progress with respect to tuberculosis where the mortality rate fell by 41 per cent between 1990 and 2013.[34] Goal 8 (to develop a global partnership for development) includes the target to provide for access to affordable essential medicines for developing countries, by working in cooperation with pharmaceutical companies. By 2015, 58 per cent of public health facilities and 67 per cent of private-sector facilities in low-income and lower-middle-income countries had access to generic medicines.[35]

---

30 UN General Assembly. Resolution 60/251. Human Rights Council. 60th Session General Assembly, 3 April 2006.

31 Human Rights Council. Resolution 6/29. paragraph 1.

32 UN General Assembly. Resolution 55/2. UN Millennium Declaration. 51st Session General Assembly, 18 September 2000.

33 United Nations (2015) *The Millennium Development Goals Report 2015, New* York: United Nations.

34 The different starting points may have been used to make the effect look more dramatic, but nonetheless it is clear that substantial progress has been made.

35 United Nations, *The Millennium Development Goals Report 2015*, 67.

In 2015, a new programme of development was launched as *Transforming Our World: The 2030 Agenda for Sustainable Development.*[36] This set out the Sustainable Development Goals to be achieved by 2030. There are 17 goals and 169 associated targets, one of the more ambitious objectives was stated to be:

> To promote physical and mental health and well-being, and to extend life expectancy for all, we must achieve universal health coverage and access to quality healthcare. No one must be left behind. We commit to accelerating the progress made to date in reducing newborn, child and maternal mortality by ending all such preventable deaths before 2030. We are committed to ensuring universal access to sexual and reproductive health-care services, including for family planning, information and education. We will equally accelerate the pace of progress made in fighting malaria, HIV/AIDS, tuberculosis, hepatitis, Ebola and other communicable diseases and epidemics, including by addressing growing anti-microbial resistance and the problem of unattended diseases affecting developing countries. We are committed to the prevention and treatment of non-communicable diseases, including behavioural, developmental and neurological disorders, which constitute a major challenge for sustainable development..[37]

In contrast to the Millennium Development Agenda which was essentially about improving the situation in developing countries, the Sustainable Development Agenda is more inclusive and includes targets relevant to both the developed and developing world.

The Sustainable Development Goals include Goal 1 (End poverty in all its forms everywhere), although the target is more modest than the goal appears to anticipate. The first target is to eradicate extreme poverty everywhere by 2030.[38] It is to 'reduce at least by half the proportion of men, women and children of all ages living in poverty in all dimensions according to national definitions'.[39] Thus, a person's living standards in one country could be considered as living in poverty, whereas someone with worse living standards in another country might not be so considered. While this may make sense when considering comparisons between, for example, the United States and Rwanda, it could equally apply where the comparisons are between two countries with comparable levels of development.

Goal 3 (Ensure healthy lives and promote well-being for at all ages), the targets include reducing maternal mortality, reducing deaths of newborns and ending the epidemics of AIDS, tuberculosis, malaria and neglected tropical

36 Resolution 25 September 2015: *Transforming our world: the 2030 Agenda for Sustainable Development*, 21 October 2015.
37 A/RES/70/1, paragraph 26,
38 Target 1.1 (extreme poverty are those people living on less than $1.25 a day – although this target does not take into account the variable value of the dollar).
39 Target 1.2.

diseases.[40] It also addresses global, rather than purely developing issues, such as road safety,[41] promoting mental health and well-being, treatment and prevention of addiction,[42] and strengthening tobacco control.[43]

The right to access to medicines

In the Report to the 59th Session of the UN General Assembly,[44] the Special Rapporteur noted the prominence of health in the MDGs and maintained that a specific entitlement to access to treatment information is understood within the broader inclusive right to health. Paragraph 16 of the Report states: 'The right to health includes the right to healthcare, but it goes beyond healthcare to encompass safe-drinking water, adequate sanitation and access to health-related information.'[45] Further, the right 'includes entitlements, such as the right to a system of health protection … and access to essential drugs'.[46] Access to essential medicines is therefore identified by the OHCHR as a specific entitlement within the inclusive right to health.

However, three years earlier in 2001, the Commission on Human Rights adopted a resolution[47] recognising access to medication in the context of pandemics to be a fundamental aspect of the fulfilment of the right to health. Paragraph 1 of the Resolution:

> Recognizes that access to medication in the context of pandemics such as HIV/AIDS is one fundamental element for achieving progressively the full realization of the right of everyone to the enjoyment of the highest attainable standard of physical and mental health.[48]

Resolution 2001/33 calls upon the international community to cooperate with developing countries towards fulfilling this element and upon states to pursue policies to promote and improve access to medicines in the treatment of pandemics and to refrain from legislative or other actions that might impede that access.

In 2006, the 61st Session of the UN General Assembly considered the report of the Special Rapporteur on the relationship between the right

40 Target 3.4.
41 Target 3.6 (halve global deaths from road traffic accidents)
42 Target 3.5.
43 Target 3.a.
44 UN General Assembly. Report of the Special Rapporteur of the Commission on Human Rights, on the right of everyone to the enjoyment of the highest attainable standard of physical and mental health. 59th Session. 8 October 2004. A/59/422.
45 Ibid., paragraph 16.
46 Ibid., paragraph 16.
47 Commission on Human Rights. Access to medication in the context of pandemics such as HIV/AIDS. Resolution 2001/33.
48 Ibid., paragraph 1.

to health and access to medicines.[49] The report notes the importance of improved access to medicines to the achievement of several MDGs, including infant mortality and maternal health: 'Crucially, implementation of the right to the highest attainable standard of health can help to achieve the health-related Goals.'[50] The Special Rapporteur refers to the right to medicines as a specific and integral entitlement within the inclusive right to the highest attainable standard of health:

> Medical care in the event of sickness, as well as the prevention, treatment and control of diseases, are central features of the right to the highest attainable standard of health. These features depend upon access to medicines. Thus, access to medicines forms an indispensable part of the right to the highest attainable standard of health.[51]

Indeed, as identified in the Report, the right to medicines has been enforced in several jurisdictions. The results of successful individual and public interest litigation in health were analysed by the director, Dr Hans Hogerzeil, and members of the WHO Department of Medicines Policy and Standards.[52] Examining successful litigation in developing countries, the authors investigate the use of the courts to fortify the circumstances necessary to fulfil the right to health, noting that litigation should not be the mechanism by which to ensure that standards of health are met, but rather 'should preferably be used as a measure of last resort'.[53] In each case the litigation was supported by the ratification of, or accession to, the ICESCR.[54] In addition, almost all recognised the right to health in the national constitution (with the exception of Argentina and India). Notably, the study considered only developing countries and endorses the recognition of the important link between the right to health and development. Furthermore, in conjunction with support from civil society organisations, these cases show the persistent need for individual and public interest litigation in these regions to address

49 UN General Assembly. Report of the Special Rapporteur of the Commission on Human Rights, on the right of everyone to the enjoyment of the highest attainable standard of physical and mental health. 61st Session. 13 September 2006. A/61/338.

50 Ibid., paragraph 39, page 11.

51 Ibid., paragraph 40, page 11.

52 The WHO Department of Medicines Policy and Standards is lead in developing and setting medicines policies, norms and standards as well as contributing to the overriding responsibility to provide information and guidance to Member States and other stakeholders in global health.

53 Hogerzeil HV, Samson M, Casanovas, J, and Rahmaniocora L (2006)'Is Access to Essential Medicines as Part of the Fulfilment of the Right to Health Enforceable through the Courts?' 368 *The Lancet* 22 July: 305 at 311. This article was also considered in the Special Rapporteur's Report to the 61st General Assembly.

54 With the exception of South Africa, which is only a signatory to the ICESCR and has not yet ratified it.

the possibly greater impact of inequities in access with respect to the specific life chances of citizens in developing countries.

Like the Millennium Development Agenda before it, the Sustainable Development Agenda addresses the issue of access to medicines in Target 3.b:

> Support the research and development of vaccines and medicines for the communicable and non-communicable diseases that primarily affect developing countries, provide access to affordable essential medicines and vaccines, in accordance with the Doha Declaration on the TRIPS Agreement and Public Health, which affirms the right of developing countries to use to the full the provisions in the Agreement on Trade-Related Aspects of Intellectual Property Rights regarding flexibilities to protect public health, and, in particular, provide access to medicines for all.

As the implementation of TRIPS, as far as it applies to pharmaceuticals, is not required to be implemented in the least-developed countries until after 2033 the full range of flexibilities will be available in the poorest countries and so it is likely to be more significance, at least in terms of intellectual property, in the developing countries which have progressed further in their development.

Pharmaceutical companies

In 2008, the UN Special Rapporteur published Human Rights Guidelines for Pharmaceutical Companies in relation to Access to Medicines.[55] The guidelines indicate[56] that pharmaceutical companies should respect the right of countries to use the flexibilities in TRIPS, respect the Doha Declaration, not impede those countries who wish to use WTO Decision on Paragraph 6, and not lobby for least-developed countries to comply with WTO rules earlier than the deadline (then 2016, now 2033).[57] The guidelines included some practical requirements, such as suggesting companies consent to the use of their test data in least-developed countries (and so not rely on data exclusivity rights[58]) and, crucially, that companies should issue non-exclusive voluntary licences in low- and middle-income countries to all medicines along with transparency requirements. In addition to guidelines on patents, there was a requirement that companies give a commitment to research and development in relation to neglected diseases[59] and to using differential prices (i.e. drugs cheaper in poor countries and more expensive in richer ones) and the donations of drugs in accordance with the WHO Guidelines for Drug Donation.[60]

55 Included in the Report to the General Assembly (A/63/263).
56 See Guideline 26 to 29.
57 Compulsory licensing, the Paragraph 6 system and other efforts to wards improving access are considered in detail in Part IV: Access.
58 Guideline 30: Discussed in Part IV: Access.
59 Guidelines 23 to 25.
60 Guidelines 33 to 37.

In 2003 Wim Leereveld set up the Access to Medicines Foundation,[61] which is supported by the Dutch Ministry of Foreign Affairs, the Bill & Melinda Gates Foundation, and the UK Department for International Development amongst others. Every two years since 2008, the foundation has monitored and ranked the performance of the 20 leading pharmaceutical companies in terms of their commitment to access to medicines. The ranking looks at seven areas of behaviour: strategy; governance; R&D; pricing; licensing; capacity building; and donations. In 2017, it introduced the Access to Vaccines Index and it is now beginning to consider antibiotic resistance. The leading company in 2016 was GlaxoSmithKline, which had led the index since it began, with Johnson & Johnson, Novartis and Merck following closely behind. These reports provide details of the things that pharmaceutical companies have done, the diseases they are researching and how they are trying to make drugs more accessible. The basic premise being that companies will want to be high up in the index for reputational reasons and this will lead to such companies taking appropriate steps to implement policies compatible with the facilitation of access to medicines.

Declaration of Alma-Ata and the primary healthcare approach

The Declaration of Alma-Ata was agreed at the International Conference on Primary Healthcare, 12 September 1978. The conference was concerned with the urgent need to address public health priorities through the establishment of primary healthcare in countries throughout the world. This Declaration of Alma-Ata is very significant as the first international declaration in primary healthcare and global health. The primary healthcare approach, where efforts are made to resolve health needs at the source of immediate access between practitioners and consumers, is identified as integral to WHO's approach to global public health. For example, the WHO Essential Medicines List (EML)[62] identifies the importance of national expertise and information resources.[63] Similarly, training of local and traditional practitioners, educating local community and capacity-building for local infrastructure are critical aspects of WHO's global strategy.

Consistently with the WHO Constitution and the articulation of the human right to health in the ICESCR, the declaration affirms health as 'a fundamental human right', defining health as 'a state of complete physical, mental and social wellbeing, and not merely the absence of disease or infirmity'. The

61 See www.accesstomedicinefoundation.org

62 For a fuller discussion of the Essential Medicines List (EML) see Chapter 9.

63 WHO (2004) 'Equitable Access to Essential Medicines: A Framework for Collective Action'. Policy Paper. Geneva: WHO. The importance of national medicines policies is also recognised in the Sustainable Development Agenda, *Transforming Our World: The 2030 Agenda for Sustainable Development* (A/RES/70/1),paragraph 26 ('we must achieve universal health coverage and access to quality healthcare').

declaration is significant for its recognition of primary healthcare as a critical mechanism for fulfilling the right to health. Primary healthcare in a country is explained in the declaration as the broad circumstances necessary to fulfil the right to health, including economic, sociocultural and political conditions; the key health issues for that community; education and access to health-related information; related sectors including food, industry, education and communications; community and individual autonomy, self-reliance and participation; the necessary infrastructure for delivery of healthcare; and the health workers themselves.

The concept of primary healthcare articulates the individual's access to opportunities for the broader enjoyment of health and well-being, including participation and education in the public sphere. Indeed, the definition of primary healthcare articulates some of the basic principles underpinning the cohesion and formation of social and cultural identity, indicating the importance of culturally relevant healthcare and cooperation with respected practitioners within the community. This would include collaboration with traditional healers towards the delivery of information on prevention and treatment as well as encouraging the communication between patients and practitioners in public health. The importance of culturally relevant healthcare in securing meaningful access for individuals is informing a number of efforts to collaborate with traditional healers in a conventional healthcare setting.[64] Traditional medicine and culturally relevant primary healthcare will be particularly significant in delivering care that enhances group formation and identity in the face of challenging and disruptive healthcare issues.[65]

Dr Halfdan Mahler, who was WHO Director-General in 1978 at the time of the Declaration of Alma-Ata, attended the 59th WHA in 2006. At this session of

64 For instance, traditional healers in Haiti are being trained to identify HIV/AIDS symptoms and advise on treatment in order to improve delivery of healthcare to HIV/AIDS patients in rural Haiti. In view of the fact that most individuals in the region would consult traditional voodoo healers for advice, the NGO, Promoteurs Objectif Zero Sida (POZ), based in Haiti has launched projects to bridge the cultural and technical divide between traditional medical knowledge and Western medicine. POZ also provides referral cards to the 30 healers trained in treatment and prevention advice. At the time of writing, traditional healers had referred 360 patients to the conventional HIV testing centre and clinic. This collaborative work was recognised at the 2008 XVII International AIDS Conference in Mexico City, where POZ was awarded the UNAIDS/UNDP Red Ribbon Award. This is consistent with the CESCR's General Comment on the implementation of Article 12, where it was considered necessary to introduce special measures to improve the access of indigenous peoples to healthcare, including traditional medical knowledge: CESCR. General Comment No 14, paragraph 27.

65 For instance, see the discussion of traditional medicine and cultural factors underpinning the delivery of HIV/AIDS care in Malawi in Lwanda JL (2002) "Politics, Culture, and Medicine: An Unholy Trinity? Historical Continuities and Ruptures in the HIV/AIDS Story in Malawi" in Kalipeni E, Craddocl S, Oppong J and Ghosh J (eds) *HIV & AIDS in Africa: Beyond Epidemiology*, Malden, MA: Blackwell, 29.

the WHA, Dr Hani Serag of the People's Health Movement (PHM) called for the WHO to reaffirm the principles of the Declaration of Alma-Ata.[66] In 2008, the current Director-General of the WHO, Dr Margaret Chan, advocated a return to the principles of the Declaration of Alma-Ata noting, among other aspects, its emphasis on 'local ownership' of the facilities and benefits of health.[67] This is significant as the emphasis of primary healthcare, in other words general medicine, is frequently at odds with the international programmes addressing particular diseases or epidemics.[68] The power of primary healthcare is that it links 'different sectors and disciplines, integrating different elements of disease management, stressing early prevention, and the maintenance of health'.[69] Critically, it emphasises local and community sovereignty in terms of individual healthcare and, importantly, in terms of the motivations to participate in research (such as participating in the collection of samples in population studies) and to recognise legitimacy in the models for innovation and diffusion of scientific research (particularly in terms of sharing of benefits and data from research projects with participating individuals and communities).[70]

HIV/AIDS and human rights

The issue of HIV/AIDS, including its impact on the rights of individuals as well as the relevance of rights to the campaign against the pandemic, is part of the formal agenda of the Human Rights Council and the OHCHR.

In 1994, the UN Economic and Social Council (ECOSOC) adopted a resolution[71] establishing the Joint United Nations Programme on HIV/AIDS (UNAIDS), which finally launched in January 1996. The programme is co-sponsored by ten UN system organisations, including the WHO, UNESCO, the International Labour Organisation (ILO), and the United Nations Development Programme (UNDP).[72] In 1998, the OHCHR and UNAIDS published the International Guidelines on HIV/AIDS and Human

---

66 WHO (2006) WHO called to return to Alma-Ata Declaration; see further Serag H (2006) 'Addressing Unhealthy Policies'. Presentation to 59th World Health Assembly.

67 Chan M (2008) "Return to Alma-Ata," *The Lancet*, 13 September 2008, 372 (9642), 865–866.

68 See Gilliam S (2008) "Is the Declaration of Alma Ata Still Relevant to Primary Healthcare?" *British Medical Journal*, 336 (536).

69 See Gilliam, "Is the declaration of Alma Ata still relevant to primary healthcare?", 536 at 538.

70 For instance, see the discussion of the MalariaGEN project in Chapter 7.

71 UN General Assembly. Resolution 1994/24 on the Joint and co-sponsored United Nations programme on the human immunodeficiency virus/acquired immuno-deficiency syndrome (HIV/AIDS). E/1994/L.18/Rev.1. 26 July 1994.

72 The collaborating organisations are the WHO, UNESCO, the UN High Commissioner for Refugees (UNHCR), the UN Children's Fund (UNICEF), the World Food Programme (WFP), the UN Development Programme (UNDP), the UN Population Fund (UNFPA), the UN Office on Drugs and

Rights[73] to assist states with the development and implementation of effective and relevant national responses to the HIV/AIDS pandemic. Guideline 6 deals specifically with access to medicines, services and information, including antiretroviral medicines and was revised in 2002 following a Third International Consultation in 2002:

> **GUIDELINE 6 (as revised in 2002):** States should enact legislation to provide for the regulation of HIV-related goods, services and information, so as to ensure widespread availability of quality prevention measures and services, adequate HIV prevention and care information, and safe and effective medication at an affordable price.
>
> States should also take measures necessary to ensure for all persons, on a sustained and equal basis, the availability and accessibility of quality goods, services and information for HIV prevention, treatment, care and support, including antiretroviral and other safe and effective medicines, diagnostics and related technologies for preventive, curative and palliative care of HIV and related opportunistic infections and conditions.
>
> States should take such measures at both the domestic and international levels, with particular attention to vulnerable individuals and populations.[74]

The recommendation for implementation of Guideline 6 calls for states to enact legislation to strengthen access and affordability of prevention measures, medicines and services. Recommendations for implementation include the need for attention to the social, economic, cultural, political and legal factors affecting access: 'States should review and, where necessary, amend or adopt laws, policies, programmes and plans to realize universal and equal access to medicines, diagnostics and related technologies, taking these factors into account.'[75] Further, the guidelines recommend that states allocate funds to the promotion and protection of sustainable access to affordable medicines and treatment, including the possibility of contributions to the Global Fund to Fight AIDS, Tuberculosis and Malaria (GFATM)[76] or similar mechanisms.

Crime (UNODC), the International Labour Organisation (ILO) and the World Bank.

73 OHCHR/UNAIDS (2006). International Guidelines on HIV/AIDS and Human Rights. The Guidelines were revised slightly in 2002 to account for a revision of Guideline 6 and consolidated in 2006. All references are to the consolidated 2006 version.

74 Ibid., 18.

75 Ibid., 39 (paragraph 29).

76 The GFATM is public–private partnership between governments, the private sector, civil society and affected communities. It is a financial instrument concerned solely with the attraction, management and distribution of funds for programmes to address HIV/AIDS. In this way, it is a purely fiscal organ as distinct from developing programmes in its own right.

The implementation recommendations also acknowledge that flexibilities in intellectual property frameworks, such as provisions for compulsory licensing of essential medicines, provision of market exclusivity periods, monopoly periods and patentability thresholds are often at stake in bilateral and regional trading agreements: 'States should, in light of their human rights obligations, ensure that bilateral, regional and international agreements, such as those dealing with intellectual property, do not impede access to HIV prevention, treatment, care and support, including access to antiretroviral and other medicines, diagnostics and related technologies.'[77]

Free trade agreements (FTA) may override flexibilities available regarding access as well as oblige contracting parties to offer higher standards of protection than those set out in TRIPS.[78] By virtue of the most-favoured nation principle of TRIPS,[79] which prohibits discrimination between nationals, those same advantages must be extended to all other members trading within that jurisdiction. In other words, the principle of most-favoured nation will oblige the contracting party to an FTA to offer the same trade advantages to all other member countries of the WTO. In this way, free trade agreements undermine the multilateralism of human rights through the private contractual development of 'international' intellectual property laws.

In June 2001, the UN General Assembly staged the first Special Session (UNGASS) on HIV/AIDS . At this first UNGASS, the 189 Member States unanimously adopted the Declaration of Commitment on HIV/AIDS.[80] The Declaration of Commitment on HIV/AIDS recognises the human rights of all persons living with HIV/AIDS and, in particular, Paragraph 58 calls for the elimination of discrimination in ensuring access to, inter alia, healthcare, prevention, support and treatment. The declaration also includes the recommendation for international cooperation between states and with NGOs and other partners on the monitoring of the pricing of medicines and the exploration of mechanisms to improve equitable access to essential medicines.[81]

At the 2006 High Level Meeting on AIDS of the UN General Assembly, member states adopted unanimously the Political Declaration on HIV/AIDS.[82] The political declaration reaffirms access to medicines as a central element to the fulfilment of the right to health: 'access to medication in

77 OHCHR/UNAIDS, International Guidelines on HIV/AIDS, 48 (paragraph 52).
78 For instance, see the discussion in O'Hearn D & McCloskey S (2008) "Globalisation and Pharmaceuticals: Where is the Power? Where to Resist?" in O'Donovan O & Glavanis-Grantham K (eds) *Power, Politics and Pharmaceuticals*, Cork: Cork University Press 9 at 23–25. For example, see the provisions for data exclusivity protection mandated in the US–Chile Free Trade Agreement (Chapter 17: Article 17.10) and the US–Dominican Republic Central America Free Trade Agreement (DR-CAFTA) (Chapter 15: Article 15.10).
79 Article 4 of TRIPS.
80 UNGASS. Declaration of Commitment on HIV/AIDS. 25–27 June 2001.
81 Ibid., paragraph 103.
82 UN General Assembly. Resolution 20/262. Political Declaration on HIV/AIDS. 60th Session. 15 June 2006.

the context of pandemics, such as HIV/AIDS, is one of the fundamental elements to achieve progressively the full realization of the right of everyone to the enjoyment of the highest attainable standard of physical and mental health'.[83] Further, the political declaration declares the need to 'do everything necessary to ensure access to life-saving drugs and prevention tools'.[84]

At subsequent meetings, more ambitious declarations were adopted. In 2011, the General Assembly adopted the political declaration on HIV/AIDS: 'Intensifying our Efforts to Eliminate HIV/AIDS'[85] which identified 'that discontinued treatment is a threat to treatment efficacy, and that the sustainability of providing life-long HIV treatment is threatened by factors such as poverty, lack of access to treatment and insufficient and unpredictable funding'[86] and the 'pivotal role of research'[87] in HIV prevention and treatment.

In 2016, a political declaration on HIV and AIDS: 'On the Fast Track to Accelerating the Fight against HIV and to Ending the AIDS Epidemic by 2030' was adopted.[88] Like earlier such declarations it re-affirms previous declarations in 2001, 2006 and 2011[89] and links itself to the Agenda for Sustainable Development with its target of ending the AIDS epidemic by 2030, stating 'health is a precondition for and an outcome and indicator of all three dimensions of sustainable development, and that sustainable development can be achieved only in the absence of a high prevalence of debilitating communicable and non-communicable diseases, including emerging and re-emerging diseases'.[90]

The response to AIDS in the 2016 declaration demonstrates outstanding global solidarity and shared responsibility[91] and sets targets that by 2020 fewer than 500,000 people per year will die from AIDS-related causes and there will be fewer than half a million new infections each year.[92] There were also agreements to increase funding for the AIDS response[93]

Importantly, the political declarations since 2006 have all made specific provision for the relationship between the right to public health and TRIPS. The 2016 declaration recognises the importance of affordable medicines and states that the TRIPS Agreement 'should be interpreted and implemented in a manner supportive of the right of Member States to protect public health and,

83 Ibid., paragraph 12.
84 Ibid., paragraph 15.
85 UN General Assembly: Resolution 65/277. Political Declaration on HIV/AIDS: Intensifying our Efforts to Eliminate HIV/AIDS, 10 June 2011
86 Ibid., paragraph 33.
87 Ibid., paragraph 34.
88 UN General Assembly: Resolution 70/266. Political Declaration on HIV and AIDS: On the Fast Track to Accelerating the Fight against HIV and to Ending the AIDS Epidemic by 2030, 8 June 2016.
89 Ibid. paragraph 2.
90 Ibid., paragraph 12.
91 Ibid., paragraph 31.
92 Ibid., paragraph 56.
93 Ibid., paragraph 59.

in particular, to promote access to medicines for all'.[94] In a paragraph dealing with removing obstacles for developing countries to provide affordable HIV prevention, the declaration reiterates, as has become routine in international statements relating to access to medicines, that 'the use, to the full, of existing flexibilities under [TRIPS] is specifically geared to promoting access to and trade in medicines, and, while recognizing the importance of the intellectual property rights regime in contributing to a more effective AIDS response, ensure that intellectual property rights provisions in trade agreements do not undermine these existing flexibilities'.[95]

The 2016 political declaration also addresses the economic framework for innovation and affordable access to the extent that it calls for greater public–private partnerships towards technology transfer[96] as well as the bilateral, regional and international cooperation on pooled procurement programmes.[97] If progress towards greater access is to be fortified, this indicates the importance of the respect for the 'moral' framework within intellectual property itself and the translation of human rights obligations within the moral logic of the system.

One such innovation in access recognised by the 2016 political declaration is the International Drug Purchase Facility (UNITAID). UNITAID is a mechanism hosted within the WHO intended to fulfil a sustainable demand for drugs, thus influencing the market itself, leading to increased supply and availability and ultimately cheaper prices. Section 1 of the UNITAID Constitution declares its mission 'to contribute to scale up access to treatment for HIV/AIDS, malaria and tuberculosis for the people in developing countries by leveraging price reductions of quality drugs and diagnostics, which currently are unaffordable for most developing countries, and to accelerate the pace at which they are made available'.[98] The UNITAID business model is to 'use strategic approaches (such as purchasing power and negotiation) in order to continuously reduce the prices of products to the lowest sustainable level in developing countries'.[99] Under its eligibility criteria, all developing countries should be granted access to the favourable pricing terms thus negotiated.[100]

The issue of transmission of HIV/AIDS is important as it points to the broader context in which the human right to health is facilitated. That is, the underlying social and cultural determinants will be material to the

94 Ibid., paragraph 60(j).
95 Ibid., paragraph 60(l)(i).
96 Ibid., paragraph 46.
97 Pooled or bulk procurement programmes are considered further in Part IV: Access.
98 UNITAID Constitution. Adopted the UNITAID Executive Board, 6 July 2011: Section 1.
99 Ibid., Section 3.
100 UNITAID Constitution. Endorsed by the UNITAID Executive Board, 9 May 2007: Section 5.

full realisation of the right, including accessibility of information and the acceptability of the delivery of education in prevention. Furthermore, it indicates the significance of commercial and political considerations in determining the success of programmes in health and human rights and the performance of the right in a cultural context.

Access to information and the right to participate in the benefits of scientific research and progress will be instrumental in the achievement of high standards of health. This is important in terms of the goods available to individuals, including access to quality medicines. But it is also critical that individuals have access to adequate information delivered in a culturally relevant and meaningful context. Indeed, the significant relationship between development, poverty and health is crucial to understand in the broader context for health, including the right to development and the right to cultural life. The relationship between the cultural life of scientific research and progress and the human right to health is arguably fundamental. Furthermore, the delivery of the right to development rests upon cultural participation and health as essential components of development itself. For these reasons, it is not mere related to but rather critical to the characterisation of the right to health to examine the relationship with development and culture.

4 Health, development, culture

Introduction

The right to health, being a broad inclusive right to the circumstances necessary for physical as well as social and mental well-being, is fulfilled where there is meaningful access and availability to healthcare goods and services.[1] The previous chapter examined the way in which the full realisation of the right to health includes fulfilment of the underlying cultural, social and political determinants relevant to health. Further, the broader right to health is linked to programmes in development, with the fulfilment of the right to health directly implicated in socio-economic development. This necessarily invites consideration of human rights to development and culture in the context of medicine and public health, and the operation of these rights on the framework of intellectual property.

Health and the right to development

The Declaration on the Right to Development

The UN General Assembly adopted the Declaration on the Right to Development, by Resolution 41/128, in its 41st Session, 1986.[2] Article 1.1 declares the right to development to be an inalienable human right:

> The right to development is an inalienable human right by virtue of which every human person and all peoples are entitled to participate in, contribute to, and enjoy economic, social, cultural and political development, in which all human rights and fundamental freedoms can be fully realized.[3]

1 ICESCR Article 12; CESCR. General Comment No 14 (2000). The right to the highest attainable standard of health (Article 12 of the International Covenant on Economic, Social and Cultural Rights. 22nd Session. E/C.12/2000/4. 11 August 2000.

2 UN General Assembly. Resolution 41/128 Declaration on the Right to Development. A/RES/41/128. 4 December 1986.

3 UN General Assembly. Resolution 41/128, paragraph 1.1.

This character of the right to development is articulated with respect to health in Article 8. Article 8.1 provides for health as one of the underlying determinants for the full realisation of the right to development:

> States should undertake, at the national level, all necessary measures for the realization of the right to development and shall ensure, inter alia, equality of opportunity for all in their access to basic resources, education, health services, food, housing, employment and the fair distribution of income.[4]

In effect, the fulfilment of the right to development necessarily addresses the life chances of all citizens and provides for opportunities for all individuals to these fundamental human rights. As such, the declaration also provides that the right to development necessarily supports the right to self-determination in Article 1.2, including the right to sovereignty over genetic resources:

> The human right to development also implies the full realization of the right of peoples to self-determination, which includes, subject to the relevant provisions of both International Covenants on Human Rights, the exercise of their inalienable right to full sovereignty over all the natural wealth and resources.

Importantly, beyond the primary nature attributed to the value of property in democratic systems, the right to development and its implication of the right of self-determination articulate democracy upon principles of the collective. This is significant not only for human rights discourse but also for the social and political dimension of individual human rights as safeguarding the individual's opportunities to participate in the public sphere: 'States should encourage popular participation in all spheres as an important factor in development and in the full realization of all human rights.'[5]

This resonates with earlier examinations of the importance of the individual's life chances and access to the public sphere. Habermas emphasises the communicative value of the law and the legitimating force of addressing the circumstances for that social cohesion. In other words, in addressing not only access, in terms of availability, but also use in terms of genuine participation, 'governmental authority derives from the power produced communicatively in the civic practice of self-determination, and it finds its legitimation in the fact that it protects this practice by institutionalizing public liberty'.[6] The right to development articulates this 'use' of the public sphere as an inalienable human right and characterises the value of the fulfilment of that right to the social collective:

4 UN General Assembly. Resolution 41/128, paragraph 8.1
5 UN General Assembly. Resolution 41/128, paragraph 8.2
6 Habermas J (1997/[1992]) *Between Facts and Norms: Contributions to a Discourse Theory of Law and Democracy*, Rehg W (trans), Cambridge: Polity Press, 270.

> [D]evelopment is a comprehensive economic, social, cultural and political process, which aims at the constant improvement of the well-being of the entire population and of all individuals on the basis of their active, free and meaningful participation in development and in the fair distribution of benefits resulting therefrom ... everyone is entitled to a social and international order in which the rights and freedoms set forth in that Declaration can be fully realized.[7]

The Vienna Declaration and Programme of Action

In 1993, the World Conference on Human Rights considered the right to development at length and adopted by consensus of the 171 member states the Vienna Declaration and Programme of Action.[8] Paragraph 10 of the declaration 'reaffirms the right to development, as established in the Declaration on the Right to Development, as a universal and inalienable right and an integral part of fundamental human rights'.[9] Indeed, the right to development is inextricably and necessarily implicated in the realisation of fundamental human rights,[10] including the human right to health[11] and freedoms and entitlements contained within that human right. This includes access to benefits of scientific research and development as part of the meaningful fulfilment of the right to development, arguably incorporating access to medicinal products. Paragraph 11 provides that:

> Everyone has the right to enjoy the benefits of scientific progress and its applications. The World Conference on Human Rights notes that certain advances, notably in the biomedical and life sciences as well as in information technology, may have potentially adverse consequences for the integrity, dignity and human rights of the individual, and calls for international cooperation to ensure that human rights and dignity are fully respected in this area of universal concern.[12]

---

7 UN General Assembly. Resolution 41/128, Preamble. See further paragraph 2.

8 World Conference on Human Rights. Vienna Declaration and Programme of Action. A/CONF.157/23. 12 July 1993.

9 World Conference on Human Rights, paragraph 10. See further paragraph 72 which declares that the right, as established in the Declaration on the Right to Development, must be implemented and realised. Further, the Declaration recommends the participation of civil society and NGOs in normative developments and cooperation with State Actors (paragraph 38; paragraph 73) and notes the necessary cooperation between actors in the field of development (Part C), compatible with the principles of cooperation for achievement of the MDGs. The relevance of civil society activity is considered further in Part IV: Access.

10 World Conference on Human Rights, paragraph 74.

11 World Conference on Human Rights, paragraph 31.

12 World Conference on Human Rights, paragraph 11.

The Vienna Declaration reaffirms the right of self-determination of all peoples in Paragraph 2 and explains its basis for the free pursuit of economic, social and cultural development.[13] This is related to Paragraph 20, which calls for the facilitation of indigenous peoples' full social, political and cultural participation:

> The World Conference on Human Rights recognizes the inherent dignity and the unique contribution of indigenous people to the development and plurality of society and strongly reaffirms the commitment of the international community to their economic, social and cultural well-being and their enjoyment of the fruits of sustainable development. States should ensure the full and free participation of indigenous people in all aspects of society, in particular in matters of concern to them.

Again, the link between development and access to the public sphere is instrumental and fundamental to the full realisation of human rights, with self-determination being a critical mechanism through which to achieve development. The Vienna Declaration 'recommends that priority be given to national and international action to promote democracy, development and human rights'[14] and thus 'reaffirms that the universal and inalienable right to development, as established in the Declaration on the Right to Development, must be implemented and realized'.[15]

Implementation of the right to development

The Intergovernmental Working Group on Development was established by the Commission on Human Rights by Resolution 1998/72[16] and ECOSOC Decision 1998/269[17] to monitor and review progress on the implementation of the right to development at national and international levels. Its first session was held in 2000 and it has held them annually ever since. A high-level task force was created pursuant to Resolution 2004/7 of the Commission on Human Rights to assist the working group in fulfilling its mandate by providing expertise and making appropriate recommendations to implement to right to development.

The high-level task force started its work in 2004 and its mandate ended in 2010, over which time there were six sessions. Its original mandate was to examine two aspects of implementation: obstacles and challenges to the Millennium Development Goals (MDGs).[18] It narrowed its work to consider

13 World Conference on Human Rights, paragraph 2.
14 World Conference on Human Rights, paragraph 66.
15 World Conference on Human Rights, paragraph 72.
16 Commission on Human Rights. Resolution 1998/72. The Right to Development.
17 ECOSOC. Decision 1998/269. The Right to Development.
18 See the discussion of the Millennium Development Goals (MDGs) and the targets defined within the eight MDGs in Chapter 3.

in detail MDG Goal 8 (develop a global partnership for development) and in particular Target 17 (access to affordable essential drugs in developing countries) which comes within the global partnership goal.[19] Part 3 of its Consolidated Findings relate to access to essential medicines and in particular, the findings were:

> the reference in the strategy and plan to the constitutional commitment of the World Health Organization (WHO) to the right to health ... It was noted with concern that the strategy and plan do not caution against adoption of Trade-Related Aspects of Intellectual Property Rights (TRIPS)-plus protection in bilateral trade agreements, or refer to the impact of bilateral or regional trade agreements on access to medicines. Nevertheless, these documents contain elements of accessibility, affordability and quality of medicines in developing countries, corresponding to the normative content of the right to health. ... States parties should ensure that their legal or other regimes protecting intellectual property do not impede their ability to comply with their core obligations under the rights to food, health and education ... Regarding the role of the pharmaceutical industry, the task force and WHO saw the potential of exploring with stakeholders the Human Rights Guidelines for Pharmaceutical Companies in relation to Access to Medicines and the right to health.[20]

The task force made additional findings in relation to the Special Programme for Research and Training in Tropical Diseases, where it suggested its rights-based approach was empowering for developing countries, albeit transparency and accountability needed to be improved.[21] Its findings on the Global Fund to Fight AIDS, Tuberculosis and Malaria were that it was consistent with the development principles although it did not take a rights-based approach.[22] The work of the high-level task force was considered by twelfth session of the intergovernmental working group. There were suggestions from some countries that future work should involve civil society and the private sector.[23] Others suggested the task force did not take adequate account of international perspectives and trade rules.[24] The EU suggested that only states can move

19 A full list of the goals and the targets comprising each goal in the Annex to the road map towards the implementation of the United Nations Millennium Declaration, UN General Assembly, 56th Session, 6 September 2001 (A/56/326).

20 Consolidation of findings of the high-level task force on the implementation of the right to development, 25 March 2010 (A/HRC/15/WG.2/TF/2/Add.1), paragraph 45.

21 Consolidation of findings of the high-level task force, paragraph 48.

22 Consolidation of findings of the high-level task force, paragraph 51.

23 Report of the Open-ended Working Group on the Right to Development on its twelfth session (14–18 November 2011) (19 December 2011), paragraph 22.

24 Report of the Open-ended Working Group, paragraph 20.

the right to development from commitment to development practice.[25] Over subsequent sessions, aspects of the high-level task force's findings have been considered by the working group as it works toward the development of the draft right to development criteria on the implementation of the right to development.

The WHO Intergovernmental Working Group on Public Health, Innovation and Intellectual Property

The WHO Intergovernmental Working Group on Public Health, Innovation and Intellectual Property (IGWG) was established in 2006 by resolution WHA 59.24[26] at the 59th World Health Assembly (WHA) of the WHO. The IGWG was given a mandate to develop and prepare a global strategy and work programme, with particular regard to the special issues for developing countries.

Following the report of the IGWG, at the 61st WHA in 2008 the meeting adopted the Global Strategy and Plan of Action by resolution,[27] reaffirming the right to health as a fundamental right and prioritising the importance of addressing the health needs of developing countries in the research and development agenda of developed countries. Furthermore, the promotion of research and development is understood to include not only support to governments in the development of national programmes, but also the promotion of accessibility to research benefits in order to build capacity and innovation in developing countries. Mechanisms by which to achieve this advocated in the global strategy include open-source methods and the identification of incentives and barriers to research and development, including intellectual property.[28] Access to knowledge and technology is emphasised throughout the strategy and includes mechanisms both within the intellectual property system (such as patent pools[29]) and through competition to improve availability and accessibility of products.

In establishing the IGWG, Resolution WHA 59.24 emphasises critical issues in global health in the context of the freedom to participate in the cultural life of the community and characterises the broader context in which

25 Report of the Open-ended Working Group, paragraph 21.

26 WHA. Resolution WHA59.24. Public health, innovation, essential health research and intellectual property rights: towards a global strategy and plan of action. 27 May 2006.

27 WHA. Resolution WHA61.21. Global strategy and plan of action on public health, innovation and intellectual property. 24 May 2008: Element 1.

28 Element 2 of the Global Strategy and Plan of Action includes 'promoting upstream research and product development in developing countries' a component of which includes the support of scientific research capacity and discovery including, 'where feasible and appropriate, voluntary open-source methods'. See Global Strategy and Plan of Action on Public Health, Innovation and Intellectual Property, adopted at the 59th Session of the World Health Assembly by Resolution WHA61.21, 24 May 2008.

29 Considered further in Chapter 8.

the right to health is realised, also reflected in the global strategy ultimately adopted by the WHA. This broader context includes concerns related to pricing and access to medicines and the need for new models and initiatives to encourage and promote innovation. This is an important articulation of the interaction between various human rights and the critical question of social, cultural and political access.[30] In this context, the resolution links questions of access and public health to the underlying determinants for public health, including the commercial environment in that the WHA urges member states:

1. to make global health and medicines a priority sector, to take determined action to emphasize priorities in research and development addressed to the needs of patients, especially those in resource-poor settings, and to harness collaborative research and development initiatives involving disease-endemic countries;
2. to consider the recommendations of the report and to contribute actively to the development of a global strategy and plan of action, and to take an active part, working with the Secretariat and international partners, in providing support for essential medical research and development;
3. to work to ensure that progress in basic science and biomedicine is translated into improved, safe and affordable health products – drugs, vaccines and diagnostics – to respond to all patients' and clients' needs, especially those living in poverty, taking into account the critical role of gender, and to ensure that capacity is strengthened to support rapid delivery of essential medicines to people;
4. to encourage trade agreements to take into account the flexibilities contained in the Agreement on Trade-Related Aspects of Intellectual Property Rights and recognized by the Doha Ministerial Declaration on the TRIPS Agreement and Public Health ...[31]

The holistic approach to human rights advocated throughout the documents on development indicates that the right to culture should be considered in the context of intellectual property and health. Indeed, it is through the interrogation of human rights frameworks that the cultural life of patents is becoming particularly clear.

The impact of the right to development

The right to development led to an agreement between the European Economic Community (now EU) and the African, Caribbean and Pacific countries known as the EEC–ACP Lomé Convention. This convention

30 WHA. Resolution WHA59.24, Preamble.
31 WHA. Resolution WHA59.24, paragraph 2.

ran from 1974 to 2000 and specifically adopted human rights norms. This convention was, however, the exception as Tahmina Karimova explains:

> The right to development rarely informs mainstream developments or human rights NGOs and remains entirely outside of development thinking. Its role, rather, has been confined to platitudinous wording in the declarations, action plans and other outcome documents adopted in the framework of financing for developing countries.[32]

Others, have suggested that the right to development adds little value to other human rights norms and so could be dissolved into them without any substantial effect on state or other practice.[33] While its practical significant may be limited it remains a powerful rhetorical device.

Health and the right to culture

Arguably the right to culture has been somewhat overlooked in the context of its role in relation to the right to health. Although it is thought of as relevant, in the context of rights to health and access to medicines, it has been suggested as ancillary to the right to health.[34] However, arguably its relevance in this area is much more significant and indeed it is an interpretive framework for the right to health itself. Article 15 of the ICESCR provides for right to culture, broadly speaking:

> 1. The States Parties to the present Covenant recognize the right of everyone:
>   a. To take part in cultural life;
>   b. To enjoy the benefits of scientific progress and its applications;
>   c. To benefit from the protection of the moral and material interests resulting from any scientific, literary or artistic production of which he is the author.
> 2. The steps to be taken by the States Parties to the present Covenant to achieve the full realization of this right shall include those necessary for the conservation, the development and the diffusion of science and culture.
> 3. The States Parties to the present Covenant undertake to respect the freedom indispensable for scientific research and creativity activity.

---

32 Karimova, T (2016) *Human Rights and Development in International Law*, London: Routledge, 113.

33 See Vandenbogaerde A (2013) 'The Right to Development in International Human Rights Law: A Call for its Dissolution' 31(2) *Netherlands Quarterly of Human Rights*, 209.

34 For instance, see the discussion in Hestermeyer H (2007) *Human Rights and the WTO: The Case of Patents and Access to Medicines*, Oxford: Oxford University Press, 112.

4. The States Parties to the present Covenant recognize the benefits to be derived from the encouragement and development of international contacts and co-operation in the scientific and cultural fields.[35]

The text of Article 15 has been considered in detail with respect to the right to benefit from one's creative output (largely interpreted as being facilitated through the mechanism of intellectual property rights). Nevertheless, the broader entitlements and freedoms within this right are importantly relevant to providing for equal opportunities for all citizens to take part in cultural life[36] and enjoy the benefits of scientific progress,[37] regardless of individual life chances. Significantly, this would indicate the right to access the benefits of medical research and development, including medicines. Further, it would also indicate the need for attention to possible obstacles to incentives to scientific research that may be posed by excessive intrusion of intellectual property monopolies.[38]

Equality of access

On the greater relevance of Article 15 to the right to health, the General Comment No 16 on the implementation of Article 3[39] is important. Article 3 concerns equality of access for men and women to economic, social and cultural rights:

> The States Parties to the present Covenant undertake to ensure the equal right of men and women to the enjoyment of all economic, social and cultural rights set forth in the present Covenant.[40]

The significance of this right is that it is a "non-derogable standard for compliance with the obligations of States parties as set out in Articles 6 through 15 of ICESCR"[41] and is of particular relevance to the access to healthcare and information in many developing countries. Further, the General Comment's approach to the eradication of discrimination and the promotion of equality of opportunities for all individuals to access economic, social and cultural rights is important. In particular, it takes account of

35 ICESCR, Article 15.
36 Article 15.1(a).
37 Article 15.1(b).
38 For instance, consider the specific nature of patents for gene-related inventions, where the classical interpretation of patent protection may preclude further commercialisation of products for other uses based on the same gene sequence, and the relevance of purpose-bound protection in these areas. See the discussion in Chapters 2 and 6.
39 CESCR. General Comment No 16 (2005). The equal right of men and women to the enjoyment of all economic, social and cultural rights (art 3 of the International Covenant on Economic, Social and Cultural Rights). E/C.12/2005/4. 11 August 2005.
40 ICESCR, Article 3.
41 CESCR. General Comment No 16 (2005), paragraph 17.

discrimination both within the law and in a broader social context, citing failure to address the total context for the realisation of economic, social and cultural rights being a violation of those rights:

> The principle of equality between men and women is fundamental to the enjoyment of each of the specific rights enumerated in the Covenant. Failure to ensure formal and substantive equality in the enjoyment of any of these rights constitutes a violation of that rights. Elimination of de jure as well as de facto discrimination is required for the equal enjoyment of economic, social and cultural rights. Failure to adopt, implement and monitor effects of laws, policies and programmes to eliminate de jure and de facto discrimination with respect to each of the rights enumerated in rights 6 to 15 of the Covenant constitutions a violation of those rights.[42]

Health as culture

In May 2008, during its 40th Session, the CESCR organised a Day of General Discussion (DGD) on the right to take part in cultural life (Article 15.1(a)). A DGD is a public meeting open to international UN institutions, governments, intergovernmental organisations and NGOs and civil society. The meeting on Article 15.1(a) structured discussions around four themes: the definition of cultural life within the human rights framework; analysing the right to cultural life itself and access to that right; exploring and identifying the interaction between the right to cultural life and other universal human rights; and the individual and collective character of the right. The last theme is particularly relevant in the context of discussions throughout this book of the need to interpret the full realisation of human rights through participation in the public sphere as an important aspect of the social formation of human collectives. In a background paper to the DGD, Elissavet Stamtopoulou, Secretariat of the Permanent Forum on Indigenous Issues (PFII) welcomed the DGD, describing the right to participate as a neglected human right.[43]

Contributions by participants explicitly explored the link between the right to cultural life and the right to health. The International Commission of Jurists argued that health is in fact an aspect of cultural life, acknowledging the importance of cultural acceptability and relevance in the implementation and realisation of human rights throughout the work of the CESCR:

> The right to participate in cultural life is closely connected with many other human rights. Some other human rights are particularly significant for the right to participate in cultural life ... However, the exercise of many

42 CESCR. General Comment No 16 (2005), paragraph 41.

43 Stamatopoulou E (2008). 'The Right to Take Part in Cultural Life'. Background paper. Day of General Discussion on the right to take part in cultural life (article 15(1)(a) of the Covenant). E/C.12/40/9. 9 May 2008: page 2.

> other human rights also entails cultural components, relevant to assess the enjoyment of the right to take part in cultural life. The Committee on Economic, Social and Cultural Rights has adequately captured this concept in several of its General Comments referred to specific economic and social rights, through the notion of 'acceptability,' 'cultural adequacy' or 'cultural appropriateness.' The Committee has employed this notion to define the normative requirements of other rights set forth by the International Covenant on Economic, Social and Cultural Rights (ICESCR) – such as the right to adequate house, the right to adequate food, the right to the highest attainable standard of health and the right to water. This, in turn, implies that *food, housing, health and water can be, inter alia, significant components of cultural life.*[44]

Indeed, towards achieving accessibility to the right, Article 15.1(a) should be interpreted with respect for cultural relevance and acceptability. Recalling that this principle of culturally relevant implementation has been recited throughout the CESCR's general comments on the ICESCR, it seems clear that the effective implementation of all the provisions of Article 15 will take heed of this requirement. In the context of traditional medical knowledge, the right to cultural life is significant not only in terms of access to participate and practice traditional knowledge, but also in terms of achieving relevant protection for the holders of that knowledge, pursuant to Article 15.1(c).

Traditional and indigenous medical knowledge

Traditional medicine is a particularly significant public health resource for many communities and regions in the world.[45] With respect to medical research and public health, both the transfer of traditional medical knowledge in research and development as well as its cultural and social relevance to adequate healthcare in many regions raise the issue of the right to culture as it interacts with health.

Current intergovernmental discussions towards the equitable management and benefit sharing of traditional knowledge and genetic resources are immediately relevant to health and access to medicines in the community concerned.[46] In particular, the critical social and cultural dimension to medicine and medical practice in many indigenous and traditional communities is

44 International Commission of Jurists (2008). Background Paper. Day of General Discussion on the right to take part in cultural life (article 15(1)(a) of the Covenant). E/C.12/40/9. 9 May 2008: page 2. Emphasis added.

45 WHO. Fact Sheet no. 134. Traditional Medicine.

46 In particular, see the documents of the WIPO Intergovernmental Committee in Intellectual Property and Genetic Resources, Traditional Knowledge and Folklore. For a full discussion of the cultural and legal conflicts between traditional knowledge and intellectual property frameworks, the work of WIPO and international initiatives towards protection, see Gibson J (2005) *Community*

significant to delivering culturally relevant and effective healthcare (such as through collaborations between western and traditional practitioners) as well as fulfilling the cultural participation of the groups involved. Furthermore, the potential research and commercial value in genetic resources and associated traditional knowledge indicates the importance of developmental concerns in conjunction with the expropriation of knowledge through the possible creation of intellectual property rights in products derived from that knowledge.

From these discussions, a broader understanding of the importance of cultural specificity and relevance in delivering healthcare will offer insight into the efficacy of primary healthcare. Indeed, sharing of benefits, delivery of public healthcare and access to medicines in traditional and indigenous communities directly implicates the importance of culture to medicine and medical systems. As well as the question of access to medicines in broader populations in developing countries, associated prevention and treatment must be prepared and available within a respected and trusted infrastructure, which includes cooperation with traditional healers. The WHO Traditional Medicine Strategy 2002–2005 outlined its main objectives with respect to traditional medicine, including the integration of traditional medicine in national health systems,[47] implementation of international standards and clinical guidelines and the facilitation of knowledge transfer.[48] Its more recent Traditional Medicine Strategy 2014–2023 aims to support countries by harnessing the potential contribution of traditional medicines to health, wellness and people-centred healthcare as well as promoting the safe and effective use of such medicine by regulating, research and integrating traditional medicine into health systems where appropriate.

As discussed in this and the previous chapter, the right to public health arguably incorporates cultural identity as part of 'a state of complete physical, mental and social wellbeing'. Indeed, health is a component of cultural life. Traditional medicine is extremely important to the social, cultural and economic circumstances of many countries and it is often the only affordable treatment available to poor people or remote communities. According to the WHO, up to 8 per cent of the population in developing countries depends upon traditional medicines; the global market for herbal medicines is more than USD 60 billion annually in 2003[49] and Chinese materia medica was valued at USD 83.1 billion in 2012.[50] Traditional knowledge of the medicinal value of plants has also informed

Resources: Intellectual Property, International Trade and Protection of Traditional Knowledge, Aldershot: Ashgate.

47 As discussed in the previous chapter, traditional medicine is also an important aspect of the full realisation of Article 12 of the ICESCR. See CESCR. General Comment No 14 (2000). The right to the highest attainable standard of health (article 12 of the International Covenant on Economic, Social and Cultural Rights. 22nd Session. E/C.12/2000/4. 11 August 2000: paragraph 27.

48 WHO traditional medicine strategy 2002–2005.

49 WHO Fact Sheet no. 134. Traditional Medicine (2003).

50 WHO Traditional Medicine Strategy 2014–2023, paragraph 3.1.1.

research for modern medicine. Indeed, the use of traditional knowledge in this way has been the subject of concerns over biopiracy and calls for access and benefit-sharing for communities contributing the critical starting material.[51]

Protection for traditional knowledge is currently being discussed within the WIPO Intergovernmental Committee on Intellectual Property and Genetic Resources, Traditional Knowledge and Folklore (IGC). However, at present there is no internationally agreed definition or framework for traditional knowledge. While much work has been done, it can be seen from the Draft Articles for the Protection of Traditional Knowledge promulgated in 2014[52] that there is still disagreement as to the potential beneficiaries. In the section, "Policy Objectives," it states:

> This instrument should aim to:
>
> Provide Indigenous [Peoples] and [local communities] [and nations]/[beneficiaries] with the [legal and practical/appropriate] means, [including effective and accessible enforcement measures/sanctions, remedies and exercise of rights]...

As can be seen, while it is agreed it should benefit indigenous peoples, there is less certainty whether it should benefit local communities or nations or both. This uncertainty is continued in the definition of traditional knowledge:

> Traditional knowledge [refers to]/[includes]/[means], for the purposes of this instrument, knowhow, skills, innovations, practices, teachings and learnings of [indigenous [peoples] and [local communities]]/[or a state or states].
>
> [Traditional knowledge may be associated, in particular, with fields such as agriculture, the environment, healthcare and indigenous and traditional medical knowledge, biodiversity, traditional lifestyles and natural resources and genetic resources, and know-how of traditional architecture and construction technologies.]

As a result of this continuing lack of an internationally agreed definition, any reference to traditional knowledge in free trade agreements could have the effect of defining the concept within such agreements without international consensus on that definition and its application.[53] As a result,

51 See further the discussion of starting-material and a beneficial interest in the invention in Chapter 7.

52 WIPO (2014), *The Protection of Traditional Knowledge: Draft Articles* (WIPO/GRTKF/IC/28/5).

53 See the discussion in Rodriguez Cervantes S (2006) 'FTAs: Trading Away Traditional Knowledge' GRAIN Briefing Paper; and International Centre for Trade and Sustainable Development (ICTSD) 'IP Standards In US-Peru FTA To Affect Talks with Colombia and Ecuador?' 10(2) *Bridges Weekly Trade New Digest*, 25 January 2006.

traditional knowledge systems are potentially vulnerable within such trade initiatives. Because of the importance of traditional medicine to many of the communities this is a further public health issue raised by such agreements.

Cultural life and access to scientific benefits

The Convention on Biological Diversity (CBD) is administered by the United Nations Environment Program (UNEP) towards the conservation of biodiversity and the equitable sharing of benefits arising from the access to genetic resources, over which each country enjoys national sovereignty. The text of the CBD adopted 22 May 1992 and opened for signature 5 June 1992. The TRIPS Agreement was not signed until two years later, 15 April 1994.[54]

Access to genetic resources can include individual genetic resources, cell-lines, virus samples and other resources of critical value as essential starting material for the development of vaccines and other medicines. For example, the controversies surrounding Indonesia's reluctance to share avian influenza virus samples has shown the need to account for the sharing of benefits with developing country donors given the prevalence of this infection in these regions.[55] Many of the arguments raised by donor countries refer to the virus sample as a genetic resource over which that country can exercise national sovereignty (given that it is specific to the people of that region),[56] at the same time emphasising the principles of access and fair and equitable benefit sharing as set out in the CBD.[57] The government of the Lao People's Democratic Republic established the Traditional Medicines Resource Centre (TRMC)[58] as a means by which to promote documentation and preservation together with

---

54 The relationship between TRIPS and the CBD is a current topic being discussed by the Council for Trade-Related Aspects of Intellectual Property Rights (TRIPS Council), pursuant to paragraph 19 of the WTO Ministerial Declaration, adopted on 14 November 2001 (WT/MIN(01)/DEC/1).

55 Avian influenza and the sharing of virus samples is discussed in detail in Part IV: Access.

56 For instance, see Indonesia's proposal to the WHO Intergovernmental Meeting (IGM) on Pandemic Influenza Preparedness (PIP) for terms of reference for a new system of virus sharing. The preamble states 'It is now recognized by the international community of the need for concrete, effective, operational and transparent international mechanisms for fair and equitable sharing of benefits arising from the use of viruses which cannot be present within the current system, including GISN, when the states' sovereign rights and their respective governing laws are taken into consideration." See Fundamental Principles and Elements for the Development of a New System for Virus Access and Fair and Equitable Benefit Sharing Arising from the Use of the Virus for the Pandemic Influenza Preparedness. Proposed by Indonesia. IGM-PIP. 20–23 November 2007. See further the discussion of avian influenza and virus sharing in Chapter 8.

57 CBD. Article 15: Access to Genetic Resources.

58 For a discussion of the initiative see the CBD Ad Hoc Open-Ended Inter-Sessional Working Group on Article 8(j). 3rd Meeting. Regional report: Australia, Asia and the Middle East. UNEP/CBD/WG8J/3/INF/4. 8 September 2002: 36.

knowledge exchange.[59] This centre provides technical assistance and expertise to local traditional healers in order to document all traditional medicines. As well as the documentation of knowledge towards its preservation,[60] the TRMC aims to facilitate sharing of knowledge and practices with the wider healthcare community as well as sharing benefits with all contributors to the centre. Recalling the earlier discussions of fair and equitable benefit sharing, the TRMC collaborates with the International Cooperative Biodiversity Group (ICBG) towards developing medicinal products on the basis that future benefits and royalties would be shared fairly and equitably with the communities involved in contributing the initial knowledge.

Both in terms of the use of traditional knowledge in conventional patentable inventions and in terms of its inclusion in bilateral agreements, the central issues are protection against misappropriation of a community's traditional knowledge (and traditional medical knowledge) and the possible conflict between subsequent intellectual property rights and customary knowledge rights to that knowledge within the community. In a very real sense, the impact of expropriation of genetic resources and related traditional knowledge and the creation of intellectual property rights in subsequent benefits derived from those resources, introduces the interference of trade rules with the right to cultural life of the knowledge holders. In this context, the provisions of the CBD pertaining to benefit sharing and prior informed consent are very significant.

As set out in Article 15, the principle of access based on prior informed consent and mutually agreed terms providing fair and equitable benefit sharing is critical in the context of access to traditional medical resources and knowledge:

1. Recognizing the sovereign rights of States over their natural resources, the authority to determine access to genetic resources rests with the national governments and is subject to national legislation.
2. Each Contracting Party shall endeavour to create conditions to facilitate access to genetic resources for environmentally sound uses by other Contracting Parties and not to impose restrictions that run counter to the objectives of this Convention.
3. For the purpose of this Convention, the genetic resources being provided by a Contracting Party, as referred to in this Article and Articles 16 and 19, are only those that are provided by Contracting Parties that

59 See also the Report of the Commission on Intellectual Property Rights, UK (2002). *Integrating Intellectual Property Rights and Development Policy*: 82.

60 Although documentation of traditional knowledge has certain advantages in terms of defensive protection against patents (establishing traditional knowledge as prior art), there are serious limitations, including exposing knowledge to bioprospecting and disclosing knowledge without reference to the cultural differentiation within the community of knowledge-holders themselves. For further discussion of the limitations of documentation, see Gibson J (2007) 'Audiences in Tradition: Traditional Knowledge and the Public Domain', in Waelde C & MacQueen Q (eds), *Intellectual Property: The Many Faces of the Public Domain*, Cheltenham, Edward Elgar: 174–88.

are countries of origin of such resources or by the Parties that have acquired the genetic resources in accordance with this Convention.

4. Access, where granted, shall be on mutually agreed terms and subject to the provisions of this Article.
5. Access to genetic resources shall be subject to prior informed consent of the Contracting Party providing such resources, unless otherwise determined by that Party.
6. Each Contracting Party shall endeavour to develop and carry out scientific research based on genetic resources provided by other Contracting Parties with the full participation of, and where possible in, such Contracting Parties.
7. Each Contracting Party shall take legislative, administrative or policy measures, as appropriate, and in accordance with Articles 16 and 19 and, where necessary, through the financial mechanism established by Articles 20 and 21 with the aim of sharing in a fair and equitable way the results of research and development and the benefits arising from the commercial and other utilization of genetic resources with the Contracting Party providing such resources. Such sharing shall be upon mutually agreed terms.[61]

The CBD also takes account of intellectual property rights, providing that access and transfer of genetic resources should be consistent with the adequate and effective protection of intellectual property rights. This is usually interpreted as establishing that national governments have an obligation to provide access to national genetic resources on mutually agreed terms that take account of prior rights to knowledge in those resources, including rights to traditional medicine. In particular, the creation of subsequent patent rights on inventions based on that traditional knowledge should not compromise the achievement of the objectives of the CBD.

At the Sixth Conference of the Parties to the CBD, 2002, the governing body of the CBD agreed the Bonn Guidelines on Access to Genetic Resources and Fair and Equitable Sharing of the Benefits Arising out of their Utilisation.[62] These guidelines are accepted as the basic framework to be considered when drafting relevant national legislation.

In the European Union, this relevant starting point is the Biotechnology Directive[63] recital (26):

> if an invention is based on biological material of human origin or if it uses such material, where a patent application is filed, the person from whose body the material is taken must have had an opportunity of expressing free and informed consent thereto, in accordance with national law.

61 CBD. Article 15.

62 Bonn Guidelines on Access to Genetic Resources and Fair and Equitable Sharing of the Benefits Arising out of their Utilisation. 2002.

63 Directive 98/44/EC.

The reference to national law in this recital has removed most of the impact of this provision. This is particularly the case as the European Patent Office, which grants most the relevant sorts of patents in Europe, has taken the view that there is no requirement of prior informed consent or benefit sharing under the European Patent Convention[64] and so the recital is not given any effect before the grant of the patent.[65]

There have been debates within the World Trade Organisation (WTO) as to the relationship between the TRIPS Agreement and CBD with respect to the disclosure of origin. A group of member states led by Brazil and India, supported (amongst others) by the Africa Group, have argued for amendment to TRIPS (Article 29*bis*) to include mandatory disclosure of origin of biological resources and associated traditional knowledge in the patent system.[66] Their proposed Article 29*bis* would oblige members to require, under national patent laws:

> that applicants provide information including evidence of compliance with the applicable legal requirements in the providing country for prior informed consent for access and fair and equitable benefit-sharing arising from the commercial or other utilization of such resources and/or associated traditional knowledge.[67]

The proposed amendment thus introduces provisions to realise sovereignty over genetic and biological resources and to materialise an important reciprocal relationship based upon prior informed consent and the sharing of benefits, that is, upon the relationship to use. Other nations have suggested different approaches. Switzerland suggested an amendment to the Patent Law Treaty to require disclosure during the prosecution of patents. The EU takes the view that the sanction for failure to disclosure the obligation should fall outside patent law. And the United States suggests it should be through

64 See *Breast and ovarian cancer/UNIVERSITY OF UTAH* (T 1213/05) (27 September 2007).

65 It might be possible to revoke it for lack of consent in contracting states once the European patent has been granted. However, this is only likely to be possible if it becomes a substantive, rather than formal requirement of patentability (see Patent Law Treaty, article 10).

66 Council for Trade-Related Aspects of Intellectual Property Rights (TRIPS Council), Doha Work Programme: The Outstanding Implementation Issue on the Relationship between the TRIPS Agreement and the Convention on Biological Diversity. Communication from Brazil, China, Colombia, Cuba, India, Pakistan, Peru, Thailand and Tanzania, 5 July 2006 (IP/C/W/474). In the 2007 report, it was noted that Venezuela, the African Group, Paraguay and the LDC Group had jointed the list of co-sponsors for the proposal. See Council for Trade-Related Aspects of Intellectual Property Rights (TRIPS Council), Annual Report (2007) of the Council for TRIPS, 7 December 2007 (IP/C/48).

67 Proposed Article 29*bis*.2 of TRIPS.

national law or contract. The absence of agreement means that the issue has gone into the long grass over the last decade.

National effectuality is arguably critical to delivering within territories intellectual property systems that are culturally and politically relevant. That is, legitimacy is derived from a system that is actually meaningful to the development of national industry and technical expertise, as distinct from the illegitimacy of a system that appears to promote external interests over and above those subjects to which the law is to apply. In this way, local expertise and consultation is deployed to implement the law so as to motivate legitimacy and promote national interests.

Throughout these frameworks for dealing with resources for culture and development, there is a clear relationship between use and the creation of a beneficial interest in the resources and benefits of scientific and medical research and development. That use necessitates the safeguarding of the beneficial enjoyment of scientific research as distinct from any legal rights created in those benefits through intellectual property systems. This central value of use is critical questions of morality in the application and exercise of patent law. When examining the concept of use in patent rights, not only the scope of patent (the legal rights in the invention) but also the accessibility for users (the beneficial interests in the invention) will be manifest. This characterisation of use is critical to an appreciation of the cultural life of patents.

5 Patent morality

> [T]here is no shortage of significant political issues that in fact touch on questions of justice. They're mostly cloaked as juridical deliberations, but they're also occasionally directly discussed as what they are: as moral and practical questions.[1]

Introduction

The cultural and physical health and well-being of the individual underpins the full realisation of the right to cultural life. The previous chapter examined the right to culture, and health as a component of that right, as comprising the individual's access to the public sphere and to the institutions within that sphere, including the institution of medicine and health care. The ongoing cultural and legitimate constitution of that institution's normative and legal order indicates the role of access by the individual and the collective in its maintenance and reproduction. Classical definitions of health and well-being suggest a state of harmony and order: 'being well means to be capable of ordered behavior … How very important the regaining of order is for recuperation can be seen from the fact that the organism seems primarily to have the tendency to preserve, or gain, such capacities that make this possible.'[2]

Intellectual property and medicine are institutional components of the knowledge economy. These institutions are characterised by manifest order and functional unity, without necessarily deriving that unity from public consensus, that is, from access.[3] The institution of intellectual property is presented as a functional organic unity, but achieves that unity and presents as a public institution arguably without the consensus of the collective participants in the system. Instead, the democratic character of the public sphere and the institutions within it are organised around the principle of proprietary relationships and individual legal rights to, and manifest in, property. The

1 Habermas J (1994/[1991]) *The Past as Future*, Pensky M (trans), Cambridge: Polity Press, 109.
2 Goldstein K (1995/[1934]) *The Organism: A Holistic Approach to Biology Derived from Pathological Data in Man*, New York: Zone, 332–33.
3 Weber M (1975/[1903–6]) *Roscher and Knies: The Logical Problems of Historical Economics*, Oakes G (trans), New York: The Free Press.

apparent unity of the system suggests an inherent logic based upon the will (expressed through ownership) of its individuals. Challenges to that logic are, as it were, 'illogical' and 'undemocratic'. The entitlements of freedoms of the individual are articulated through property and the market. Within this logic then, the significant influence of the market on health research agenda threatens to compromise access (in the broader sense of use) to the system and the accessibility of benefits for many, particularly in developing countries.

Despite this 'crisis' in access and the creation of limitations on the benefits of these institutions, intellectual property and medicine and health care themselves are arguably, importantly and necessarily public goods rendered excludable by specific technical, but not consensual, intrusions. For instance, knowledge can become excludable simply by preserving it as a secret. Indeed, this is not only the motivation behind the maintenance of personal confidential information but also the economic reasoning behind the creation of value in trade secrets.[4] Therefore, the patent system takes non-excludable knowledge and produces an excludable good as an alternative to secrecy. It creates, therefore, legal rights in the invention that subsist alongside beneficial interests in the diffusion of that technology.

Despite this character of excludability, it would be difficult to argue that, in doing so, the patent system itself is designed to prevent access to consumption collectively agreed by society. Rather, the economic models built upon the opportunities for exclusion provided by the patent system may provoke collective engagement with the institution and 'the consensually valid chance of coercive intervention by *all* the members of the community in the event of an infringement of a valid norm'.[5]

Access to these institutions therefore underlies an individual's right to cultural life, not merely in terms of the accessibility to the benefits of those institutions but the use of those benefits to all regardless of individual life chances. Similarly, as a public good, the research and development that inputs into the institution of medicine and health care comprises not only the economic functioning of that institution but also the cultural life.

Therefore, the cultural life of patents comprises not only the research culture that produces the resources of the institution of medicine, but also the ethical oversight for medicines (including both the ethical context for patents and the regulatory framework for medicines).

Health as a public good

Public goods are by definition non-excludable, that is, use by one cannot limit the benefits to others. Clean air and water, the underlying determinants for

4 Fiedman DA et al (1991) 'Some Economics of Trade Secrets Law' 5(1) *Journal of Economic Perspectives* 61.

5 Weber M (1968/[1956]) *Economy and Society: An Outline of Interpretive Sociology, Volume 3*, Roth G & Wittich C (eds), New York: Bedminster Press, 317.

realisation of the right to health, are indeed classic public goods. However, recalling the earlier discussion of health, both in terms of medical sociology and history[6] and the right to health,[7] health itself demonstrates the character of a public good. The benefits of achieving well-being in the individual are not exclusive, but are relevant to all other individuals in society. This relationship between the health of individual's and the economic, social and cultural development of the greater society is indicated not only generally, throughout the WHO work programme and the MDGs, but also specifically in the characterisation of health as a component of the right to development. The health of individuals is instrumental to the health of the entire social organism. Therefore, individual health provides benefits to developing countries and ultimately to industrialised trading partners. Health is indeed a public good.

Research and development

Research and development is one of the most critical concepts both in the modelling of investment and the appropriation of value in the pharmaceutical industry. Its contribution, quantification and qualification are some of the most contested topics in debates over intellectual property, patents and access to medicines. As a contribution to the production of knowledge in the institution of science and technology, it is a significant component of the knowledge economy. This is especially in terms of its demonstration of the apparent functional unity of the knowledge economy in terms of its deployment in analyses and projections of the public benefit of (increased) innovation. As distinct from patents as indices of innovation (the acquisition of goods), research and development expenditure is applied as a benchmark for the remuneration in profits. Indeed, this is the classic model of capitalism:

> A 'drive to acquire goods' has actually nothing whatsoever to do with capitalism, as little as has the 'pursuit of profit,' money, and the greatest possible gain ... capitalism is distinguished by the striving for *profit*.[8]

Indeed, the quantification of innovation through research and development introduces an ethical priority to the expectations of profit in that it is constructed as driven by investment in research not the product itself.

The research and development business model thus ties investment to potential markets, suggesting possible issues in public health, in that markets for a medicine arguably drive the research and development agenda. In this context, it is the creation of a 'market' in developing countries that underpins the arguments by largely industrialised nations and their dominant industries for

---

6 See further the discussion in Chapter 1.
7 This is considered further in Chapter 3.
8 Weber M (2002/[1904–05]) *The Protestant Ethic and the Spirit of Capitalism*, Kalberg S (trans), Oxford: Blackwell, 152 (original emphasis).

stronger intellectual property rights. These arguments betray the presumption that the rights themselves are perceived as defining the opportunities of a region to participate in the health economy, rendering the market the starting-point for innovation and the circumstances necessary for development, as distinct from articulating research agenda on the specific cultural and social needs and values of a region. In other words, the necessary circumstances for innovation, according to this discourse, are the opportunities to render a public good (knowledge) excludable and thus registrable as innovation.

Thus, the narrative of intellectual property as a measure for innovation (and patents taken as indices of innovative activity) suggests a link between economic development and transfer of technology, causality between technology and industrialisation and economic advancement.[9] The entire body of innovation is therefore incorporated, arguably misleadingly, within the narrative provided by intellectual property rights notably after the event.[10] Further, this construction of innovation maintains the colonial discourse of the developed North's delivery of civilisation and development through the transfer of technology to the developing south. Intellectual property rights are therefore skilfully and problematically constructed as the mechanism not merely by which to protect innovation but the mechanism by which to deliver 'civilisation' to the South.

The translation of intellectual property rights (based upon a technologically advanced social capability) to developing countries (in the process of developing that technological capacity) appears to conflict with the democratic concept of legitimate law as law developed in consultation with those to be made subject to it.[11] It is this imposition of intellectual property that arguably interferes with the motivations and circumstances by which to develop that technical capacity,[12] compromising opportunities for knowledge transfer and the development of local expertise. Thus, the legitimacy and indeed morality of intellectual property laws imposed under such conditions is undermined, being distanced from original bases in commercially, developmentally and morally justifiable policies: 'Legitimate law is compatible only with a mode of legal coercion that does not destroy the rational motives for obeying the law.'[13]

---

9 See further Gibson J (2006) *Creating Selves: Intellectual Property and the Narration of Culture*, Aldershot: Ashgate.

10 See further Gibson, *Creating Selves.*

11 Further on this point, the move from multilateral negotiations in the context of intellectual property to bilateral arrangements is similarly totalitarian in that the partner to the agreement is bound to third parties to provide the same higher standards and greater advantages by virtue of TRIPS Article 4, principle of most-favoured nation. Therefore, local intellectual property law and policy can be imposed by stronger contracting parties in an 'international' way without true consensus at the multilateral level.

12 For instance, patents for chemical substances were prohibited in the British patent system for a period deemed necessary to develop the technical capacity and expertise in this area (see the discussion in Chapter 2).

13 Habermas J (1997/[1992]) *Between Facts and Norms: Contributions to a Discourse Theory of Law and Democracy*, Rehg W (trans), Cambridge: Polity Press, 121.

The legal framework thus overwrites the collective cultural expertise and practices of the lifeworld with proprietary relationships:

> The lifeworld is constituted from a network of communicative actions that branch out through social space and historical time, and these live off sources of cultural traditions and legitimate orders no less than they depend on the identities of socialized individuals.[14]

The colonisation of the lifeworld is reproduced in its overwriting by the intellectual property system.[15] Indeed, this 'undemocratic' colonisation of the international knowledge economy is suggested also in the mapping of the economy through bilateral trading agreements.

On this point, the move from multilateral negotiations in the context of intellectual property[16] to bilateral arrangements is similarly totalitarian in that the partner to the agreement is bound to third parties to provide the same higher standards and greater advantages by virtue of TRIPS Article 4, principle of most-favoured nation. Therefore, local intellectual property law and policy can be imposed by stronger contracting parties in an 'international' way without true consensus at the multilateral level. This is a direct challenge to the possibility of truly international frameworks for socio-economic development according to regional specificity, and indeed to composing health agenda responsive to the social, economic and cultural issues in a particular country: The crises in accessibility and research agenda facing global health present a cultural and colonial dissensus that has genuinely generated litigious if not political battles, but the system with equipping the responses to those battles are arguably geographically and politically specific:

> Are the principles of international law so intertwined with the standards of Western rationality – a rationality built in, as it were, to Western culture – that such principles are of no use for the nonpartisan adjudication of international conflicts?[17]

Problematically, if research and development is determined by the market alone, legitimate concerns may be raised regarding research into rare and

---

14 Habermas, *Between Facts and Norms*, 80.

15 See the discussion of Habermas's concept of lifeworld in Chapter 1. In the present sense, Habermas's notion of the colonisation of the lifeworld explains the way in which the cultural uncertainty of international trade is generalised by its organisation within the institution of intellectual property. See in particular Habermas J (1987/[1981]) *The Theory of Communicative Action: Volume 2 Lifeworld and System: A Critique of Functionalist Reason*, McCarthy T (trans), Cambridge: Polity Press.

16 Indeed, the latest discussions on the Doha round of trade negotiations in the WTO were characterised by breakdown, provoking major concerns in the media that the round will be abandoned (for instance, see Politi J (2008) "Top US Official Sees 'No Alternative' to Doha," *Financial Times*, 6 August 2008).

17 Habermas, *The Past as Future*, 20.

tropical diseases as compared to research into diseases prevalent in richer industrialised nations. Thus, 'classes' with respect to accessibility to medicines are created by the life chances of the public constructed by that model and research agenda adopt a certain cultural nature with respect to the social values justified by that model. In that responses to global public health are thus dominated and driven by local markets and regional privilege, the harnessing of life chances to development makes access to health inherently an issue of development. Furthermore, healthcare, goods and services themselves become transactional resources for socio-economic advancement in a disturbing replication of colonial politics:

> the capitalistic utilisation of money resources could take place through investment in sources of potential profit which were not oriented to opportunities of exchange in a free commodity market and thus not to the production of goods.[18]

Indeed, protection specifically devised for pharmaceuticals to address the market opportunity as distinct from the process of innovation include the associated monopolies of supplementary protection certificates and data and marketing exclusivity and are incorporated into this model of compensation for the costs in developing new medicines.

Generic producers present a somewhat different business model, although recent mergers have started to change this landscape.[19] But traditionally generics have been primarily national companies operating only within the domestic market. In particular, mergers between pharmaceuticals and generic companies raise issues with respect to the possibility of controlling markets through generic subsidiaries.[20] As companies begin to develop both research-based and generic activities within a single firm, the traditional separation between pharmaceutical multinationals and generics has become less meaningful. Indeed, in the UK some independent generic manufacturers have been absorbed by multinational companies.[21] Furthermore, cooperation

18 Weber, *Economy and Society*, 113.

19 Nevertheless, this distinction between the two models is blurring through acquisition of many generic companies by pharmaceuticals. For instance, see the *Economist* report on mergers both between generics companies and between generics and pharmaceuticals: "All Together Now." Editorial. *The Economist*. 24 July 2008.

20 For instance, in June 2005, the European Commission fined AstraZeneca EUR 60 million for infringement of Article 82 EC (now Article 102, TFEU) and Article 54 EEA, having been found to guilty of abuse of market dominance so as to exclude competition of generic firms and parallel traders by a filing strategy relating to supplementary protection certificates: this was upheld by the General Court *AstraZeneca v Commission* (T-321/05) [2010] ECR II-2805.

21 Some of these are research-based, including the entry of the major UK-based pharmaceutical company, GSK into the generics market through a joint venture with South African generics firm, Aspen.

between generics firms can be equally detrimental to the accessibility of medicines.[22] More recently, it has become apparent that issues do not arise just between on- and off-patent drugs. Prior to September 2012, Pfizer sold phenytoin sodium capsules (used to prevent epilepsy) under the brand name Epanutin at a price of £2.83 per packet. In September 2012, Pfizer sold the UK distribution rights to Flynn Pharma who debranded the product, which meant it was no longer subject to price controls. Pfizer continued to sell the product to Flynn, at a substantially escalated price, and Flynn in turn sold them on to the NHS at a price of £67.50 per packet. As the branded drug was no longer available to the NHS, it was necessary to buy the generic at the much inflated price. This overnight increase in prices led to a £90 million fine from the Competition and Markets Authority.[23] As this demonstrates, the market can be manipulated by more things than intellectual property law.

The value of time

Within this market approach to developments in healthcare, health research and intellectual property are significant coercive structures, distancing the contributions of the collective public to the functioning and development of these institutions. Every aspect of investment and risk is calculable within the intellectual property model that institutes and regulates the economic monopolies that define research agenda. Thus, not only the direct financial investment but also the indirect costs and value of time are incorporated within this expanded market, leading to protection directed specifically towards the coercive institutional force of pharmaceutical science. The value of time has led to various competition law investigations into so-called 'pay to deal' agreements, whereby the patent holder has paid its rival to delay its entry into the market as part of a settlement of a patent dispute. For example, Lundbeck had a patent on the process of making citalopram (its product patent having expired), and generic manufacturers could have entered the market, albeit risking a claim for infringing the process patent. Instead of taking this risk, they took money from Lundbeck not to enter the market while the process patent was in force. The European Commission fined those involved €146 million, which was upheld by the General Court.[24]

22 For instance, consider the investigation into alleged collusion on price-fixing between Goldshield Group, Ranbaxy, Kent Pharmaceuticals, Norton Healthcare and Generics (UK) in order to maintain the generic price of amoxicillin. The Serious Fraud Office (SFO) alleged conspiracy to defraud the NHS. See *R v Goldshield Plc and others* (Unreported), Southwark Crown Court, 11 July 2008. The case was dismissed due to problems with the indictment (also see *R v GG plc & Ors* [2008] UKHL 17).

23 CMA, Press Release, 'The CMA Has Fined Pharma Companies Pfizer and Flynn Pharma nearly £90 Million for Excessive Prices to the NHS for Anti-Epilepsy Drug' (7 December 2016). The CMA has also started investigations into similar behaviour by other drug companies.

24 *H. Lundbeck v European Commission* (T-472/13) (2016) ECLI:EU:T:2016:449.

In addition to expenditure in research and development that ultimately leads to the patented invention, the associated monopolies of supplementary protection certificates and data and marketing exclusivity are incorporated into this model of compensation for the associated 'costs' to that patent involved in bringing that invention to market, quantified by time. That is, delays experienced during the regulatory process not only shorten the effective period of patent monopoly in the marketplace, but also represent an additional 'investment' over time. Supplementary protection certificates provide an extension to the patent monopoly itself to account for delays in regulatory procedures. Similarly, protection for clinical and testing data provides an additional period of data exclusivity before generics competitors can start examining the test data of pharmaceuticals. This protection is designed to compensate for these additional costs in bringing original products to market.

Supplementary protection certificates

Supplementary protection certificates are special kinds of intellectual property[25] rights in the European Union[26] that are applied only in the fields of pharmaceuticals and plant protection, due to the particular requirements for clinical trials and regulatory approval in these areas of technology. As intellectual property rights, supplementary protection certificates are based on and are similar in nature to patents, but they are dependent on the granting of marketing authorisations to sell the drug in question. In effect, they operate to extend patent protection[27] where it has not been possible for the patent owner to take full advantage of their patent rights over the period of the grant, coming into effect at the expiration of the patent.[28]

The possible limitation on the interference with the system that might be posed by supplementary protection certificates is the restriction on what is covered by this right. Compared to the broad coverage of patents, this protection is more limited. Pharmaceutical patents protect chemicals or combinations or chemicals, methods of production and new medicinal uses of products. On the other

25 In 1990 there was a Proposal by the Commission which resulted in two Council Regulations creating new rights related to patents for medicinal products and for plant protection products. In 1992, the European Commission introduced Council Regulation (EEC) No 1768/92 of 18 June 1992 concerning the creation of a supplementary protection certificate for medicinal products. This was codified in 2009 as Regulation (EC) 469/2009. The relevant regulation in plant protection products was introduced in 1996: Regulation (EC) no 1610/96 of 23 July 1996.

26 Many other countries have straightforward, patent term extension, albeit often limited to regulatory approvals: see for example, US Patents Act, s 156. Patent term extension has not presented the (unnecessary) complexities of the supplementary protection system.

27 Regulation (EC) No 469/2009, Article 5 provides the supplementary protection certificate will confer the same rights as the basic patent.

28 Regulation (EC) No. 469/2009, Article 13.1.

hand, supplementary protection certificates are defined by chemical[29] or other ingredients, limited to the physical form and limited to the intended mode of delivery;[30] that is, the product which is covered by the marketing authorisation. This relationship between the patent claim and the marketing authorisation led to a long period of uncertainty in relation to combination therapies and vaccines. This arose where the patent claim covers one drug (A), but that drug is more effective with another known drug (B) and so the marketing authorisation is for both drugs (A and B). As a marketing authorisation did not exist for drug A alone and a patent claim did not cover drug B, it appeared that protection from supplementary protection certificates could not be obtained. Eventually, the Court of Justice held that it was possible to get a supplementary protection certificate in such cases.[31] More recently, that court has held that certificates are available for second and subsequent medical indications,[32] but it remains the case that medical devices are not probably eligible.[33]

Limitations and obligations governing the rights granted under a supplementary protection certificate are the same as those applied to a basic patent.[34] In particular, it is not possible to have two supplementary protection certificates for the same product. And so, as for a patent, a supplementary protection certificate may also be subject to compulsory licences.

This form of protection will come into operation at the expiration of the patent, subject to the requirement that the patent is maintained until the end of its potential term. If the patent is permitted to lapse or is declared invalid or is revoked, the supplementary protection certificate will not come

---

29 The protection extends only to the active ingredients of a medicinal product, it does not extend to where the product is a combination of two substances only one of which has therapeutic effects: see *Massachusetts Institute of Technology* (C-431/04) [2006] RPC 34; this also applies to adjuvants (that is a pharmacological agent which modifies the effect of another agent): see *Glaxosmithkline* (C-210/13) [2014] RPC 7.

30 Protected products are usually defined by reference to their chemical or other ingredients and physical form or intended mode of delivery. A patent, on the other hand, would usually be much broader in coverage, and could in fact extend to a chemical per se or a combination of chemicals, a method of production, or a new medical use of a known product. So where a single patent could in fact cover a range of individual medicinal or plant protection products, this would not be the case for a supplementary protection certificate.

31 *Medeva* (C-322/10) [2011] ECR I-12051; *University of Queensland* (C-630/10)[2011] ECR I-12231; *University of Georgetown* (C-422/10) [2011] ECR I-12157

32 *Neurim Pharmaceuticals* (C-130/11) [2013] RPC 23; which appears to depart from *Pharmacia Italia* (C-31/03) [2004] ECR I-10001.

33 A reference on this point was made to the Court of Judtice in Merck Sharp & Dohme Corporation v The Comptroller-General of Patents, Designs And Trade Marks [2016] EWHC 1896 (Pat)

34 It does enable a supplementary protection certificate owner to object to a product which includes more than the product covered by their certificate: *Novartis v Actavis* (C-442/11) (2012) ECLI:EU:C:2012:66.

into effect.[35] The duration of protection will vary depending upon the time it took to receive regulatory approval and the kinds of delays suffered by the applicant, but the maximum time extension is five years.[36] The system also assumes that all products take five years to get to market and so this period is also not counted when calculating the period of protection. For example, consider the circumstances of a patent application with a date of filing of 1 May 2007, where the marketing authorisation was granted 1 March 2016. It took eight years and ten months to get approval. This figure is reduced by five years and so the certificate lasts three years and ten months (had this period been over five years it would have been capped).

In 2006, the European Commission revised the law on approval of paediatric medicine and one change made was to allow an additional six months of monopoly under a supplementary protection certificate for medicines in this area upon the filing of a paediatric implementation plan. Again, this protection would be awarded on the same basis as the standard supplementary protection certificate.[37]

Data exclusivity

Unlike supplementary protection certificates, data exclusivity is not part of the patent system as such and is distinct from protection under patent law. While patent protection might be understood as compensating for the innovative activity (risk, effort and investment in research and development, for instance), data exclusivity is associated with the costs and delays associated with regulatory delays and procedures.

By providing an additional period of protection for clinical test data, originators are given an extra means by which to protect their market, in that generic manufacturers cannot access safety and efficacy studies during this period in order to obtain expedited approval nor can they make an application during this time. As a result, the provision for data exclusivity protection is in effect a form of additional market protection for originator pharmaceutical firm. Furthermore, the effective period of market exclusivity that is created is in effect longer than the actual period of data exclusivity protection because of the additional time it subsequently takes to approve generics to come onto the market.

Generic producers will nevertheless undertake their own limited testing to show their version of the drug is safe,[38] but their applications rely upon

35 Regulation (EC) No. 469/2009, Article 15.1.

36 Regulation (EC) No. 469/2009, Article 15.2.

37 These changes were introduced by Regulation (EC) No 1901/2006 of the European Parliament and of the Council of 12 December 2006 on medicinal products for paediatric use and amending Regulation (EEC) No 1768/92, Directive 2001/20/EC, Directive 2001/83/EC and Regulation (EC) No 726/2004. See in particular Article 36. This has also led to the grant of negative term certificate (where the term would be positive once the six months were added): *Merck Sharp & Dolme* (C-125/10) [2011] ECR I-12987.

38 Relying on so called 'Bolar exemptions' see Part IV: Access.

the safety and efficacy data of originators to avoid repetition of costly testing with animal and human subjects. The general safety and efficacy data cannot be relied upon until after the data exclusivity period (they could, however, produce their own data but the cost is usually prohibitive). The data itself is not released to generics after the exclusivity period, but authorities will be able to evaluate generic applications against the originator's data.

Reliance on originator clinical test data can be a critical feature of the generics business model. As discussed, the business models of generics and originator pharmaceutical firms are quite different, with the former often being smaller local companies that may be ill-equipped to conduct their own safety and efficacy trials. Most applications for approval of generic medicines therefore rely on the clinical test data of originators.

Civil society organisations, patient groups and generic manufacturers criticise data exclusivity provisions as simply delaying the entry of generic competitors onto the market and providing de facto extensions to patent protection, with possible negative consequences for access to medicines and adequate public health. Nevertheless, in many cases, patent term extension or supplementary protection certificates which prohibit the selling of the product itself will last longer than the period of data exclusivity. This means data exclusivity will usually be significant where there is no patent in the first place or the patent expired long before the drug was put on the market based on the data.

The mechanics of data exclusivity

Data exclusivity protection is provided in the EU pursuant to the Directive on the Community code relating to medicinal products for human use.[39] The Medicinal Products for Human Use Directive provides for a period of eight years data exclusivity and a minimum of 10 years from initial authorisation before a generic version of the medicinal product can be placed on the market.[40] For example, if the product's patent expires within 10 years from the date of

39 Directive 2001/83/EC of the European Parliament and of the Council of 6 November 2001 on the Community code relating to medicinal products for human use as amended by Directive 2002/98/EC and 2004/27/EC (Medicinal Products for Human Use Directive). As a member of the EU, the UK has implemented the provisions of the Directive in the Medicines for Human Use (Marketing Authorisations Etc) Regulations 1994 (SI 1994/3144). European data exclusivity protection is provided for four categories under the Medicinal Products for Human Use Directive: new chemical entities (NCEs) (eight years data-exclusivity from date of approval; 10 years marketing exclusivity (Article 10.1)); new therapeutic indication during eight-year period (additional one year (Article 10.1)); change of product classification (additional one year (Article 74a)); and well-established products with new therapeutic indication (one year (Article 10.5)).

40 Directive 2001/83/EC of the European Parliament and of the Council of 6 November 2001 on the Community code relating to medicinal products for human use as amended by Directive 2002/98/EC and 2004/27/EC (Medicinal Products for Human Use Directive): Article 10.

marketing approval (due to regulatory delays and so on), the originator will still enjoy protection.[41] Therefore, although the data exclusivity period is eight years from the date of approval of the originator's product, the effective market exclusivity is for 10 years. Furthermore, there is provision for an additional one year of data exclusivity for three other categories.[42] The first is where an application is made for a new indication of a well-established substance and significant clinical benefit can be shown.[43] Second, an extension of one year is available where the classification of the product changes from prescription to over-the-counter. Finally, a further one year is available where a well-established product is granted approval for a new therapeutic indication.

The EU Paediatric Medicines Regulation,[44] provides for additional 'incentives' with respect to research and development in this area. As mentioned above, the Regulation extends supplementary protection certificates by six months for products already available on the market if their use is to be extended to children.[45] Critically, it also extends marketing exclusivity for orphan drugs by two years;[46] and creates a new category of marketing authorisation, the paediatric uses marketing authorisation, for products that are no longer within patent protection, giving such products an additional 10-year period of data and market exclusivity protection.

The Food, Drug and Cosmetic Act[47] provides for data exclusivity protection in the US under the authority of the Food and Drug Administration (FDA). To qualify for the five-year data exclusivity protection[48] in the US, the product must not contain an active moiety that has been approved previously by the FDA. An active moiety is that part of the molecule that gives it its therapeutic effect. If this molecule has been previously approved in another product, then no data exclusivity protection will be available to the originator. However,

41 Directive 2001/83/EC, Article 10.

42 Directive 2001/83/EC, Article 10.

43 This is more restrictive than the requirement in the US for the same extension of protection, as discussed later in this section.

44 Regulation (EC) No 1901/2006 of the European Parliament and of the Council of 20 December 2006 on medicinal products for paediatric use (Paediatric Medicines Regulation).

45 Regulation (EC) No 1901/2006, Article 36.1.

46 Directive 2001/83/EC of the European Parliament and of the Council of 6 November 2001 on the Community code relating to medicinal products for human use as amended by Directive 2002/98/EC and 2004/27/EC (Medicinal Products for Human Use Directive): Article 10.1. See also Regulation (EC) No 1901/2006 of the European Parliament and of the Council of 20 December 2006 on medicinal products for paediatric use (Paediatric Medicines Regulation): Article 36.5.

47 21 U.S.C. 355.

48 The US provides for several categories of protection: NCEs – five years exclusivity (may be extended to up to seven and a half years if originator commences a suit for patent infringement after the fourth year); product change (new indications, new dosing regimes, change of classification to over-the-counter, labelling changes) – additional three years; and conduct of paediatric studies at the request of the FDA – additional six months.

where that active moiety has not previously been approved, the data exclusivity is quite extensive in that generic producers are unable to apply for approval of any drug with the same active moiety during the five-year period.[49]

An additional three years protection may be granted for a very broad range of product changes including additional strengths, administration routes and other changes. The standard for determining additional protection is much less restrictive than that applied in the EU and UK, where significant clinical benefit must be shown.[50] In the US, the applicant must show that new clinical investigations were essential to the approval process and therefore should be protected.[51] Although only that test data relevant to the change that qualifies for the additional period will be protected, this is a significant mechanism by which to access incremental protection. Importantly nonetheless, generic competitors can make applications during this additional three-year period (unlike the five-year period, where no applications can be made) and so these generic products can be ready to enter the market as soon as the three-year period expires.

Finally, with respect to paediatric studies requested by the FDA, an additional six months protection may be available.[52] Unlike the three-year extension for product changes, the additional six months for paediatric studies will not just apply to the product studied in the paediatric formulation and will be extended to all of the applicant's formulations and dosage forms. If containing the same active moiety, it will also apply to products with existing exclusivity or patent protection.

Substitution – imitating biological costs

The specific value that is presented as at stake in research and development models is the lack of connection between investment costs and the security of the product in the market. Thus, as well as protection for the product itself in terms of market monopolies and data exclusivity, the possibility of imitating that product may also be captured within the regulatory process of approving new generic versions. That is, obstacles to the possible substitution of products will affect any symmetry that might be possible in that exchange as well as diminish the marginal rate of substitution.

In this context, biological medicines introduce a specific dimension to the calculation of economic monopolies for originators. With the increased

49 The five-year period may be reduced to four years if a generic claims that its product does not infringe the originator's patent or makes a claim for the originator's patent to be declared invalid and revoked. However, if the originator commences an action for patent infringement after the fourth year of data exclusivity, then the exclusivity period can be extended to up to seven and a half years.

50 Regulation (EC) No 1901/2006 of the European Parliament and of the Council of 20 December 2006 on medicinal products for paediatric use (Paediatric Medicines Regulation): Article 36.5.

51 21 CFR §314.108(b)(4)(iv).

52 21 U.S.C. 355A, this would extend (by an additional six months) the five-year period, seven-and-a-half-year period and three-year period as described earlier.

use of biotechnology in the development of medicines and health, biologics (also known as biopharmaceuticals, biological medicines or biomedicines) are becoming more common. These are medicines for which the active substance is made by or derived from a living organism. Therefore, unlike the relative simplicity of conventional chemical pharmaceuticals, biologics are much more complex and usually much larger molecules than standard drugs and, as they are usually proteins, are reportedly much less stable than conventional medicines. Biosimilar medicines or 'biosimilars' are medicines that are similar to an originator's biologic that has been previously approved. In this case, the originator's biologic is known as the 'biological reference medicine.' Just as generic producers seek to expedite approval using clinical test data of the originator's medicine, a biosimilar relies on the similarity between its active substance and that of the biological reference material.[53]

However, the reliability and relevance of this similarity is debated in the medical field.[54] Biologics, because they are derived from biological material, have the potential to produce immunogenic responses in the test subject, therefore necessitating comprehensive trials before approval. For this reason, it is often argued by the biotechnology industry that generic biologics, biosimilars, must be made subject to the same level of testing and trials before they can be approved.[55]

Further, as these medicines are complex and more unstable proteins, it is difficult to produce consistent products during manufacturing. Without access to the originator's biological material (usually cloned and maintained) and allowing for the difficulty of reproducing biological processes, leading to potential production variations, it is argued by originators that it is not always possible to guarantee equivalence in follow-on products. In other words, the originality of the product is tied not only to the invention itself, but also to the crucial starting material, in stark contrast to generic forms of conventional chemical compounds. As a result, generic forms of biologics are not authorised in the EU and US through the same abbreviated procedures available for conventional generics,[56] but there are still aspects of the information provided in the approval of the originator's biologic that is not considered necessary to reproduce.

---

53 See in particular Directive 2004/27/EC of the European Parliament and of the Council of 31 March 2004 amending Directive 2001/83/EC on the Community code relating to medicinal products for human use.

54 For instance, see Mellstedt H et al (2007) "The Challenge of Biosimilars" 19(3) *Annals of Oncology* 411; Nowicki M (2007) "Basic Facts About Biosimilars" 30 *Kidney and Blood Pressure Research* 267; Tsiftsoglou AS (2007) "Biosimilars: The Impact of Their Heterogeneity on Regulatory Approval" 6(3) *Nature Reviews: Drug Discovery* 1; and Locatelli F & Roger S (2006) "Comparative Testing and Pharmacovigilance of Biosimilars" 21 (Supplement 5) *Nephrology Dialysis Transplantation* v 13.

55 For instance, see EuropaBio (European Association for Bioindustries) Biological and Biosimilar Medicines, Healthcare Biotech Fact Sheet, January 2005; and Roche Position Paper on Similar Biological Medicinal Products, 15 March 2005.

56 See the discussion in Chapter 8.

The originator's biologic is protected by a period of data exclusivity, just as for other medicines for human use and at the end of this period, biosimilars may be submitted for marketing authorisation. However, the Medicinal Products for Human Use Directive provides that where a biosimilar does not meet the conditions in the definition of generic medicinal products (usually due to difference in raw materials or manufacturing process) then trial data must be submitted for the biosimilar.[57]

Biosimilars, like generic forms of conventional medicines, are usually cheaper than the originator's product once on the market, indicating important considerations for access to medicines and public health. This is explicitly recognised in the European Union law:

> Since generic medicines account for a major part of the market in medicinal products, their access to the Community market should be facilitated in the light of the experience acquired. Furthermore, the period for protection of data relating to pre-clinical tests and clinical trials should be harmonised.[58]

While the biotechnology industry has raised concerns,[59] the generics industry has advocated the need to ensure biotechnological therapies and medicines are also cost-effective, pointing to the need for a competitive market in safe, accessible, effective and approved medicines:

> Biosimilar medicines now offer a major opportunity to provide greater access to affordable healthcare for several life-saving medicines, at least equally significant to the emergence of generic medicines over the past two decades.[60]

The morality of patents

> Modern legal systems are constructed on the basis of individual rights. Such rights have the character of releasing legal persons from moral obligations in a carefully circumscribed manner. By introducing rights that concede to agents the latitude to act according to personal

---

57 Directive 2001/83/EC, Article 10. The type and quantity of supplementary data is set out in an Annex to the Directive (Commission Directive 2003/63/EC of 25 June 2003 amending Directive 2001/83/EC of the European Parliament and of the Council on the Community code relating to medicinal products for human use).

58 Directive 2004/27/EC of the European Parliament and of the Council of 31 March 2004 amending Directive 2001/83/EC on the Community code relating to medicinal products for human use: Recital 14.

59 EuropaBio (European Association for Bioindustries) Biological and Biosimilar Medicines, Healthcare Biotech Fact Sheet, January 2005.

60 European Generics Association (EGA) (2007) *Handbook on Biosimilar Medicines*, Brussels: EGA, 2.

> preferences, modern law as a whole implements the principle that whatever is not explicitly prohibited is permitted. Whereas in morality an inherent symmetry exists between rights and duties, legal duties are a consequence of entitlements, that is, they result only from statutory constraints on individual liberties. This basic conceptual privileging of rights over duties is explained by the modern concepts of the 'legal person' and the 'legal community'.[61]

It is possible to interpret exceptions to intellectual property rights as contributing to a broader ethical dimension instituted within the law. These are technical exceptions provided for in the law,[62] but their underlying rationale is founded upon ethical, social and developmental concerns, introducing a dynamic of legal duties in return for the constraints on the individual liberties of users accessing the public good of knowledge. Furthermore, the exception to patentability for reasons of morality and public order introduces 'an inherent symmetry' between the rights introduced by the patent system and the social duties to provide solutions of collective interest and acceptability.[63] The accountability to the moral order or public morality engages, to a limited extent, collective agreement on the desirability of an invention.

Patents and bioethical issues

With new developments in technology come new expectations as well as unanticipated concepts to be assimilated within the current patent system. The fundamental framework for determining what constitutes a new invention, what might constitute an exception to patentability and what might otherwise limit the grant and exercise of a patent can be understood as cooperating with the broader bioethical concerns within which the patent system operates. On

61 Habermas J (1998/[1996]) *The Inclusion of the Other: Studies in Political Theory*, Cronin C and de Greiff P (trans), Cambridge: Polity Press, 256.

62 Patents are provided only for inventions (TRIPS Article 27) and so certain subject matter will be excluded by definition, such as mere discoveries (EPC Article 52). TRIPS Article 27.3(a) also provides for the exclusion of methods of medical treatment, which are specifically excluded in the EPC by virtue of Article 53(c) (in the United States, medical methods are patentable but there is an exception from infringement for doctors). TRIPS also provides that member states may provide exceptions to patent rights provided this does not compromise the normal commercial exploitation of the patent (Article 30). These include private, non-commercial use (UK Patents Act 1977 s 60(5)(a)) and exceptions for research (s 60(5)(b)) (based on the Community Patent Convention (which never came into force). The breeding of patented plants and animals is also an exception to infringement under the Biotechnology Directive (98/44/EC), Article 11. A patent will also be invalid if disclosed insufficiently for a person skilled in the art to work the invention (TRIPS Article 29, EPC Article 83). This underscores the public interest of the patent document and its cultural status as a communicative instrument as distinct from a physical good.

63 TRIPS Article 27.2; EPC Article 53(a).

this point, it is important to consider the difference between ethical arguments as to whether or not research should proceed and ethical arguments concerning whether or not the outcomes should be subject to private intellectual property rights.[64] It is importantly outside the remit of the patent system to determine the programme of research, notwithstanding the possible influence of the market on driving such an agenda. As a commercial system, the patent system is not the relevant framework within which to declare the ethical nature or otherwise of research. Oliver Mills argues 'patent law is not appropriate, or, indeed, designed, to regulate biotechnology and any attempt to do so, in particular, by denying patents on the basis of morality, is misplaced'.[65] However, the decision to patent is importantly distinct from any decision on the ethical nature of the research itself. One is concerned with commercial questions and the desirability of commodification of the invention; the other would be a regulation of the field of biotechnology research itself. Indeed, the legitimacy of that system is, as discussed, necessarily constituted by the morality of that system – that is, the way in which the commercial system is overseen by the culturally relevant public policy of a particular territory confers a democratic legitimacy upon an otherwise completely external (Western) moral order. Thus, the declaration of a patent is necessarily constrained by the effects of the decision to patent a particular research product and the possible implications of commercialisation of that invention in that the latter constitutes the most meaningful communication of the system with its public.

The relevant question here is whether the patent, if exploited, will be morally and socially acceptable.[66] Any illegality applicable to the use of the invention itself is not sufficient to constitute immorality.[67] In other words, immorality is a separate question of public policy. The research has thus given rise to an invention that otherwise fulfils the criteria for patentability, but

64 For instance, the exception to patentability for reasons of *ordre public* (public policy and morality) is where commercialisation of the patent will be contrary to public morality. Therefore, the provision makes no decision as to the research itself (indeed, it does not impact upon publication of that research including publication in the patent itself), but is a commercial decision in that it impacts upon the exclusion of others from using the patent.

65 Mills O (2005) *Biotechnological Inventions: Moral Restraints and Patent Law*, Aldershot: Ashgate, 11. In particular, the fact that the application is still published indicates that this decision is specifically in terms of commercialisation and is not related to any determination of the field itself.

66 There are also broader and indirect concerns that may nevertheless contribute to the ethical context for patentability, including the ethical context in which the research that produced the invention was conducted. For instance, such questions will include whether or not subjects have provided prior informed consent (consider the discussion of the CBD in Chapter 4 and the sampling of tissue in Chapter 6) and whether there a suitable arrangement to deal with the distribution of benefits and secondary use of collected material (Chapters 4 and 6), as well as arrangements to guarantee access to products obtained from work on that material (Part IV: Access).

67 TRIPS Article 27.2; Paris Convention Article 4*quater*.

should nevertheless be refused the protection of a patent. In otherwise, the market (as the public sphere) does not recognise the invention as such if it is contrary to society's consensus on use, as it were. Thus, it does not warrant the creation of excludability in an otherwise public good.

Ordre public

The principle of *ordre public* as a basis for exclusions to patentability[68] introduces a mechanism not only for the cultural and democratic relevance of the law within it national territory, but also for the self-determination of the national subjects of that law. Indeed, this confers legitimacy upon a law that would otherwise not only regulate the access to public goods (knowledge) but also permitting legal sanctification of knowledge as innovative despite public policy objectives or objections:

> the modern legal order can draw its legitimacy only from the idea of self-determination: citizens should always be able to understand themselves also as authors of the law to which they are subject as addresses.[69]

Thus, it is the important exception of *ordre public* that confers any legitimacy upon the patent system as a consensual and culturally relevant intervention in access to public goods through the institution of the patent system: '*ordre public* is an evolutionary concept that concerns the fundaments from which one cannot derogate without endangering the institutions of a given society'.[70] Crucially, this is a crucial link to the realisation of the cultural life of patents and access to the benefits of scientific research (that are also made subject to the patent system but, despite the logic of that system, not constituted by it) as part of an individual's right to cultural life.

The application of this exception is a limitation upon the commercial framework for restricting access to the benefits of research. However, it makes no impact upon the research itself, including no restriction upon the publication of that research (including that in the patent documents themselves).[71] It is not an exercise in moral judgment of research, but an exercise in moral judgment of the rendering private a public good, arguably

68 TRIPS Article 27.2; EPC Article 53(a). Some jurisdictions, such as the United States, do not expressly have an *ordre public* exception; rather, there has been a rule that an invention must not be injurious to well-being (*Lowell v Lewis,* 1 Mason 182 (D Mass 1817). This rule, while long in abeyance, was probably abrogated by *Juicy Whip v Orange Bang*, 185 F. 3d 1364 (Fed Cir 1999).

69 Habermas, *Between Facts and Norms*, 449.

70 Gervais D (2012) *The TRIPS Agreement: Drafting History and Analysis*, 4th ed, London, Sweet & Maxwell: paragraph 2.360 (p 436) (footnote omitted).

71 However, if the publication of the research affects public safety or national security, its publication may be precluded. See, for example, UK Patents Act 1977, s 22.

within the remit of the patent system and not an inappropriate extension of the commercial framework into the morality of research as such.[72]

Nevertheless, concerns do arise about the certainty surrounding the application of this provision, particularly the capacity of technical patent examiners to judge the morality of a patent and, as such, to sit as moral arbiters of the system. In this role, examiners act in their capacity as members of the public and thus with their cultural knowledge of that collective membership:

> examiners, as members of the public in general, are as well fitted to judge this as anyone else. But if … examiners are supposed to carry out sophisticated balancing of subjective moral values as part of the examination procedure, then they are wholly incapable of the task.[73]

However, patent offices themselves generally take a different view, that examiners are not the appropriate authorities to determine ethical issues.[74] According to the Guidelines for Examination gives some insight into the approach taken by the European Patent Office:

> Any invention the commercial exploitation of which would be contrary to 'ordre public' or morality is specifically excluded from patentability. The purpose of this is to deny protection to inventions likely to induce riot or public disorder, or to lead to criminal or other generally offensive behaviour …
>
> This provision is likely to be invoked only in rare and extreme cases. A fair test to apply is to consider whether it is probable that the public in general would regard the invention as so abhorrent that the grant of patent rights would be inconceivable. If it is clear that this is the case, an objection should be raised under Art. 53(a); otherwise not. The mere possibility of abuse of an invention is not sufficient to deny

72 Objections within Europe that the exception is beyond the patent system and potentially threatening to European competitiveness in a global market (commercial disadvantage is not a relevant consideration in applying the exception, according to the Guidelines on Examination in the European Patent Office: Part IV-7, 4.4) are considered in Beyleveld D et al (2000) 'The Morality Clauses of the Directive on Legal Protection of Biotechological Inventions: Conflict, Compromise and the Patent Community', in Goldberg R & Lonbay J (eds) *Pharmaceutical Medicine, Biotechnology and European Law*, Cambridge: Cambridge University Press 157 at 161–63. The authors conclude: 'it is perfectly property for patent law to incorporate morality exclusions – not, in the final analysis, because there are only poor arguments against such provisions but because acceptance of morality points quite naturally to the incorporation of moral constraints on patentability' (163).

73 Grubb PW et al (2016) *Patents for Chemicals, Pharmaceuticals and Biotechnology: Fundamentals of Global Law, Practice and Strategy*, 6th edn, Oxford: Oxford University Press, 345.

74 See *Howard Florey / Relaxin* [1995] EPOR 541, Paragraph 6.5.

patent protection pursuant to Art. 53(a) EPC if the invention can also be exploited in a way which does not and would not infringe 'ordre public' and morality.[75]

Both the European Union and the United States have taken steps to prohibit the patenting of certain types of inventions, The Biotechnology Directive prohibits certain things on the basis they are contrary to *ordre public*:[76] the patenting of processes for cloning human beings[77] and for modifying the germ-line genetic identity of human beings;[78] uses of human embryos for industrial or commercial purposes;[79] processes for modifying the genetic identity of animals where that is likely to cause the animals unwarranted suffering (that is, suffering without any substantial medical benefit[80] to humans or animals);[81] and animals resulting from such processes of modification to their genetic identity.

The assessment of whether something is contrary to *ordre public* under the Biotechnology Directive is made at the priority date of the patent (usually its date of filing).[82] There have been numerous challenges to patents on the grounds that that they used human embryos for industrial and commercial purposes. The term human embryo is understood in a wide sense and extends to any fertilised human ovum.[83] It also extends to non-fertilised human ovum into which the cell nucleus from a mature human cell has been transplanted and a non-fertilised human ovum whose division and further development have been stimulated by parthenogenesis.[84] However, where the cells cannot lead to a fully developed human being they are outside the scope of the exclusion.[85] It could be argued that the development of a human being for the purposes of the exclusion could be traced back even further to include germ cells.[86] Anything which subsequently becomes the subject matter of a patent is considered to be an industrial or commercial use.[87] This means

75 EPO (2016) Guidelines on Examination in the European Patent Office (status November 2016): Part G-II, 4.1.; Thomas D & Richards GA (2004) "The Importance of the Morality Exception Under the European Patent Convention: The OncoMouse Case Continues ..." 97 *European Intellectual Property Review* 97–104.
76 Biotechnology Directive, Article 6.2.
77 Biotechnology Directive, Article 6.2(a).
78 Biotechnology Directive, Article 6.2(b).
79 Biotechnology Directive, Article 6.3(c).
80 Biotechnology Directive 98/44/EC, Recital 45.
81 This balancing test was first suggested in a slightly different form in *Harvard / OncoMouse* (T 19/90) [1990] EPOR 501.
82 *Transgenic animals/HARVARD* (T 315/03) [2006] OJ EPO 15 at [r 8.2]–[r 9.5] and [r 9.6].
83 Thus the legal definition is broader than the scientific one.
84 *Oliver Brüstle v Greenpeace* (C-34/10) [2012] 1 CMLR 41.
85 *International Stem Cell Corporation* (C-364/13) ECLI:EU:C:2014:2451.
86 See Biotechnology Directive, Recital 16.
87 *Oliver Brüstle v Greenpeace* (C-34/10) [2012] 1 CMLR 41, paragraph 46; also see *Use of embryos/WARF* (G 2/06) [2009] OJ EPO 306, r 25–27.

something remains unpatentable even where after the priority date it became possible to implement the invention without destroying embryos.

In the United States, the situation is equally confused. In 2004, the so-called 'Weldon Amendment' was introduced into the annual Appropriation Act. It precluded public money being spent on the issuing of a patent claim 'directed to or encompassing a human organism'. The Weldon Amendment was included in every subsequent Appropriations Act until a similar provision was enacted in the America Invents Act in 2012.[88] The Weldon Amendment was enacted to stop scientists doing 'ghoulish research'[89] as part of the pro-life policy agenda. The exclusion is meant to cover claims directed to or encompassing:

> a human organism at any stage of development, including a human embryo, fetus, infant, child, adolescent or adult, regardless of whether the organism was produced by technological methods (including, but not limited to, in vitro fertilisation, somatic cell nuclear transfer, or parthenogenesis).[90]

What is considered to be a human organism, and more importantly, what is not remains to be determined.[91] Yet it can be seen that despite a general freedom in the United States to patent inventions without regard to the morality of the invention, there is a concern in one specific area, namely patenting human organisms which may lead to similar approaches being adopted to that in the European Union. Therefore, although not harmonising morality or *ordre public*, international instruments facilitate certain interpretive tools with respect to the provision in conjunction with appropriate expectations of moral judgment as for the exercise of any law.

The morality provisions in patent law address the question as to the type of invention for which it is appropriate to attract legal rights. In other words, the provisions relate specifically to use as a justification for those legal rights. What has emerged in this discussion is the nexus between use and, on the one hand, the scope of legal rights and, on the other hand, the realisation of beneficial interests. This central value of use articulates the issues of identity and privacy that are arise in the context of biotechnology-related inventions and research. This aspect of the culture of patents is inextricably tied to questions of (biological and cultural) life in health, biotechnology and property.

88 Section 33.
89 157 Congressional Record E1178.
90 157 Congressional Record E1180.
91 See Heled, Y "On Patenting Human Organisms or How the Abortion Wars Feed into the Ownership Fallacy" (2014) 36 *Cardozo Law Review* 241.

Part 3
Life

6 The technology of life

> Every technology means violence to nature; and even where it utilizes or exploits natural energies by direct manipulation, it is able to serve its purpose only in opposition to nature. Moreover, the aim of technology is not to render the natural energies available and instrumental, but rather to protect its products against their encroachments. Around its products it builds protective walls against nature, within which nature does not function, but rather the knowledge that results from analytic procedure, culminating in the form of machines.[1]

Introduction

In the process of examining the intellectual property issues raised by patent protection in biotechnologies, it is important to consider the social and ethical dimensions to concepts like 'life form' and 'living material.' To some extent, these concepts also introduce the key ethical and cultural concerns that frame intellectual property protection and public health in this area. When dealing with medical and public health developments in biotechnology, significant issues arise with respect to the subject-matter itself. Furthermore, this subject matter reaffirms the importance of cultural differences not only in the context of the treatment and autonomy of the patient, but also in terms of the exploitation of material, the limits of use and the application of medical knowledge and traditional medical systems.

As this discussion will consider, the application of intellectual property in the area of life technologies or biotechnology has provoked tremendous controversy and condemnation of the extension of proprietary rights over inventions derived from or relating to living material. Arguably, the most critical distinction is that between property in life and property in use. Building upon the discussion in the previous chapter, the most resounding criticism seems to be articulated upon the distinction between the right to life itself, as it were, and the right to use. In that use civilises, as it were, the scope of the 'invention' with respect to the 'life' of the gene sequence, similarly use articulates the distinction between rights over life and rights over the mere invention related to that living material. It is where those rights in an

1 Goldstein K (1995/[1934]) *The Organism: A Holistic Approach to Biology Derived from Pathological Data in Man*, New York: Zone, 379.

invention limit the ordinary 'use' and practice of life that the technology appears 'dehumanising.' In this way, the ethical limits to the research itself are captured within the actual legal limits on the proprietary scope of any use. That is, if proprietary rights in one use limit the opportunity for any other use, then the patent begins to suggest an immodest commodification of life.

Recalling the discussion of the rights in the patent document as distinct from the subject, perhaps the greater controversy attaches to the way in which the patent system confers 'authorship' upon the invention.[2] In particular, inventions relating to transgenic species introduce an ownership of life, not so much in terms of a chattel (or example, as it would be for an individual pet) but in terms of ownership of life as the authority for that life. In the right to be named as the inventor in a patent document,[3] the document substantiates human authorship of the living invention. In that sense, the patent documents the charge, 'playing God'.

The technology of life

Of exactitude in science

In that Empire, the craft of Cartography attained such Perfection that the Map of a Single province covered the space of an entire City, and the Map of the Empire itself an entire Province. In the course of Time, these Extensive maps were found somehow wanting, and so the College of Cartographers evolved a Map of the Empire that was of the same Scale as the Empire and that coincided with it point for point. Less attentive to the Study of Cartography, succeeding Generations came to judge a map of such Magnitude cumbersome, and, not without Irreverence, they abandoned it to the Rigours of sun and Rain. In the western Deserts, tattered Fragments of the Map are still to be found, Sheltering an occasional Beast or beggar; in the whole Nation, no other relic is left of the Discipline of Geography.

From *Travels of Praiseworthy Men* (1658) by
J. A. Suárez Miranda[4]

Technologies, not necessarily just biotechnologies, have been described as the media through which we not only achieve new activities but also construct and recognise new identities. George J Annas likens the impact of technology as a descriptive force to a cartography of that identity.[5] It is perhaps no coincidence

2 See the earlier discussion in Chapter 2.
3 Paris Convention Article 4*ter*, EPC Article 62.
4 Borges JL (1975) *A Universal History of Infamy*, NT di Giovanni (trans), London: Penguin, 131.
5 Annas GJ (2004) 'Mapping the Human Genome and the Meaning of "Monster Mythology",' in Burley J & Harris J (ed) *A Companion to Genethics*, Malden MA: Blackwell, 127 at 134.

that the activity of locating and knowing identities through the genome is described as 'mapping'. As Annas suggests, 'maps may become particularly powerful thought transformers. Maps model reality to help us understand it.'[6]

However, the maps become useless if they attempt to coincide with the 'Empire' of knowledge 'point for point'. Habermas criticises the encroachment of the map into all aspects of the lifeworld through the overwriting of technology:

> Put bluntly: you had to pay for books, theater, concert, and museum, but not for the conversation about what you had read, heard, and seen and what you might completely absorb only through this conversation. Today the conversation itself is administered.[7]

This resonates with the overwriting of innovation and creativity by the organic unity of the intellectual property system. Indeed, in the context of biotechnologies, that overwriting is so successful that inventors are accused of 'playing God' – the intellectual property system is taken for life itself.

Owners or authors

With respect to genetic material, concerns with the notion of 'ownership' over such material are frequently raised (as created through patent rights over subsequent inventions related to that material). Article 1 of the 1997 UNESCO[8] Universal Declaration on the Human Genome and Human Rights states:

> The human genome underlines the fundamental unity of all members of the human family, as well as the recognition of their inherent dignity and diversity. In a symbolic sense, it is the heritage of humanity.[9]

According to the Nuffield Council on Bioethics discussion paper, *The Ethics of Patenting DNA*,

> many people feel that genetic information in humans warrants special treatment. Some claim that there should be no property rights in genes; others claim that … such rights should be the subject of share public ownership rather than being in private hands.[10]

---

6 Annas, 'Mapping the Human Genome', 127 at 134.
7 Habermas J (1992/[1962]) *The Structural Transformation of the Public Sphere: An Inquiry into a Category of Bourgeois Society*, Burger T (trans), Cambridge: Polity Press, 164.
8 United Nations Educational, Scientific and Cultural Organization.
9 UNESCO (1997) Universal Declaration on the Human Genome and Human Rights. Article 1.
10 Nuffield Council on Bioethics (2002) *The Ethics of Patenting Life*. Discussion Paper. London: Nuffield Council on Bioethics. 22.

Indeed, the Biotechnology Directive itself makes special provision in this regard.[11]

Related to this impression of 'common heritage' is the argument that genes and genetic material amount to public property and as such, should not be made the subject of private property rights. These arguments maintain that such private ownership would be incompatible with the concept of the 'common heritage' as well as contrary to the public good or public interest. Related to this concern is the concept of the gene as mere information pertaining to the individual (but perhaps revelatory about other members of a family). Not only does this raise issues as to the 'ownership' of that information but also as to the patentability of mere information as invention and the potential authority over genetic and genealogical identity.

This concern regarding the ownership of life is perhaps the critical moral controversy in the creation of proprietary rights in biotechnology. This is distinct from concerns regarding animal welfare and the exclusion of others from the technology, which arguably are attributable not to the laws per se but to the system itself, including the business models built upon those laws. However the ethical issue is perhaps not so much the ownership of the patent, but the inventorship of the 'life'. For example, in the context of gene sequences, discussed in Part I, it is not the ownership of genetic identity that is at stake, as it were, but the authorship of that identity. While the concept of ownership may have currency in a conventional economic model of knowledge products, it is the aspect of inventorship and the authority over the invention (when related to living material) that is perhaps more disconcerting in terms of the evolutionary interjection of the product. Although the exclusive rights conferred by the patent monopoly raise specific issues with respect to the subject matter at stake, the 'authorship' of that subject matter is what is perhaps more unsettling in the context of life technologies.

Therefore, the controversies surrounding intellectual property rights in these areas are conceptualised less in terms of ownership as in that of a chattel,[12] and more in terms of authorship, as in authority over a species. Indeed, ownership in a chattel may be defeated, interfered with and transferred, whereas authorship of a biotechnology is immutable. Regardless of the transfer of ownership in a patent, the inventorship remains untouched.

---

11 Biotechnology Directive, Article 6.

12 Nils Holtug questions the controversy over a patent over life forms: 'having "reverence for life" is not usually thought to imply that we may not own pets, livestock or crops.' He continues, 'So, although arguably the so-called Harvard mouse was harmed by being created, it is less clear that it was harmed or violated by being patented' (213). However, arguably the focus on 'ownership' is a misinterpretation of the issues. Rather, it is the question of 'inventorship' that gives rise to 'ownership' (in terms of patent rights) that creates rights to control the production, use, keeping and so on with respect to that animal. See Holtug N (2001) "Creating and Patenting New Life Forms," in Kuhse H & Singer P (eds) *A Companion to Bioethics*, Malden MA: Blackwell, 206 at 213.

The inventor retains the right to be recognised in the patent – the patent immortalises that inventorship. Therefore, it is the concept of that sovereignty over a transgenic species that encompasses the critical ethical questions. And the patent provides the necessary circumstances in which to exercise sovereignty over that species. The patent is an indicator of that authorship of the species.[13]

The invention of nature

Recalling discussions of the criteria for patentability, mere discoveries are not patentable as inventions.[14] There are important legal as well as social reasons for the exclusion of discoveries from protection. First, a mere discovery could never demonstrate the necessary inventive step to warrant protection by the patent monopoly and therefore it can be argued that nothing has been 'added' by the skill and ingenuity of the researcher. In that the patent system is described as an incentive to innovation, there is no innovation in a mere discovery. Second, a discovery already exists in nature. To grant private rights over a discovery would be to grant property in a naturally existing substance.

In this regard, many have argued that a gene is a naturally existing substance and inventions comprised of the function of particular gene sequences should be excluded from patentability as mere discoveries.[15] And indeed the United States Supreme Court has now found as such.[16]As discussed earlier, the expensive process of deciphering the function or purpose of a gene sequence

---

13 Similar concerns arise in relation to genetically modified crops and agriculture, particularly in relation to the licensing of patent-protected technology. Such agreements usually prohibit the saving of seed in that to do so would usually infringe any patent or plant variety right on the seed purchased (keeping a protected product outside the terms of the licence). These agreements also raise competition concerns related to the potential bundling of products by firms in a dominant position in the market (by tying the purchase of seed to the purchase of fertiliser and related products marketed by the dominant entity). Critics interpret this as interference with a natural system and then obligating users of that natural system to pay for that interference, removing the choice to adopt the technology and at the same time introducing a price for that technology.

14 EPC Article 52(2)(a).

15 For instance, see the discussion in Nwabueze RN (2007) *Biotechnology and the Challenge of Property: Property Rights in Dead Bodies, Body Parts and Genetic Information*, Aldershot: Ashgate, 18–19; Mgbeoji I (2006) *Global Biopiracy: Patents, Plants, and Indigenous Knowledge*, Vancouver: UBC Press, 143–4; Mills O (2005) *Biotechnological Inventions: Moral Restraints and Patent Law*, Aldershot: Ashgate, 11–17; Bently L & Sherman B (2014) *Intellectual Property Law*, 4th edn, Oxford: OxfordUniversity Press, 472; Salazar S (2003) "The World of Biotechnology Patents" in Bellmann C et al (eds) *Trading in Knowledge: Development Perspectives on TRIPS, Trade and Sustainability*, London: Earthscan. 117 at 123–4; and Scherer FM (2002) "The Economics of Human Gene Patents" 77(12) *Academic Medicine* 1348 (concerning the impact on new research).

16 *Association for Molecular Pathology v Myriad*, 133 S Ct 2107 (2013).

(the protein for which it codes and the function of that protein in the body) is considered to be worthy of reward by the patent system. Deciphering that function provides the 'industrial application' of the gene-related innovation.

In addition, gene sequences are isolated and cloned, rendering them 'outside' the individual and the integrity of the body. This brings the discussion to the question of human rights and genetic material. Isolation renders genetic material potentially legally and philosophically outside the ethical and human rights arguments regarding the sovereignty and integrity of the body and the enslaving of individuals, to which this discussion now turns.

Enslaving life

It is a fundamental human right of every individual to enjoy 'life, liberty and security of person'.[17] International human rights norms also protect against slavery. Article 4 of the UDHR mandates that 'No one shall be held in slavery or servitude; slavery and the slave trade shall be prohibited in all their forms'. This prohibition against slavery has been widely interpreted as including a prohibition against the ownership of human biological resources, particularly through the privatisation of their genetic material and unique genetic identity.

It is useful to note here that the Biotechnology Directive explicitly states that the human body cannot constitute an invention:

> The human body, at the various stages of its formation and development, and the simple discovery of one of its elements, including the sequence or partial sequence of a gene, cannot constitute patentable inventions.[18]

Nevertheless, concerns remain that once material is isolated from the body, this makes it available to be developed and for any subsequent invention to be protected. This question of isolation from the body is particularly important in the context of inventions based on tissue samples obtained for other purposes (including therapeutic) and will also arise in the context of the collection and donation of material for public health databases. Significantly, the possibility of isolation of elements of 'life' will be subject to a diversity of cultural interpretation, particularly with respect to the appropriation of genetic resources of traditional and indigenous groups.

These various issues suggest that the integrity over one's body is necessarily protected and articulated upon the vital concept and process of consent. The concept of consent recognises and affirms the autonomy of the individual and is a concept that is vital in identifying and delimiting use and addressing issues arising in the collection of tissue and genetic samples, genetic resources and traditional knowledge.

---

17 UDHR Article 3.
18 Directive 98/44/EC, Article 5.1.

The legal framework for biotechnology

As introduced earlier, the key piece of legislation regulating intellectual property in biotechnology in Europe is the Biotechnology Directive.[19] The directive was introduced to clarify and harmonise legal protection and patentability of biotechnology-related inventions in the EU, including inventions relating to human gene sequences and plant varieties. At the same time, the directive explicitly excludes from patentability process for human cloning, human germ-line modification and the commercial or industrial use of human embryos. An independent committee, the European Group on Ethics in Science and New Technologies (EGE), advises the European Commission on the ethical issues arising in these areas of technology.

Although the original proposal for the Biotechnology Directive was adopted by the European Commission in 1988,[20] due to the complex ethical issues regarding patents and life forms it was a further ten years before its final approval in 1998.[21] The significant development made in order to facilitate its adoption was to accept the patentability of human gene-related inventions if the protein coded by the gene sequence (and ideally also the function of the protein for which it codes) was disclosed in the claimed invention. Another area of significant debate was that of traditional knowledge, but a proposal for disclosure of the origin of traditional sources was rejected in the final document.[22]

In particular, the passage of the Biotechnology Directive met with opposition largely articulated upon the undesirability and immorality of proprietary rights being granted over material occurring in the natural environment. Arguments included claims that the Biotechnology Directive would be inconsistent with European patent law (rendering discoveries and naturally-occurring substances patentable) and with the Convention on Biological Diversity (there being no provision for prior informed consent in accessing genetic material, although there is mention in Recital 26). Indeed, in a press release of 27 November 1997, Greenpeace raised concerns regarding bioprospecting of genetic resources in developing countries, condemning the law as 'a new form of genetic imperialism'[23] and encouraged biopiracy.[24]

19 Directive 98/44/EC.
20 Proposal for a Council Directive on the Legal Protection of Biotechnological Inventions. COM (88) 496 final, 17 October 1988.
21 For instance, see the discussion of the rejection of the 1995 draft in Watson R (1995) "Brussels Rejects Biotechnology Directive" 11 March, *British Medical Journal*: 619.
22 Proposal for a European Parliament and Council Directive on the legal protection of biotechnological inventions COM(95) 661 final. However, disclosure of origin is included in Recital 27 of the final adopted version of the Biotechnology Directive: 'Whereas if an invention is based on biological material of plant or animal origin or if it uses such material, the patent application should, where appropriate, include information on the geographical origin of such material, if known'.
23 Greenpeace (1997). 'Greenpeace Condemns Commercialization of Life'. Press Release. 27 November 1997.
24 Greenpeace (1998). 'Biopiracy Urged by EU Biotechnology Patent Directive'. Press Release. 12 May 1998,

After the directive's adoption, the Netherlands government, supported by the governments of Italy and Norway, challenged the Biotechnology Directive on six grounds:[25] the directive was on the incorrect legal basis; the principle of subsidiarity; the principle of legal certainty; obligations of European member states at international law (including the TRIPS Agreement and the CBD); breach of fundamental rights to respect for human dignity; and procedural rules in the adoption of the proposal.

In particular, with respect to the fourth plea (obligations at international law), the Netherlands government argued that TRIPS allows member states flexibility as to the granting of patents for plants and animals,[26] and that flexibility is consequently removed by the Biotechnology Directive. Further, Article 6(1) of the Biotechnology Directive, which excludes inventions where commercial exploitation of the invention would be contrary to *ordre public*, is compatible with the comparable provision of the EPC, which excludes inventions for which the publication or exploitation would be contrary to *ordre public*.[27] With respect to obligations created by the CBD, the Netherlands argued that the Biotechnology Directive was incompatible with the principle of fair and equitable sharing of benefits, a principle central to the efficacy of the CBD. Nevertheless, the European Court of Justice (ECJ) rejected all of these grounds. Specifically, regarding the fourth plea, the ECJ determined that the risk to the principles of the CBD was not created by the provisions themselves but by the subsequent use of the patenting framework (that is, the commercial business models as distinct from the rules).

Similar considerations underpinned the decision on whether the Biotechnology Directive was contrary to fundamental rights to respect for human dignity. On this point, the ECJ considered that the directive concerned only a procedural framework for patents and not an ethical framework for research before the patent or commercialisation on the basis of the patent:

> It is clear from those provisions that, as regards living matter of human origin, the Directive frames the law on patents in a manner sufficiently rigorous to ensure that the human body effectively remains unavailable and inalienable and that human dignity is thus safeguarded … Reliance on this fundamental right [the right to human integrity] is, however, clearly misplaced as against a directive which concerns only the grant of patents

---

25 *Kingdom of Netherlands v European Parliament and Council of European Union* (C-377/98) [2001] 3 CMLR 49.

26 TRIPS, Article 27.3(b).

27 EPC, Article 53(a). The ECJ determined that the applicant did not submit adequate evidence to support this aspect of the plea and so concluded that it could not accept this argument in the absence of specific examples. *Kingdom of Netherlands v European Parliament and Council of European Union* (C-377/98) [2001] 3 CMLR 49: Paragraph 62. The European Patent Office subsequently found that anything which offends Article 6 of the Directive is automatically contrary to article 53(a): *Transgenic animals/HARVARD* (T 315/03) [2006] OJ EPO 15 at [r 6].

> and whose scope does not therefore extend to activities before and after that grant, whether they involve research or the use of the patented products.
>
> The grant of a patent does not preclude legal limitations or prohibitions applying to research into patentable products or the exploitation of patentable products, as the 14th recital of the preamble to the Directive points out. The purpose of the Directive is not to replace the restrictive provisions which guarantee, outside the scope of the Directive, compliance with certain ethical rules which include the right to self-determination by informed consent.[28]

This relationship between the commercial framework of patent law and the ethical context is important. While patent law may not be relevant as a mechanism for ethical oversight, nevertheless its application may facilitate commercial activities that might be considered contrary to sound ethical principles including respect for human dignity. Returning to the discussion of the quality of 'use' as both a limit to the scope of the patent and as a way in which to contain the impact of a commercial commodity on sensitive research questions, the relationship between use and morality emerges as a viable 'framework' for the commercial patent system.

A moral framework for the patent system

Useless immorality

The patent system is not responsible for the ethical oversight of research agenda as such. The 2002 Report of the Canadian Biotechnology Advisory Committee on the Patenting of Higher Life Forms recommended 'The patent system ought only to take account of economic considerations. While ethical and social concerns are important, they are better addressed using other means, such as regulation, criminal law, or industry best practices.'[29] However, the committee goes on to explain that this economic nature of the patent system does not preclude the addressing of ethical concerns to a limited extent within that legal framework.[30] While the patent system is not a system of ethical oversight as such, morality considerations may inform the definition of patentability, arguably in as much as the immorality of an invention would compromise its 'use-value' as a commercial product. This is articulated in the patent system through the exception of *ordre public*, crudely translated as public order and morality.[31]

28 *Kingdom of Netherlands v European Parliament and Council of European Union* (C-377/98) [2001] 3 CMLR 49: Paragraphs 77–80.

29 Canadian Biotechnology Advisory Committee (2002). P*atenting of Higher Life Forms*. Report. Ottawa: CBAC, 30.

30 Canadian Biotechnology Advisory Committee *Patenting of Higher Life Forms*, 30.

31 TRIPS Article 27(2); EPC Article 53; there is no such requirement in some notable jurisdictions, including the United States.

The *ordre public* exception is provided in Article 6 of the Biotechnology Directive, which also explicitly prohibits patent protection for processes for cloning human beings, processes for modifying germ-line identity of human beings and uses of human embryos for industrial or commercial purposes. Article 6 also specifically excludes processes for modifying the genetic identity of animals and animals themselves resulting from such processes where those processes are likely to cause suffering not balanced by substantial medical benefit to humans or animals. This provision in particular has been criticised as inadequate in its protection of animal welfare and for its provision of patent protection for transgenic animals where substantial medical benefit can be shown. However, it is noteworthy that this is the first time these specific exclusions were introduced into patent law in Europe.[32]

Recital 38 of the directive provides a general guide to the interpretation of *ordre public*, including reference to offences to human dignity (such as the production of human–animal chimeras). Recalling the discussion in Part II, the right to dignity is a central concern of basic human rights discourse. The jurisprudence of the EPO on the interpretation of this equivalent provision in the EPC[33] is that such interpretation should be undertaken in a restrictive way.

The interpretation of the provision was first considered in the 1989 *OncoMouse* decision of the EPO: *Harvard/OncoMouse*.[34] The OncoMouse case concerned the patentability of genetically modified mice and on appeal to the Technical Board of Appeal, the EPO examined both ethical and environmental issues raised by this patent. The board remitted the case to the Examining Division for reconsideration on the basis that the interpretation of Article 53(a) should be based upon a utilitarian balancing of interests – the suffering of the animals and potential environmental risks against the benefit of the invention to humanity. On this basis, the Examining Division held that the invention was patentable.

First implementation report: ordre public *in the directive*

As part of the ordinary review process of European legislation, in 2002 the European Commission provided its first review of the Biotechnology Directive.[35] Regarding the first assessment report, this was to concern the relevance of publication to research in biotechnology and, in particular, the impact of failure to publish or late publication of papers on patentable subjects. The subsequent reports are to deal with any problems concerning

32 There is also no mention of plants in this provision, which has raised some criticism of the ability to rely on *ordre public* to address possible environmental concerns. However, EPO jurisprudence establishes that the environment can be relevant to the determination of *ordre public*: *Plant Genetic Systems* (T 356/93) [1995] EPOR 357.

33 EPC, Article 53(a).

34 *OncoMouse/HARVARD* (T 19/90)[1990] OJ EPO 476

35 See Biotechnology Directive, Article 16.

the relationship between the directive and international human rights agreements. The first assessment was submitted in January 2002.[36]

In October of the same year, the first implementation report, *Development and Implications of Patent Law in the Field of Biotechnology and Genetic Engineering*[37] was produced. This document represents the Commission's first annual report on implementation of the directive. Accepting that patents and transaction costs may introduce obstacles to access for research and development, the report makes reference to the possible obstacles posed by patents in the context of research, noting that the directive is not intended to call into question the freedom of research in Europe.

The report also makes note of the exclusion of inventions where commercial exploitation would be contrary to *ordre public*, stating that the ECJ has determined that the directive is sufficiently precise on this exclusion.[38] Importantly, the application of the *ordre public* exclusion introduces questions of the cultural specificity of each member state. On this, the ECJ is noted as considering the expertise of national administrative and court authorities to be sufficient to take account of 'social and cultural context of each Member State'.[39] As the report maintains, this indicates the need for some margin of manoeuvre within each member state to apply 'the ethical, sociology or philosophical context of each country'.[40]

A moral limit to the patent

An examination of the specific ethical issues raised by stem cell research and cloning was an explicit request by the then President of the Commission, Romano Prodi, and was reported in 2000.[41] The European Group on Ethics in Science and New Technologies (EGE) has since reported on the importance of balancing the interests of the inventor and the interests of society as well as providing certainty in the limits and conditions for patentability of inventions in this area, expressly requiring precise and useful disclosure of industrial application:

> The patent system aims to keep a balance between the inventor's interest and the interests of society. That is why a fair balance between both

36 An assessment of the implications for basic genetic engineering research of failure to publish, or late publication of, papers on subjects which could be patentable as required under Article 16(b) of Directive 98/44/EC.

37 Report from the Commission to the European Parliament and Council. Development and implications of patent law in the field of biotechnology and genetic engineering. 7 October 2002. COM(2002) 545 final.

38 *Kingdom of Netherlands v European Parliament and Council of European Union* (C-377/98) [2001] 3 CMLR 49: paragraphs 35–39.

39 See further *Kingdom of Netherlands v European Parliament and Council of European Union* (C-377/98) [2001] 3 CMLR 49: Paragraph 38.

40 Report from the Commission, COM(2002) 545 final, 23.

41 As reported in Opinion No 15 Ethical Aspects of Human Stem Cell Research and Use, 14 November 2000.

> interests, meaning that the scope of the claim of the patent must be proportional to the scope of the effectively described applications of the inventions, has an ethical dimension.[42]

In maintaining that balance, the diversity of stake-holders, including other researchers and inventors, must be addressed. The ethical implications of patents as possible barriers to access to healthcare[43] and access to innovation are of critical interest:

> [T]he Group again insists on the necessity to avoid the granting of too broad patents that would impair further research and development … It is therefore the opinion of EGE that patents shall only be granted, when the claim refers to a specific and a sufficiently accurately described stem cell line and its industrial application. That involves a consistent relationship between a patent claim and the description of an invention.[44]

The first implementation report identifies the important topic of the scope of patents on inventions related to genes and stem cells.[45] The very important limitation and condition of patentability in this area is arguably that of the function disclosed in the patent.[46] These topics were considered again in the second implementation report at the end of 2005[47] and in 2016 an expert group appointed by the European Commission reported on the patentability of human stem cells.[48]

Technologies of nature: genes, stem cells, embryos

It is useful, in this context, to revisit earlier discussions regarding concerns raised by gene-related inventions, the patentability of gene sequences, the arguments regarding 'natural products' and 'discoveries,' and recent developments towards purpose-bound approaches to interpreting patent

---

42 Opinion No 16 Ethical Aspects of Patenting Inventions Involving Human Stem Cells, 7 May 2002: Paragraph 1.18.
43 On this point, Opinion No 16 notes: 'One ethical dilemma arises due to the fact that patents can encourage scientific progress which can be used to the benefit of better health care, and at the same time, patents can also impair access to the health care' (Paragraph 2.2)
44 Opinion No 16, Paragraph 2.7.
45 Report from the Commission, COM(2002) 545 final.
46 See further the discussion of use, purpose-bound protection and gene patents in Chapter 2.
47 Report from the Commission to the European Parliament and Council. Development and implications of patent law in the field of biotechnology and genetic engineering. COM(2005) 312 final.
48 European Commission (2016), Final Report of the Expert Group on the development and implications of patent law in the field of biotechnology and genetic engineering (17 May 2016), Part B.

protection in this area of technology. In particular, it is relevant to reaffirm the moral efficacy of use as a constraining value for the invention.

Earlier discussion in Part I also introduced the importance of consumer information in the context of medicines and the capacity of such use-directed labelling as a potential limit on what can be interpreted as 'infringing activity'. In other words, a medicine may produce beneficial side effects not claimed in the original patented invention, but it is possible that production for purposes of the side effect may not infringe the original patent if that use is explicitly disclaimed on the packaging.[49] While this is still a very unclear and volatile area in the law of patents and medicines, it is a very important example of the way in which a defined purpose can potentially limit the reach of the patent monopoly. Such developments introduce consumer-led approaches adding importance and relevance to questions of corporate accountability.

Rights to life or rights to use

The second Commission implementation report[50] addresses the patenting of inventions based on gene sequences isolated from the human body and inventions relating to stem cells. Responding to the work of the group of experts, the Commission addressed two key topics: the patenting of gene sequences isolated from the human body; and the patenting of inventions relating to stem cells. This issue has subsequently been considered by the ECJ as well as by the expert group in 2016. Nevertheless, the difficult issues remain.

Life limits: stem cells

Regarding the patentability of human embryonic stem cells and cell lines, the second implementation report distinguishes between totipotent stem cells and pluripotent embryonic stem cells. The former can develop into a human being, rendering totipotent stem cells inappropriate subject matter for patent protection on the grounds of human dignity.[51] Pluripotent embryonic stem cells, however, do not (yet) have the capability to develop into human beings and so they might be the subject of a patent.[52] Adult stem cells, as such, are not excluded from patentability.[53] Reiterating discussion elsewhere in this book, the scope of research permitted is not a concern of patent law,[54] but the application of commercial monopolies to the invention is. Approaches

49 Assuming such a disclaimer precludes the use for the patented purpose from being reasonably foreseeable.

50 Report from the Commission, COM(2005) 312 final.

51 See *Brüstle v Greenpeace* (C-34/10) [2011] ECR I-9821.

52 See *International Stem Cell Corporation* (C-354/13) (2014) ECLI:EU:C:2014:2106.

53 European Commission, Final Report of the Expert Group, 142.

54 Save where the research would infringe the patent and then there is usually a patent exception to permit some forms of research.

to research in this area will therefore be influenced by the ethical and philosophical positions of the particular member state.

Authoring life

Transgenic animals raise several critical issues. First, there are the significant concerns regarding animal welfare and animal suffering (particularly in animals bred for expression of a particular disease) and the process by which such animals are produced (by introducing extraneous human genetic material into a mammalian embryo). Second, there is the question of the commodification and ownership of species seen to be effected by the patent law system. This presents not only ethical and moral concerns with respect to dominion over a species (as distinct from an individual) but also commercial and research issues with respect to obstacles to research practice, breeding and keeping subjects and related issues.

Transgenic animals have been developed in medical research and development for various purposes including the expression or predisposition for a particular human defect or disease state; and expression of commercial quantities of a particular human protein.

One of the most famous and protracted examples of litigation in transgenic species is that of the Harvard OncoMouse. First patented in the US,[55] the Harvard OncoMouse is an invention involving a mouse genetically modified to develop cancer. The OncoMouse is created by injecting the 'oncogene' into the fertilised mouse ovum, which is then implanted in a female host. Mice born with the oncogene (founder mice) are then mated with normal mice and the offspring carrying the oncogene are then used for cancer studies.

The patent application concerned the process to produce the OncoMouse and the products themselves (the founder mice and the second-generation offspring carrying the oncogene).[56] Patent protection of the mice themselves gives Harvard the exclusive patent rights over the mice themselves (such as the right to manufacture or license for manufacture, to store and keep the mice, and so on). Harvard licenses the patent to Du Pont for manufacture and sale.

The issue of patentability

The patentability of this invention has been challenged in several jurisdictions. Earlier discussion introduced the opposition to the OncoMouse in the EPO, but ultimately the invention was found to be patentable over a decade later,

55 US Patent No 5, 567,607.

56 Note, Recitals 46–50 and Article 11 of the Biotechnology Directive deal with the use of animal reproductive material. Farmers are permitted to use such material for agricultural purposes but not for commercial activity.. See further the discussion Roughton A, Johnson P and Cook T (2014) *Roughton, Johnson and Cook: The Modern Law of Patents* (3rd edn), London: LexisNexis, paragraph 7.155 to 7.156

although various narrowing amendments were required.[57] Nevertheless, the conclusion in Europe is that there is no general exclusion in this jurisdiction with respect to the patentability of animals.[58] The patent is also protected in Australia and Japan.

However, in Canada, the jurisdiction considered in this case study, the litigation led to some very significant results. In Canada, the claims for patent protection of the animals themselves were ultimately rejected, making it the only industrialised country to prohibit patents on higher life forms.

The challenge in Canada

The process patent was originally granted in 1993 by the Canadian Intellectual Property Office (CIPO) but the application for protection of the mice themselves was refused. This decision was upheld by the Commissioner of Patents in 1995 and the Trial Division of the Federal Court in 1998.[59] However, in 2000 the Federal Court of Appeal allowed the appeal and determined that both the process and product patents were valid, maintaining that although patents could not be granted on human beings, patents on lower animals may be possible.[60]

The government of Canada (Commissioner of Patents) then served and filed an application to seek leave to appeal the Federal Court of Appeal's decision in the Supreme Court. In a press release, the CIPO stated that 'The Patent Office has consistently held the view that the current Patent Act does not allow for the patenting of higher life forms such as plants and animals.'[61] Of further note, the CIPO declared that public dialogue is necessary because of the important public interest, which resonates with the significance of the exception for *ordre public*.

The appeal to the Supreme Court[62] became an important test case to determine the scope of protection in this field. The patent claims on the process itself were upheld in the Supreme Court, but the patents on the mice themselves were rejected. In refusing patent protection for the mice, the court decided that the mouse could not constitute an invention because it was not fulfil the definition in the Act: 'any new and useful art, process, machine, manufacture or composition of matter, or any new and useful improvement in any art, process, machine, manufacture or composition of matter'.[63] In that only 'manufacture' and 'composition of matter' could apply

57 *Transgenic animals/HARVARD* (T 315/03) [2006] OJ EPO 15..
58 This presents the strange proposition that animal varieties are not patentable, but all varieties in a species are patentable: *Oncomouse/HARVARD* [1990] OJ EPO 476.
59 *Harvard College v Canada (Commissioner of Patents)* [1998] 3 FC 510.
60 *Harvard College v Canada (Commissioner of Patents)* [2000] 4 FC 528.
61 Canadian Intellectual Property Office (CIPO) 'The Government Seeks Leave to Appeal the Federal Court of Appeal's Decision on the Harvard Oncomouse Case to the Supreme Court.' Press Release. 4 October 2000.
62 *Harvard College v Canada (Commissioner of Patents)* [2002] SCC 76.
63 Canada Patents Act, RSC 1984, s 2.

to the mouse, the Court focused on these concepts, ruling that 'manufacture' refers to non-living, mechanistic processes and the latter could not be read as applying to higher life forms.[64]

On this point, the concept of life form itself indicates the possibility of autonomy, autopoeisis and capacity for self-reproduction, something which ethically and philosophically distinguishes the mouse from mechanistic manufacture. This autonomy of living things (including plants) also informs current debate in genetic modification in other areas (such as food crops) because of the capacity to respond to environmental changes and to ensure the perpetuation of genetic material through reproduction.

While Canada provides patent protection for simple life forms (single-celled organisms or microorganisms) it is now established that ownership of higher life forms raises more serious moral and ethical issues so as to exclude such subject matter from patent protection.[65]

Pharming

In addition to the development of particular species for the purposes of medical research, animals have also been developed as hosts for medicinal products. Pharming refers to the use of host animals (and also plants) to express certain medicinal product (for example, in milk). The development of such animals, sometimes described as 'animal factories', has attracted a great deal of criticism, not only with respect to potential safety issues, but also in terms of ethical concerns regarding the use of animals in this way.[66] So-called pharm animals are being described as 'revolutionising' the pharmaceutical industry. In particular, pharming is especially valuable for producing product in substantial quantities (as in milk), usually for proteins.

The first example[67] to be approved in Europe and the United States is the use of genetically modified goats to express a product, ATryn, in their milk. ATryn is a recombinant form of human antithrombin (ATIII), used in the treatment of hereditary antithrombin deficiency (HAD), where the individual is missing the gene responsible for making the protein, antithrombin. HAD can lead to various problems, including deep-vein thrombosis, because the blood clots too easily. ATryn is marketed as a much safer way by which to

64 See generally Section B of the Supreme Court's judgment: *Harvard College v Canada (Commissioner of Patents)* [2002] SCC 76.

65 The Canadian Supreme Court revisited the issue in *Schmeiser v Monsanto* [2004] SCC 34.

66 See further the comprehensive treatment of public views and attitudes as well as considerations of animal welfare in Rehbinder E et al (2009) *Pharming: Promises and Risks of Biopharmaceuticals Derived from Genetically Modified Plants and Animals*, New York: Springer.

67 For a review of the sorts of projects being undertaken, see Lievens A et al (2015) 'Genetically Modified Animals: Options and Issues for Traceability and Enforcement' 44 *Trends in Food Science and Technology* 159.

deliver the missing copy of the gene than other methods, such as through human blood plasma (which carries the risk of vCJD (Variant Creutzfeldt-Jakob disease). Antithrombin is administered to HAD patients during times when the usual treatment by warfarin is too risky (such as during childbirth and surgery).

GTC Biotherapeutics, the company responsible for developing the drug, applied for European Market Authorisation in January 2004. However, in February 2006 the European Medicines Agency (EMEA) refused the application to license ATryn, calling for more evidence on the benefits of the drug.[68] After reversing this decision and deciding to issue the licence in June 2006,[69] as set out in its positive opinion, the EMEA Committee for Medicinal Products for Human Use (CMPH) gave approval to the drug. It was approved by the US Food and Drug Administration (FDA) in 2009.[70]

The various applications of life technologies have introduced the very critical relationship between use and authority. Indeed, while this provokes anxiety with respect to the creation of proprietary rights in inventions based upon living materials, it also introduces the authority of the beneficial interest in those inventions and in the accessibility and availability of these benefits in the area of biotechnology research. The nature of this 'trust' is further complicated where identity is tied to invention and to resources for research, especially in the context of public health databases – life's libraries.

68 EMEA. 'Committee for Medicinal Products for Human Use'. Press Release. 23 February 2006. (EMEA/69276/2006).

69 EMEA. 'European Medicines Agency Adopts First Positive Opinion for a Medicinal Product Derived from Transgenic Biotechnology'. Press Release. 2 June 2006 (EMEA/203163/2006).

70 Approval 6 February 2009 (Reference: BL 125284/0).

7 Life's libraries

Introduction

Privacy is a contested and contentious zone. Not only does it concern the personal freedom of individuals within their own domestic space, but also the legitimate secrecy and privacy of the commercial private enterprise. In the context of medicine, the concept of privacy arguably compels new language and a reconfiguration of the bases. When considered in the context of the intrusion of that space by intellectual property laws, the pirates become chameleonic. The range of controversy attached to intellectual property over benefits derived from genetic resources, tissue samples and related personal material introduces a new configuration of players – the privateers of the private space are the same as those 'victims' of personal 'piracy'.

The advance of genomics in medicine and medical research has raised specific issues with respect to the creation of proprietary interests in inventions based upon donor material, databases compiling samples and related information and genetic resources specific to a particular community. These developments in medical technologies interfere with the conventional division between the public good (as distinct from goods) of medical research, and development and the privacy of the individual, the family and identity. The operation of intellectual property within this area raises complex ethical as well as legal issues with respect to sovereignty over genetic resources (including those of the individual) and indeed the concept of life in the context of the invention as product.

Privateers and the piracy of the private sphere

Habermas has previously articulated the eighteenth-century public sphere[1] as a social assemblage characterised by its privileged perspective upon enlightenment and proposed as a kind of manifestation of the consensus on enlightened ideals of progress and innovation. In this way, it is valorised by the rationalism and efficiency of scientific and progressive discourse –

1 See in general Habermas J (1989/[1962]) *The Structural Transformation of the Public Sphere*, Burger T (trans), Cambridge: Polity Press.

the scientific basis of research and development, the immutable value of innovation and creativity. This is especially clear in the ethical priority afforded to an undifferentiated 'research and development' at the 'cost' or devaluation of the private:

> The identification of the public of 'property owners' with that of 'common human beings' could be accomplished all the more easily, as the social status of the bourgeois private persons in any event usually combined the characteristic attributes of ownership and education. The acceptance of the fiction of *one* public, however, was facilitated above all by the fact that it actually had positive functions in the context of the political emancipation of civil society from mercantilist rule and from absolutist regimentation in general. Because it turned the principle of publicity against the established authorities, the objective function of the public sphere in the political realm could initially converge with its self-interpretation derived from the categories of the public sphere in the world of letters; the interest of the owners of private property could converge with that of the freedom of the individual in general.[2]

Habermas identifies the public sphere as taking on political functions during this period,[3] maintaining that

> The self-interpretation of the public in the political realm, as reflected in the crucial category of the legal norm, was the accomplishment of a consciousness functionally adapted to the institutions of the public sphere in the world of letters.[4]

Indeed the politicising of the public sphere is a critical characteristic of civil society activity in campaigns dealing with intellectual property and the right to public health. For example, the WHO identifies the role of civil society in creating a 'norm cascade' with respect to an explicit rights agenda on access to medicines.[5]

Indeed, much of the rhetorical conflict in the contemporary intellectual property debates in this area reflects the conflict between the purported scientific rationalism and commercial efficiency of the supposed public sphere of substantial medical benefit and the specific interests of the private sphere where such efficiency is not necessarily of material relevance. In particular, this is arguably related to the historically personal nature of the freedom that is socially and politically accommodated in the private sphere, while the public sphere is

2 Ibid., 56.
3 Ibid., 73
4 Ibid., 55.
5 WHO CSDH (2008), *Closing the Gap in a Generation: Health Equity Through Action on the Social Determinants of Health*, Geneva: WHO, 164.

subject to greater oversight and duty. Furthermore, in gender studies scholarship, the distinction is of critical importance in characterising the value attached to public sphere activities as distinct from the devaluing of that production within the private sphere.[6] Similarly, a certain privilege attaches to those purporting to speak for the public sphere in terms of the ethical priority credited to those speaking from the perspective of substantial medical benefit. On the other hand, defence of the private is perhaps devalued as unscientific and uncivilised.

This resonates more broadly in current intellectual property debates in the apparent curtailment of liberties enshrined as exceptions within the law, such that users who have been more systematically pursued in what is otherwise seemingly uncommercial litigation.[7] The 'costs' being pursued are clearly outside the conventional model of business efficiency, and the 'private' activity is becoming more and more incorporated within the overall economic model of innovation. In other words, the characteristic personal freedom of the private sphere is at odds with the privateering of the 'public benefit' of private intellectual property rights in that private space. Those seen to be interfering with the ordinary exploitation of intellectual property rights (particularly the re-use of information in a digital but non-commercial context) are interpreted as acting contrary to the genuine public benefit (that of creativity and innovation). However, arguably, such examples of private use (in the social rather than strictly legal sense) are examples of enjoyment of the personal freedom of private and uncommercial activity. Similarly, challenges for intellectual property frameworks with respect to the privatisation and commercialisation of medical information, whether incorporated in a tissue-based invention or traditional knowledge, are to protect against the expropriation of that information and to ensure the sharing of benefits derived from that privateering of the private sphere.

When it comes to individual sovereignty over one's body or a community's sovereignty over its natural resources, this is co-opted into the dominant discourse of public–private. The attempt to be compensated for access to the private sphere (the individual's tissue, the community's genetic resources, Indonesia's bird flu samples) is immediately condemned as the immodest commodification of the private. That is, it challenges the very human dignity, as a fundamental element of human rights, incorporated in the physical identity of human life.[8] Yet the commodification of inventions derived from those products, and the containment of the benefits from those inventions

6 For instance, see the discussion in Rössler B (2004) 'Gender and Privacy: A Critique of the Liberal Tradition' in Rössler B (ed) *Privacies: Philosophical Evaluations*, Stanford, CA: Stanford University Press, 52.
7 For instance, the rise in copyright suits against individual consumers: Peel M (2008) 'Woman Faces £16000 penalty after Sharing Computer Game' *Financial Times* 19 August. These sorts of claims are now brought in the IPEC Small Claims Court.
8 See further the discussion of dignity and human rights in Beyleveld D & Brownsword R (1998) 'Human Dignity, Human Rights and Human Genetics'

within the commercial firm, is exonerated as properly public. Therefore, at once both the intrusion in the private sphere and the commercialisation of benefits derived from that intrusion are justified by the 'public' created in intellectual property rhetoric.

Legal privacy

Trade secrets and breach of confidence

Trade secrets law protects information rendering it unlike other areas of intellectual property law, despite its inclusion within the TRIPS Agreement.[9] The subject matter of protection – information – is not defined in and of itself. There is no fixation of the information as a formal requirement of protection.[10] The quality of confidence confers greater value in the goods is by virtue of the circumstances surrounding its acquisition, as distinct from the good, protected by trade secrets laws and actions for breach of confidence.

Trade secrets and confidential information will have commercial relevance for the protection and licensing of know-how, business information and related information of commercial value. Importantly, of course, this legal characterisation of information relationships will also concern patient information and medical treatment. Indeed, it is this overlap between commercial confidential information and privacy that has raised some difficulty in practice.[11] Its rationale is founded in both moral (the duty to observe the confidence, that is, to fulfil obligations of trustworthiness as created by the trust placed within the relationship) and economic judgment (the market may direct that the cost of a patent is beyond the value of the information maintained as a secret; or the information simply may not constitute an invention).

Data protection

In addition to trade secrets law it is possible that there will be protection available under data protection laws. The role of data protection law is to protect personal data, whereas the purpose of trade secrets is to prevent the disclosure of industrial information. In Europe, the law relating to data protection was harmonised in accordance with the Data Protection Directive,[12]

---

in Brownsword R et al (eds) *Law and Human Genetics: Regulating a Revolution*, Oxford: Hart, 69.

9 TRIPS Article 39.

10 There is a strict requirement of particularisation of the information to avoid the imposition of vague obligations.

11 See for example, *R v Department of Health ex p Source Information* [2001] QB 424.

12 Directive 95/46/EC of the European Parliament and of the Council of 24 October 1995 on the protection of individuals with regard to the processing of personal data and on the free movement of such data.

which will be replaced in 2018 by a General Data Protection Regulation.[13] The EU data protection regime requires certain principles to apply, known as the 'Data Protection Principles.'[14] In practice, data protection operates in conjunction with trade secrets and privacy laws.

Property and human tissue

Property in one's own tissue remains a significant issue in current developments, particularly in the increased emphasis on genetic sampling and collection, genomic databases and the bioprospecting and exploitation of genetic material. Individual interests in personal tissue samples and the impact of subsequent commercialisation of developments based on such samples raise specific ethical issues and possible constraints upon the scope and treatment of inventions. Relevant to this discussion is the question of proprietary rights in personal genetic resources and the ethical and proprietary implications of organ transplants.

Some have argued that individual sovereignty must be protected by the recognition of proprietary rights in one's own body.[15] The appropriation of tissue for the purposes of research might therefore be governed by the concept of compulsory purchase or, as it is termed in the US, the eminent domain.[16] Compulsory purchase or eminent domain is the inherent right of government to compulsorily acquire property for the purposes of public benefit, usually on the basis of fair and just terms. Therefore, the compulsory acquisition of that property and the development of projects upon that property would be governed by the principle that those projects must be for the development of

13 Regulation (EU) No 2016/679 on the protection of natural persons with regard to the processing of personal data and on the free movement of such data, and repealing Directive 95/46/EC (General Data Protection Regulation). It comes into force on 25 May 2018.

14 These include: Personal data shall be processed fairly and lawfully and, in particular, shall not be processed unless at least one of the relevant conditions is met, and in the case of sensitive personal data, at least one of the special conditions is also met: Personal data shall be obtained only for one or more specified and lawful purposes, and shall not be further processed in any manner incompatible with that purpose or those purposes; Personal data shall be adequate, relevant and not excessive in relation to the purpose or purposes for which they are processed; Personal data shall be accurate and, where necessary, kept up to date; Personal data processed for any purpose or purposes shall not be kept for longer than is necessary for that purpose or those purposes; Personal data shall be processed in accordance with the rights of data subjects; Appropriate technical and organisational measures shall be taken against unauthorised or unlawful processing of personal data and against accidental loss or destruction of, or damage to, personal data.

15 For instance, see the discussion in Nwabueze RN (2007) *Biotechnology and the Challenge of Property: Property Rights in Dead Bodies, Body Parts, and Genetic Information*, Aldershot: Ashgate, 225–31.

16 Stanton A (2008) 'Forfeited Consent: Body Parts in Eminent Domain' in Gibson J (ed) *Patenting Lives: Life Patents, Culture and Development*, Aldershot: Ashgate, 95.

public resources and for the public benefit. This indicates suggestions of access and benefit-sharing, as distinct from the privatisation and commercialisation of benefits as in business models based on patent monopolies.

These kinds of arguments characterise the rights of the individual as legal rights in private property. However, the beneficial interest in knowledge as a public good is not only more defensible but also more effective in safeguarding access to benefits of scientific research. This tension between personal and property rights is fundamental to debate in the commodification of the body and indeed in scientific research more broadly as a public good.

Personal rights or property rights

The debate over rights in one's own tissue is complex. As the exclusive rights conferred upon a patentee show, proprietary rights in this context amount to a bundle of rights.[17] However, it is not necessary that all manifestations of a proprietary right inevitably confer the full bundle of rights; indeed, intellectual property rights themselves are characterised by their partial nature as distinct from granting full sovereignty over its subject matter. As Dickenson suggests, the misapprehension over property in the body is linked to an incorrect perception that of property 'as an all-or-nothing concept'.[18] It is to this concern, therefore, that Dickenson attributes the conservative approaches to proprietary rights in the context of the human body.

At the same time, arguments for the recognition of self-ownership in the body or attempts to derive benefit from the sharing of genetic resources are condemned, by the very same logic, as an undesirable and deplorable commodification of the private sphere. Arguably this renders not only the individual, but also indigenous and traditional communities in particular, especially vulnerable when the entire possibility for conceptualising this relationship is premised upon property (whether in terms of the legal scope of rights if property in the body is to be determined or whether in terms of the moral scope of commodification of the body). That is, if the democratisation of the public sphere is premised solely upon proprietary relationships and rights to property, then the possibility for considerations outside that model is limited. The system appears logically and inherently consistent, functioning upon the concept of (market) freedom exercised and understood through rights to private property.

In the case of *Moore v Regents of the University of California*,[19] Arabian J stated that to grant property in body tissue would be 'to regard the human vessel – the single most venerated and protected subject in any civilized society – as equal with the basest commercial commodity'.[20] John Moore was

17 TRIPS Article 28.
18 Dickenson D (2007) *Property in the Body*, Cambridge: Cambridge University Press, 14.
19 *Moore v Regents of the University of California*, 51 Cal. 3rd 120 (Californian Supreme Court 1990).
20 *Moore v Regents of the University of California*, 141.

a patient of David Golde at the University of California Medical Center, and was diagnosed with hair-cell leukaemia in 1976. As part of his treatment, Dr Golde recommended to Mr Moore that his spleen should be removed. Mr Moore consented to this treatment. Because of the rare form of Mr Moore's leukaemia it was likely that his cells would be of some research value. Therefore, prior to the procedure, Dr Golde arranged for a co-researcher, Shirley Quan, to collect samples of the spleen once it was removed. The significance of this collection is that the samples were not required for Mr Moore's treatment. Instead, the samples were intended for use in research (possibly with the potential for commercial application of the results of that research).

The question of subsequent use is significant because it is the value of use to which any consent applies. Therefore, use is the critical determining factor not only in the case of tissue samples from the individual but also in terms of access to genetic resources of a community. Use is instrumental to reciprocal trust and mutual benefit in access, as distinct from mere exchange and remuneration. In the present case, Mr Moore had not been consulted regarding this collection nor had he consented to this subsequent use.

This issue of subsequent use is important also from the perspective of the scope of that use. While some uses may be anticipated, it is not always possible to limit the application of collected samples or to revisit donors for fresh consent for new applications (for reasons of privacy, anonymity and so on). Mr Moore was consulted much later in the research to provide consent to the research. However, obviously this could not constitute prior informed consent.

Golde subsequently developed a cell-line based upon Moore's cells in 1979 and a patent on the cell-line was granted to the University of California in 1981.[21] In order to commercialise the cell-line, the university partnered with Genetics Institute Inc and Sandoz Pharmaceuticals. Mr Moore objected to the subsequent commercialisation of research based upon his tissue samples and commenced proceedings against Golde, Quan, the Regents of the University, Genetics Institute Inc and Sandoz Pharmaceuticals. His action included: breach of fiduciary duty and lack of informed consent; and conversion. The second action is interesting in that it concerns an intentional tort to personal property. This would necessitate the conceptualisation of the body as a chattel with which Golde had interfered. It would suggest that the sampling of tissue amounted to a deprivation of possession on the part of Moore. Therefore, the dispute articulated the body in terms of personal rights (consent) and property rights (conversion).

The majority of the Supreme Court of California accepted the claim for breach of fiduciary duty, holding that 'a physician must disclose personal interests unrelated to the patient's health, whether research or economic, that may affect the physician's professional judgement'.[22] However, the claim for conversion was more problematic. Moore had consented to the removal

21 US Patent No 4,438,032.

22 *Moore v Regents of the University of California*, 129.

of his spleen and so the action in conversion as a protection of possession did not apply. It was therefore a question of conversion as a protection of the spleen itself as Mr Moore's property after removal from his body. The court had to consider whether an individual has an ownership interest in tissue after removal from the body. The majority of the court decided that there was no such issue in the tissue once it was isolated from the body.

Nevertheless, the two minority judges argued that failure to protect self-ownership in tissue samples would not prevent others from creating proprietary rights in that tissue after it was isolated from the body. Broussard J maintained that a 'no-property' rule in the body is too simplistic and general, arguing that the court would easily find conversion in cases where samples might be stolen from a laboratory. Mosk J argued that a refusal to recognise ownership of the body actually creates the opportunity for it to become property of another. Indeed, Mosk J considered the relevance of proprietary rights to fulfilling the 'profound ethical imperative to respect the human body as the physical and temporal expression of the human persona'. This approach has been considered relevant to efforts to limit the vulnerability of the individual body to commodification: 'Self-ownership immunises against potential ownership by others'.[23]

The approach in *Moore* was followed subsequently in *Greenberg v Miami Children's Hospital Research Institute*,[24] where individuals donated human tissue and fluids to a doctor, who subsequently isolated the gene causing Canavan disease and then obtained a patent[25] and sought to license it. The patients sued the doctor for conversion of their biological materials, the court once more holding that there is no

> property interest for the body tissue and genetic information voluntarily given to Defendants. These were donations to research without any contemporaneous expectations of return of the body tissue and genetic samples, and thus conversion does not lie as a cause of action[26]

It went on to find

> the property right in blood and body samples also evaporates once the sample is voluntarily given to a third party.[27]

---

23 Davies M & Naffine N (2001) *Are Persons Property? Legal Debates About Property and Personality*, Aldershot: Ashgate, 12. See further Nwabueze, *Biotechnology and the Challenge of Property* 'the recognition of a limited property interest in the human body provides some safeguards against the concerns raised by advocates of a no-property regime … it is in the remedification of injuries resulting from misuse or misappropriation of corpses or body parts that the no-property argument becomes glaringly indefensible and absurd' (92).

24 264 F. Supp 2d 1064 (SD Fla 2003).

25 There was no issue as to the validity of the patent. It may be that the mere isolation of the gene was not actually patentable.

26 264 F. Supp 2d 1064, 1074 (SD Fla 2003).

27 264 F. Supp 2d 1064, 1075 (SD Fla 2003).

These two findings were followed once more in *Washington University v Catalona*[28] where the court held that the donation of tissue was a gift to the University. In this case it is not clear whether the property right came into being once it was in the possession of the doctor (and no longer in the patient) or there was a property right of the patient which was subsequently gifted. Nevertheless, in each of the cases it is clear that there is no proprietary right in the research derived from the biological material.

A slightly different issue arose in the English case of *Yearworth v North Bristol Trust*.[29] The claimants were diagnosed with cancer and invited by the hospital to store samples of semen in case chemotherapy made them infertile. One of the issues before the English Court of Appeal was whether sperm could be owned once it has left the body. In contrast to the other cases, this was not an issue of donation of tissue for research and then a reach through conversion claim, but rather a claim relating to the body part itself. The English court, albeit quite briefly, looked at a range of issues relating to the ownership of the human body, in particular the common law as to the ownership of a living body, a corpse and its parts.

It began by reiterating that a living body cannot be owned or even possessed by anyone including oneself.[30] As a person did not own their own body they also could not destroy it.[31] A human corpse, or part of it, is similarly unownable.[32] However, this rule changes where a person has lawfully dealt with a body differentiating it from a mere corpse awaiting burial.[33] So, for example, the removal of preserved body parts from the Royal College of Surgeons could be theft of property as the preservation of parts of the corpse turned them into property.[34] Significantly, the court went on to refer to *Hecht v Superior Court*,[35] where the Californian courts considered whether sperm stored by an individual fell within the ruling of *Moore*. It concluded that it did. The Californian court held that the distinction between the two situations was the intention to continue to exercise dispositional control. In *Moore*, once the spleen was removed the patient (originally) had no further

28 437 F Supp 2d 985 (ED Missouri 2006).
29 [2009] EWCA Civ 37, [2010] QB 1.
30 Ibid., paragraph 30; the possession point stemmed from the decision of the House of Lords in *R v Bentham* [2005] UKHL 18, [2005] 1 WLR 1057 where it was held that a person could not possess their hand (so when it was used as to imitate a gun it could not be possession of an imitation firearm).
31 Ibid., paragraph 30.
32 Ibid., paragraph 31.
33 See *Doodeward v Spence* (1908) 6 CLR 406 at 414 (a still-born two-headed baby was preserved and then exhibited as a curiosity. The preservation gave the body a proprietary nature).
34 *R v Kelly* [1999] QB 621. The court also distinguished *Dobson v North Tyneside Health Authority* [1997] 1 WLR 596 where a brain removed from autopsy was preserved for further study then destroyed. The difference being that there had been no requirement on the pathologist to retain the brain.
35 (1993) 20 Cal Rptr 2d 275.

interest in what happened to it, but in *Hecht*, there was a continuing interest in the sperm.[36] The Court of Appeal therefore concluded that the cancer patients had ownership of the sperm.[37]

The critical question in both jurisdictions therefore appears to be whether the person intended to keep control of their biological material after its removal. Absent any continuing right to control the biological material, either by the patient or the doctor at the time of its separation from the body, there is no property right in it.

The hierarchy of invention

Starting materials and 'co-invention'

The contribution of tissue and other bodily samples raises a further critical issue that has arisen in the contribution of genetic resources in other contexts as well. For example, the sharing of virus samples in the development of avian influenza schemes indicates several key considerations including access to genetic resources, the provision of essential starting material, the sharing of benefits, production capacity and supply of product. Where tissue or other genetic resources are contributed and subsequent research and labour produces an invention, an important question includes the kind of 'recognition', if any, that is possible for the original contributing individual or population. Fundamentally, these kinds of controversies in sovereignty over individual and community genetic resources and the provision of tissue and other genetic resources raise the issue of the essential nature of this contribution to the ultimate invention. In this context, one of the key concerns arises as to what type of contribution might be considered 'inventive' for the purposes of rights to the subsequent invention.

This is a very important issue in the area of bioprospecting, genetic resources and traditional knowledge. Where individuals or populations provide crucial starting materials, there are compelling moral and social argument for ensuring access to the subsequent invention for the original donor and the sharing of benefits. In the case of Moore's spleen and Greenberg's biological material, the cell-line was the crucial starting material, forming the basis of an invention that was subsequently patented. In both cases, the court held that the patients had no proprietary interests in the inventions.

As well as no property in the cells themselves, courts also held that neither Moore nor Greenberg had property rights in the genetic information encoded in his cells. This is instructive about genetic information itself as well. In Moore's case, the court noted that everyone's genetic material contains information for the manufacture of lymphokines, and as a result Moore's cell-line was considered 'no more unique to Moore than the number of vertebrae

36 He committed suicide and left it in his will to enable his partner to have children.
37 [2009] EWCA Civ 37, [2010] QB 1, paragraph 45.

in the spine'.[38] In other words, it is mere information and, as discussed in earlier chapters, there is no intellectual property protection in mere information.[39] Recalling the discussion of this in the context of gene sequences, the 'use' of the gene sequence is immediately relevant in the context of inventiveness, and the labour and investment in the deciphering and disclosure of function fulfils the industrial applicability and inventiveness of the invention.

Of particular interest is the distinction between the contribution of Moore and Greenberg, in terms of the provision of starting materials, and the inventive contribution of the researchers. The *Moore* court contrasted the mundane nature of the source materials with the skills of the researchers. The court noted that the 'adaptation and growth of human tissues and cells in culture is difficult – often considered an art'. Recalling the controversies regarding the ownership as distinct from the authorship of the invention, earlier discussions about the inventor as creator or author are relevant to these issues. In particular, the characterisation of the invention by patent law as well as the hierarchising of importance of contributions with respect to the body found in the *Moore* decision indicates potential cultural conflicts regarding the significance of 'inventive' contributions. For intellectual property law, and in this case patent law, the inventor is privileged as a kind of author – the source of the important value in the 'invention'. On the other hand, Moore is simply the base materials, whose contribution does not reflect skill and therefore does not reflect authorship.

Bioprospecting identities

The issues in *Moore* and *Greenberg* therefore provide some insight into the issues raised by bioprospecting in broader contexts. The relevance of those cases to this discussion is their commentary on the value placed on those contributing starting material. Are such contributions considered to be merely 'base material' and therefore 'not inventive'? Should such contributions in fact be considered inventive? These kinds of questions are especially relevant in the context of traditional medicine and genetic resources, and the contributions of indigenous peoples in these cases. In general, the contribution of information fundamental to an invention is unlikely to amount to co-inventorship within patent laws. This is particularly the case when the information is considered to be in the public domain.

The case of the 'Hagahai patent' is one which shares much of the same ethical questions with respect to the use that defines the relationship between researcher and donor with respect to an indigenous community. During research into malaria in the Hagahai people in Papua New Guinea, many members of which were dying from the disease, local researchers from Papua New Guinea's

38 *Moore v Regents of the University of California*, 139.
39 In the context of US patent law, see *Association of Molecular Pathology v Myriad Genetics*, 133 S Ct 2107 (2013).

Institute of Medical Research were joined by virologists from the US National Institutes of Health (NIH), who requested to survey the Hagahai for variants of retroviruses. Blood tests revealed that although the population carried a human T-cell leukaemia virus, none of the population was affected.[40]

The case has much in common with the earlier discussion of the *Moore* and *Greenberg* cases regarding the nexus between donation and purpose, and the proximity between donor and subsequent benefits. One unidentified Hagahai male contributed a sample from which a cell line was established and in 1991 a patent application was made. However, it appeared that at no time were the Hagahai people informed as to the purpose and subsequent use of the sample.

In 1995 the US Patent,[41] 'Papua New Guinea human T-lymphotropic virus,' was granted to the inventors and assigned to the United States of America as represented by the Department of Health. The patent abstract describes the invention as follows:

> The present invention relates to a human T-cell line (PNG-1) persistently infected with a Papua New Guinea (PNG) HTLV-I variant and to the infecting virus (PNG-1 variant). Cells of the present invention express viral antigens, type C particles and have a low level of reverse transcriptase activity. The establishment of this cell line, the first of its kind from an individual from Papua New Guinea, makes possible the screening of Melanesian populations using a local virus strain. The present invention also relates to vaccines for use in humans against infection with and diseases caused by HTLV-I and related viruses. The invention further relates to a variety of bioassays and kits for the detection and diagnosis of infection with and diseases caused by HTLV-I and related viruses.

There was no evidence of any arrangement between the Hagahai people and the Department of Health with respect to future benefits or royalties from the invention. The condemnation of the creation of proprietary rights over this starting-material included the rejection of the subject matter as mere discovery of material appearing in nature, the objection to the sampling of material for purposes other than the therapeutic benefit of the Hagahai people with respect to their suffering from malaria and with no mechanism for prior informed consent or fair and equitable sharing of benefits and royalties with the Hagahai people. The last two points are important in the context of the international framework in place. Although the CBD necessarily does not extend to human genetic resources (it would be inappropriate for these to be considered national resources), nevertheless the principles underpinning systems of access and benefit sharing are important. In particular, the CBD

---

40 See further the discussion of the Hagahai patent in Maser C (1999) *Ecological Diversity in Sustainable Development: The Vital and Forgotten Dimension*, London: CRC Press, 241–2.

41 US Patent No 5 397 696.

sets out a framework for consultation and consent with local peoples, however, it appears that the access took place before the CBD was even concluded, leaving the Hagahai community vulnerable.

The Rural Advancement Foundation International[42] led an international campaign against the granting of the patent, joined by civil society organisations around the world.[43] The dispute was ultimately resolved by the widely reported decision of the NIH to disclaim the patent and abandon the property in the face of enormous international objection.[44] Again, this is a significant example of the context in which the patent system is used and the relevance of the public interest and civil society activity, where civil society activity is instrumental in driving normative developments in these areas.

The significance of civil society participation is demonstrated by the recognition of its role within the WHO, where civil society is welcomed formally in its structure in the form of the established Civil Society Initiative (CSI).[45] More generally also, the WHO has affirmed the importance and growing role of civil society activity in global public health, particularly in compelling accountability of actors in the system.[46]

Property in misinformation

> A leech and an earthworm were talking beneath the ground. The leech knew that the earthworm couldn't go to the surface where the sun was very hot. So the leech told the earthworm, 'It's raining on the surface of the earth. You don't need to worry. I'll take care of everything.' When the earthworm got to the surface there he found a big hot sun and he died.[47]

This story comes from the opening scenes and the title itself of *The Leech and the Earthworm*, a 2003 documentary concerning the colonising impact on

42 Now re-named Action Group on Erosion, Technology and Concentration (ETC).

43 For further discussion on the Hagahai issues see the following: Kirsch S (2002) 'Property Limits: Debates on the Body, Nature and Culture,' in Hirsch E & Strathern M (eds) *Transactions and Creations: Property Debates and the Stimulus of Melanesia*, Oxford: Berghahn, 21; Resnik DB (2004) *Owning the Genome: A Moral Analysis of DNA Patenting*, New York: SUNY Press, 157–8; and Pottage A (1998) 'The Inscription of Life in Law: Genes, Patents and Bio-politics,' in Brownsword R et al, *Law and Human Genetics*, 148.

44 Ropp A von der & Taubman T (2006) 'Bioethics and Patent Law: The Cases of Moore and the Hagahai People' 5 *WIPO Magazine* October: 16. For reports contemporary with the decision, see the following: Lehrman S (1996) 'US drops Patent Claim to Hagahai Cell Line' *Nature* December: 500; and Robie D (1997) 'Cell Lines and Commodities: The Hagahai Patent Affair' 4(1) *Pacific Journalism Review* November.

45 Discussed again in Chapter 8.

46 WHO (2008) *Effective Aid: Better Health*. Report. 3rd High Level Forum on Aid Effectiveness. 2–4 September, Accra, Ghana. See in particular pp 6 and 33.

47 *The Leech and the Earthworm* (2003) Silver M & Pugh M (dir & scr) Harry D (prod).

indigenous peoples of Western science and genetic research. The tale itself is one of tragic misinformation, with the leech ultimately triumphing through the mechanism of misinformation. This story highlights the particular values at issue in bioprospecting not only in the individual but also the community. The film's producer, Debra Harry,[48] explains:

> We're not inviting geneticists to come out and look at our DNA. We're not inviting them to come out and look at our plants. It's a completely unwanted advance of colonisation just like all other previous acts of colonisation have been.[49]

Māori lawyer, Moana Jackson,[50] describes the priority attached to genetic research in terms similar to those recognised elsewhere in this book. The misinformation, as it were, is 'cloaked in scientific truth' which he likens to the earlier colonising imperative of ;religious truth'.[51] These links between scientific rationalism and religious progress resonate with the religious rhetoric attaching to intellectual property incentives as distinct from the immorality assigned to those seen to be interfering with research proposed for the wider social benefit. Jackson identifies this rhetoric as key to the central concern of acquiring possession – not only of things and knowledge, but also the dispossession of people:

> Genetic modification is the ultimate rape and plunder of the human spirit. So part of the reason that it has to be now cloaked in so much scientific truth is the same reason why four centuries ago the dispossession of our people was cloaked in religious truth – it's to ease the conscience of those who wish to do the dispossessing.[52]

Arguably, the concept of dispossession is much more critical to debates concerning proprietary rights in living material than the concept of possession, as such, in that the suspicion is related to potentially 'tragic misinformation' and the disavowal of sovereignty over cultural, genetic and community identity.

---

48 Debra Harry is the Executive Directive of the Indigenous Peoples' Council on Biocolonialism (IPCB), a US-based non-profit non-governmental organisation concerned with assisting indigenous peoples' in dealing with the protection of their genetic resources and traditional knowledge in the context of biotechnology encroachments upon their knowledge territories. Debra is Northern Paiute, from Pyramic Lake, Nevada. In 1994 she received a Kellogg Foundation leadership fellowship, during which she examined the practices and cultures of human genetic research in indigenous peoples.

49 *The Leech and the Earthworm.*

50 Moana Jackson is a Māori lawyer specialising in the Treaty of Waitanga and constitutional law.

51 Moana Jackson, interviewed in *The Leech and the Earthworm.*

52 *The Leech and the Earthworm.*

Property and genetic identity

With regard to genetic sampling and collection, of particular significance for public health research and population studies are the large public sector health databases being developed in various jurisdictions.[53] These databases raise specific questions about the issues elaborated in this section: consent; privacy; right to access genetic material and resources; sampling and rights to sample material; inventions and the rights to commercialise those inventions; and the fair and equitable sharing of benefits.[54] Genome-wide association studies have become especially valuable to studies on the contribution of both environmental and genetic factors in the development of disease.

UK Biobank

UK Biobank is a large long-term study in the United Kingdom (UK) targeting the prevention, diagnosis and treatment of major adult diseases in 500,000 volunteers aged 40–69, who are followed by the study for 25 years.[55] In addition to collecting the genetic samples some Biobank volunteers have worn activity monitors, had their diet monitored and so forth. As a genome-wide population study, the data collected by UK Biobank will be of primary relevance to the study of contributions to disease development from both genetic predisposition and environmental exposure.[56] Its data is available to any bona fide researchers anywhere in the world.

Although participants will be given feedback on blood pressure and other standard indicators of health, it is not currently proposed to notify participants of any later findings (including genetic predispositions and the like).[57] There are many reasons the project cannot provide this kind of diagnostic benefit to participants, including the tremendous resources necessary to undertake such a duty to participants (not only cost, but also human and other resources). However, one of the most important of these reasons is the necessary

53 Examples from the UK, Iceland as well as international consortia (MalariaGEN) are considered later in this section.

54 See further the discussion in Merz JF (2007) 'Are Human Gene Banks Worth It?' in Steinberg D (ed) *Biomedical Ethics: A Multidisciplinary Approach to Moral Issues in Medicine and Biology*, Hanover, NH: University Press of New England, 161.

55 UK Biobank (2006) *UK Biobank: Protocol for a Large-Scale Prospective Epidemiological Resource*, Protocol No: UKBB-PROT-09–06 (Main Phase), Stockport: Biobank Coordinating Centre, 3. The funding currently runs to 2022 (and so it would need extending to reach 25 years).

56 UK Biobank, *UK Biobank*, 3–4.

57 UK Biobank, Test Results, Information Paper. See further, UK Biobank, *UK Biobank* and UK Biobank Ethics and Governance Framework, Version 3.0, October 2007. For a detailed consideration of feedback and its value or otherwise, see People Science & Policy Ltd (2002) *BioBank UK: A Question of Trust: A Consultation Exploring and Addressing Questions of Public Trust*. Report prepared for The Medical Research Council & The Wellcome Trust.

anonymity of participants' samples as they proceed through the project. Therefore participants are genuinely treated and participate as donors.[58]

The act of contribution as a one-off donation rather than an ongoing relationship between health practitioner and patient is an important aspect of the project to consider for the present discussion. In particular, the concept of charitable donation is significant when considering the question of sovereignty over samples and subsequent sharing of benefits arising from the study (both on an individual and on a population-wide basis). Data researchers will be able to apply to use the database. Importantly, as well as the anonymisation of the data, researchers will not have access to the volunteers themselves.[59]

Icelandic database

deCODE genetics, Inc is an Icelandic biopharmaceutical company based in Reyjavik. It was founded in 1996 in order to undertake a nationwide population study to identify human genes linked to common diseases and ultimately to apply this research in drug development.[60]

In 2001, the Icelandic Act on Biobanks[61] came into force,[62] making it possible for deCODE to access to samples collected and stored in hospitals and other settings without the need for consent from the donors themselves.[63] This enabled deCODE to establish the Icelandic Health Sector Database (HSD), which would contain all the medical records, genealogical and genetic information of the entire population of Iceland (around 270,000 people).

This legislation introduced the especially controversial aspect of deCODE's project because of its approach to participant consent and its possible implications for individual privacy. In order to effect broad participation, the project was structured so that the medical data of all citizens of Iceland would automatically be included in the project unless a citizen specifically opted out. In other words, rather than seeking informed consent the project relied upon the concept of assumed consent.[64] Arguably this undermined the relationship of trust and any opportunity for building cohesion in participation in the project, ultimately undermining the commercial value of the project.[65]

---

58 UK Biobank Ethics and Governance Framework, Version 3.0, October 2007.

59 UK Biobank, *UK Biobank*, 99.

60 For further commentary on the project, see Arnason E & Wells F (2006) 'deCODE and Iceland: A Critique,' in Clarke A & Ticehurst F (eds) *Living with the Genome: Ethical and Social Aspects of Genetics*, Basingstoke: Palgrave Macmillan, 56.

61 No 110/2000.

62 The act came into force 1 January 2001: Article 18.

63 It should be noted that the act was not established for deCODE, but deCODE was a licensee in accordance with Section II.

64 Act on Biobanks, No 110/2000: Article 3.6 (definition) and Article 7.

65 Webster A (2007) *Health, Technology and Society: A Sociological Critique*, Basingstoke: Palgrave Macmillan, 60.

Early in the development of the database, one Icelandic woman requested that the information of her deceased father not be included. Her request was refused by the HSD, which maintained that there was no provision for relatives to prevent the inclusion of the data of deceased persons. She took the dispute to the Icelandic Supreme Court[66] and argued that, despite procedures in place to anonymise the data, the inclusion of her father's information could be used to predict information about her own health and therefore invade her right to privacy under the Icelandic Constitution to enjoy the privacy of life, home and family.[67] The Supreme Court agreed and declared the enabling Act to be unconstitutional. As a result, the HSD could not proceed on the basis of assumed consent essentially making it impossible to continue as the burden of obtaining consent in all those circumstances would be extremely onerous.

This is a significant decision in that it is instructive on the possible application of the right to privacy in other jurisdictions, at least in Europe. The constitutional right understood to be threatened by structuring the project in this way is very similar to Article 8 of the European Convention on Human Rights (ECHR), the right to respect for private and family life. Article 8 provides:

> 1. Everyone has the right to respect for his private and family life, his home and his correspondence.
> 2. There shall be no interference by a public authority with the exercise of this right except such as is in accordance with the law and is necessary in a democratic society in the interests of national security, public safety or the economic well-being of the country, for the prevention of disorder or crime, for the protection of health or morals, or for the protection of the rights and freedoms of others.[68]

This is very important in the context of the earlier discussion regarding consent to obtain samples and the possible need for fresh consent for later uses of that sample and is an important articulation of the relationship between health in the private sphere and institutions of health research in the public sphere.

Eventually, instead of getting the medical histories of all 277,000 Icelandic people, the company managed to get 140,000 volunteers to provide their genetic information.[69] It always struggled financially, and particularly when it

66 Icelandic Supreme Court, No 151/2003. For a discussion of the decision see Gertz R (2004) 'An Analysis of the Icelandic Supreme Court Judgement on the Health Sector Database Act' 1(2) *SCRIPTed* 241.

67 Constitution of Iceland, Article 71.1.

68 Convention for the Protection of Human Rights and Fundamental Freedoms as amended by Protocol No. 11. Rome, 4.XI.1950. Article 8.

69 Carmichael, M (2010) 'Can DeCode, A BioTech Star Gone Bust, Come Back': *Newsweek*, 11 February.

invested most of its money in Lehman Brothers (which was lost in the 2008 financial crisis). Since that time the company has been bought and resold a number of times, but it continues its work to try and identify genes relevant to particular diseases.

MalariaGEN

The Malaria Genomic Epidemiology Network (MalariaGEN) is an important example of international cooperation in over 20 countries (including partners in developing countries) towards developing genome-wide association data, led by the Ethox Centre, University of Oxford. Funded by a grant from the Grand Challenges in Global Health initiative (GCGH),[70] the project launched in July 2005 and will collect malaria samples from children and parents and collect these together with control samples.

A key component of its operation is the provision of informed consent for all donors. To that end, the project is conscious of the need for culturally relevant and appropriate processes of collection according to the various different network locations. Therefore, there is a diversity of collection sites, including paediatric and maternity facilities in urban areas as well as loci for primary health care in rural communities and villages.

Informed consent follows a set template[71] that includes identification of the researchers and the definition of the problem the research is addressing, as well as the exact nature of the approach to this research problem through the use of genetic material. Information is also provided as to the process of donation and sampling, risks, benefits and treatment of the sample, including the protection of the anonymity of the donor participant. The process of obtaining consent is assisted by the publication of Supporting Guidelines for Informed Consent.[72]

The project is particularly aware of the importance of data-sharing as part of the overall commitment to sharing the benefits of the research, especially in the context of capacity building.[73] Drawing upon the principles developed in the Bermuda meeting on the Human Genome Project (Bermuda Accord)[74]

70 The Grand Challenges in Global Health initiative is funded by the Bill and Melinda Gates Foundation and Wellcome Trust with participatory management by the Foundation for the National Institutes of Health (US) and Canadian Institutes of Health Research (CIHR).

71 MalariaGEN. Informed Consent Template.

72 MalaraiGEN. Supporting Guidelines for Informed Consent. The guidelines are structured in two sections: practical ethical concerns (such as obtaining consent) and considerations concerning the content of information provided to participants (information sheet).

73 Chokshi DA et al (2006) 'Data Sharing and Intellectual Property in a Genomic Epidemiology Network: Policies for Large-Scale Research Collaboration. 84(5) *Bulletin of the World Health Organization*, May 382.

74 Human Genome Organisation (HUGO). Policies on Release of Human Genomic Sequence Data. Bermuda 1996–7.

and revised in 2003 at a Wellcome Trust meeting in Fort Lauderdale,[75] data-sharing is explained in the project as a priority for the GCGH funders as well as for meeting the important dimension of the project concerned with capacity-building.[76]

Although the project is not likely itself to develop new medicines or vaccines for which patent protection might be relevant, it is nevertheless instructive in the way in which such projects can realise the beneficial interests of the public. This sharing of benefits includes the provision of free health care in consultation with ethics committees, diffusing research outputs and resources to contributing communities and participants, sharing data with members of the research consortium and contributing to the development of technical expertise and capacity in all research sites (including those in developing countries). Thus, there is a commitment not only to report on information and outputs but also to develop clinical infrastructure in the project sites.[77]

Importantly, where there is potential to develop products in developing country markets that may not be of interest to commercial firms, initiatives for production and supply are developed in order to avoid delays in supply:

> When the potential market is not a sufficient incentive for companies to invest, the options for product development are: (1) liaising with non-profit drug developers or public–private partnerships (PPPs), or (2) technology transfer to developing-world institutions.[78]

The opportunity to license with developing-country partners is recognised not only as a mechanism by which to avoid delays or failure to market but also as an important contribution to local innovation and development.

These principles underpinning the project confer custodianship upon the participants and communities themselves with respect to the specimens. Importantly, this community custodianship is generated by the socially cohesive qualities of the project, as distinct from conferring any process of 'community consent' and the risks this might introduce.[79] The presumption of community consent has also been criticised as a kind of 'biocolonialism'[80] in that it generalises and obscures the individual's autonomy for the purposes

75 The Wellcome Trust. 'Sharing Data from Large-Scale Biological Research Projects: A System of Tripartite Responsibility'. Report of a meeting organised by the Wellcome Trust and held on 14–15 January 2003 at Ford Lauderdale, USA.

76 Nyan O (2008) 'Case Study 2: Ethnicity' Presentation to the Genome-Wide Association Studies and Ethics Meeting, The Wellcome Trust, 24 July 2008.

77 Ibid.

78 Chokshi 'Data Sharing and Intellectual Property', 382 at 385.

79 For instance, the deCODE project, discussed earlier, was compromised by the severance of this link with individuals (created through consent).

80 Reilly PR (2006) 'Informed Consent in Human Genetic Research' in Clarke A & Ticehurst F (eds) *Living with the Genome*, 64 at 68.

of amassing data, ultimately distancing the individual from the project. On the other hand, by engaging individuals in a way that is culturally and socially relevant, the project itself is cohesive and compatible with community interests through that relationship with the individual. The commitment to report benefits and outcomes to participants as well as members of the consortium introduces an important reciprocal relationship of trust and motivates community input and self-recognition in the potential benefits of the project.[81] Indeed, with respect to the Bermuda Accord and commentator, Sir John Sulston explains: 'The principle of data availability had to be endorsed at the Bermuda meeting or else mutual trust would have been impossible.'[82] That is, by introducing a relationship of confidence, similar to that described in trade secrets, an obligation to fulfil that trustworthiness is met by the partners in that relationship.

Thus, access and use anatomise relationships of trust in the context of the research environment, addressing some of the critical concerns for such projects with respect to motivating participation and donation of material. MalariaGEN arguably demonstrates a greater relationship with participants not only in terms of clinical feedback but also in terms of building local infrastructure. This dynamic construction of trust is crucial to relationships of access and introduces some of the key considerations relevant in access debates, including the sharing of genetic resources and the potential exclusion from subsequent benefits.[83] This project is an important negotiation of the distance between users and institutions that characterises debates in access and the viability of responses in use. Furthermore, in this relationship built upon the sharing of data and information, the custodianship to the samples is maintained. This not only supports the beneficial interest created in this research on the part of communities and participants, but also builds the necessary relationship of trust with the institutional research framework for access and use.

---

81 This feedback to participants is similar to other participatory studies that facilitate mutually beneficial partnerships between researchers and participants. For instance, see the discussion of participatory diagramming in HIV/AIDS research in Africa in Kesby M (2004) 'Participatory Diagramming and the Ethical and Practical Challenges of Helping Africans *Themselves* to Move HIV Work "Beyond Epidemiology"' in Kalipeni E et al (eds) *HIV & AIDS in Africa: Beyond Epidemiology*, Malden MA: Blackwell 'Participants are not simply providers of information but enter into reciprocal relations with researchers and become increasingly active in the whole research process' (217 at 220).

82 Sulston, Sir J (2002) 'Heritage of Humanity,' *Le Monde diplomatique*, December.

83 For instance, see the problems in the global system of virus sharing currently being faced in the case of avian influenza, discussed in Chapter 8.

Part 4
Access

8 Access

Introduction

The international Campaign for Access to Essential Medicines, having its early foundations in Médecins sans Frontières (MSF), demonstrates the significance of civil society in international norm-setting towards guaranteeing the realisation of the right to health across a diversity of national and regional circumstances. As well as pricing, access to medicines and health care is also influenced by public awareness and education. Therefore, mechanisms by which to deliver that knowledge to local communities in an effective and meaningful way is also an aspect of civil society collaboration with local groups and lobbying of national governments.[1] Indeed, the cultural relevance of programmes (acceptability) is an important element of the right to health.

In the framework of the current pharmaceutical business models, influences upon research and development are perhaps necessarily the markets that might be available for the medicines once produced. As a result, medicinal products for diseases of the poor in developing countries, unlikely to make a profit, might not receive the same priority of investment as though for which a wealthy market might already exist. In other words, the life chances of individuals not only affect the accessibility of medicines on the market but also the availability of medicines yet to be developed. As a result of this dominant business model, there is arguably less research into diseases in developing countries that affect a large proportion of the world's poor. This is often referred to as the 10–90 gap in the literature, meaning that a mere 10 per cent of global investment in research and development in health is directed towards health problems of the developing world, 90 per cent of the global population.[2] As early as 1990, the Commission on Health Research for Development (COHRED) estimated that only 5 per

1 For instance, recall the discussion in Chapter 3 of current programmes of cooperation between traditional and religious communities and medical practitioners on training in the identification, prevention and treatment of HIV/AIDS. Issues of price and education are of particular concern in the prevention and treatment of HIV/AIDS. In particular, delivery of prevention and treatment advice must be culturally appropriate so as to ensure its relevance and acceptability.

2 The development of the term, '10/90 gap', is attributed to statistical work of the Global Forum for Health Research undertaken in the 1990s. See Global Forum for Health Research (1999). *The 10/90 Report on Health Research*, Geneva: GFHR.

cent of global investment in health was addressing problems of developing countries, problems which were preventable through adequate diffusion of health technology and research benefits.[3] This again recalls the problematic connection between the market and innovation, motivating initiatives not only to ensure the availability and accessibility of products after the innovation process, but also indicating how critical to the very concept of availability that very process is. In other words, in order to deliver the right to health, not only must the possible limitations on access to products be addressed, but also the influences and factors relevant to the innovation process itself. This is not simply a question of trade rules applied after the event, but an issue of the very cultures of innovation that are being motivated by a market-based system of incentives. Initiatives to address this by innovating beyond the current framework are considered in the following chapter, including proposals to address research and development models and to provide for prize incentives and related interruptions to the present values of the system.

Some countries have introduced specific legislation to address these issues of research and development in essential medicines and orphan drugs, legislating for 'legitimate' models for access to respond to these needs.[4] Further, there are initiatives to facilitate access within the present intellectual property framework, not by reforming the law as such but by addressing the business models built upon the law. Such examples include bulk procurement programmes and patent pooling schemes.

One such recent proposal is the Health Impact Fund, from the NGO, Incentives for Global Health (IGH).[5] The Health Impact Fund is an initiative directed specifically at addressing the market influences on research and development. The fund literally creates markets for less profitable medicines by linking clinical benefit to remuneration. Originators are encouraged to contribute to the fund by agreeing to sell their product at a lower price designated by the fund and based upon manufacturing costs (rather than marketing and other costs unrelated to the clinical value of the medicine). In exchange, the patentee is remunerated by a fixed amount from the fund, which is the 'profit' for the product based upon the global 'health impact' of the product.[6] Over ten years since its launch, there is still a struggle to demonstrate the viability of the project and so a mini-HIF proposal was launched in 2015 to try and get funding for a small-scale viability testing project.

These various initiatives are significant in signalling the relationship between the legal rights and the advantages built upon those rights. That is, access is

3 COHRED (1990) *Health Research: Essential Link to Equity in Development*, Oxford: Oxford University Press, 29.

4 For instance, see the discussion of US responses in Chapter 9.

5 Incentives for Global Health (IGH) is led by Dr Thomas Pogge, Leitner Professor of Philosophy and International Affairs at Yale University, and supported by the BUPA Foundation and Australian Research Council.

6 For more detail on the initiative see Hollis A & Pogge T (2008) *The Health Impact Fund: Making New Medicines Accessible for All*, New Haven, CT: Incentives for Global Health; see further www.healthimpactfund.org

not necessarily restricted by the intellectual property framework itself. Indeed, arguably the patent system provides for access in industries where the same knowledge would otherwise be protected by trade secrets. Rather, many of the key issues are fundamental to the business models, albeit facilitated by that framework. Thus, these initiatives indicate the necessity for political and commercial will in reform to business models based upon those rights. In this way, the functional exploitation of the system is the integral basis upon which to facilitate relationships between users of the system in a way that contributes to the realisation of the right to health rather than derogates from it.

This broader interpretation of the capacity for autonomy and use can be recognised in the application of intellectual property rules together with the contribution of civil society action in the examples below. These specific examples are chosen for their significance in demonstrating the way in which norm-setting activity can lead to structural changes not only in the law itself (considered in the Chapter 9), but also in the interpretation of present frameworks and in the very access to the market itself. If the participation in the democratic system is premised upon private property and the market, these examples are critical in their material impact on the market itself as the locus for freedom in Western-style democracy.

Civil society and communicative action in the public sphere

As the genealogy of the Access to Medicines Campaign demonstrates, civil society activity has a critical role in normative changes in health and international development. Further, the campaign demonstrates the way in which civil society expertise developed on a particular issue not only drives rights agenda but also informs developments in related questions, such as the Access to Knowledge movement.[7] Thus, civil society facilitates communication between the lifeworld of users of the institutions in the public sphere and institutional change:

> Civil society is composed of those more or less spontaneously emergent associations, organizations and movements that, attuned to how society problems resonate in the private life spheres, distill and transmit such reaction in amplified form in the public sphere. The core of civil society comprises a network of associations that institutionalizes problem-solving discourses on questions of general interest inside the framework of organized public spheres. These 'discursive designs' have an egalitarian, open form of organization that mirrors essential features of the kind of communication around which they crystallize and to which they lend continuity and permanence.[8]

7 See the discussion of the background to the Access to Knowledge movement in Chapter 1.

8 Habermas J (1997/[1992]) *Between Facts and Norms: Contributions to a Discourse Theory of Law and Democracy*, Rehg W (trans), Cambridge: Polity Press. 367.

The role of civil society is explicitly identified by international institutions, including the WHO, as performing a relevant and significant role not only in normative aspects of global health but also in facilitating the implementation of work programmes and specific commitments. The WHO Civil Society Initiative (CSI) is a programme within the WHO specifically mandated with the role of connecting the WHO with civil society and NGOs. As the WHO explains: 'Lacking the coercive or regulatory power of the State and the economic power of market actors, civil society provides the social power of its networks of people.'[9] That is, civil society specifically addresses the opportunity for users to access and communicate with the WHO, as a public sphere institution. As the WHO has also identified, social exclusion may be itself an issue in developing countries and a significant obstacle in address agenda in global health equity: 'As there has been a shift towards a more rights based approach to development, more prominence has been given to civil society roles in raising, advancing and claiming the entitlements of different social groups.'[10]

Civil society therefore fulfils a significant role in global health policy and development in that this cooperation constitutes the genuine mechanism by which individual users may participate in the actual development of systems to which they are to be made subject. It is this opportunity that will contribute to the legitimacy upon future programmes in public health: 'It is only participation in the practice of *politically autonomous* law-making that makes it possible for the addressees of the law to have a correct understanding of the legal order as created by themselves.'[11] Indeed, this introduces the necessary condition for trust in the law in that cooperation in the public sphere generates communication as the basis for that trust.[12]

Access and trust

Incorporated in four principles of the right to health[13] and the significance of primary health care is trust. The concept of trust not only suggests the cultural and social acceptability of the healthcare services and goods, but is

9 WHO (2002). Civil Society Initiative. Understanding Civil Society Issues for WHO. Discussion Paper No. 2. CSI/2002/DP2, 4.

10 WHO (2001). Civil Society Initiative. Strategic Alliances: The Role of Civil Society in Health. Discussion Paper No. 1. CSI/2001/DP1, 4.

11 Habermas, *Between Facts and Norms*, 121.

12 This emphasis on global cooperation and collaboration not only between governments and UN agencies, but also civil society and academia, is emphasised in the most recent WHO World Health Report 2007. See further WHO (2007) *Global Public Health Security in the 21st Century*, Geneva: World Heath Organisation.

13 CESCR. General Comment No 14 (2000). The right to the highest attainable standard of health: article 12 of the International Covenant on Economic, Social and Cultural Rights. 22nd Session. E/C.12/2000/4. 11 August 2000: Paragraph 12.

also an integral component of the fuller concept of use. Indeed, in feudal principles of tenure, the practice of use in and of itself constituted the holding of land in trust for the benefit of future generations – that is, that both legal and equitable interests could be held in the one property – forming the basis of modern personal equitable obligations to deal with property for the benefit of another class of persons (that is, a beneficial interest other than the legal interest of the owners). This is what will be referred to here as 'The Global Medicines Trust.'

The Global Medicines Trust

While the goods comprising the resources necessary to the realisation of the right to health might incorporate private property interests (in the form of the patent), the knowledge contained within those goods might be seen as held in equitable trust to which all are entitled as beneficiaries under Article 15.1(b) of the ICESCR.[14] Therefore, although the private property holder has certain legal rights to the invention defined within the patent, the invention itself is a public good. In principle, this can be interpreted as a beneficial interest in the invention held by each individual. In other words, there are two simultaneous interests in an invention – one is the legal interest defined by the patent; the other is the equitable interest in the invention as a public good.

Where the rights in the patent interfere with the beneficial interest in the public good to such an extent that the human right to health and to enjoy the applications of scientific research are compromised, then it must be possible to address this. That is, where the exercise of those rights begins to pose real and material obstacles to the capacity of governments to fulfil the right to health, then there may be a right against the 'trustee'. This human rights qualification on the exercise of trade-related intellectual property rights is found not only in instruments towards the interpretation and application of the right to health,[15] but also in instruments concerning the full implementation of the right to development[16] and in the TRIPS Agreement itself. Article 8 provides:

---

14 In the 1920s and 1930s, the idea of a medicines trust to which all inventions relating to medicines would be transferred was proposed by the British Medical Association: see Johnson, P (2012) 'Access to medicines and the growth of the pharmaceutical industry in Britain' in Dinwoodie, G (ed.), *Methods and Perspectives in Intellectual Property*, Cheltenham: Edward Elgar, 339–46.

15 OHCHR/UNAIDS (2006). International Guidelines on HIV/AIDS and Human Rights: Paragraph 52, p. 48.

16 Commission on Human Rights. 61st Session. Review of Progress in the Promotion and Implementation of the Right to Development: Consideration of the Report of the High-Level Task Force on the Implementation of the Right to Development. Report of the high-level task force on the implementation of the right to development. E/CN.4/2005/WG.18/2. 24 January 2005: Paragraph 45. See further Human Rights Council. 8th Session. Report of the high-level task force on the implementation of the right to development in its fourth session. A/HRC/8/WG.2/TF/2. 31 January 2008. Paragraph 85(a).

1. Members may, in formulating or amending their laws and regulations, adopt measures necessary to protect public health and nutrition, and to promote the public interest in sectors of vital importance to their socio-economic and technological development, provided that such measures are consistent with the provisions of this Agreement.
2. Appropriate measures, provided that they are consistent with the provisions of this Agreement, may be needed to prevent the abuse of intellectual property rights by right holders or the resort to practices which unreasonably restrain trade or adversely affect the international transfer of technology.[17]

Indeed, it is contended that the law itself recognises this beneficial interest of the public in the invention in the form of provisions for compulsory licensing. While the limitations imposed upon compulsory licensing by the TRIPS Agreement[18] have been criticised,[19] arguably the recent amendment to TRIPS (discussed below) redresses this. That is, where the beneficial interest is obstructed by the exercise of the legal interest, the balance is addressed by compulsory licensing. The central value of the trust, as it were, is that of use. Use not only constitutes the possessory relationship to knowledge, but also is the mechanism by which to fulfil the trust. This was seen in earlier discussions regarding the controversies of biotechnology and gene-related inventions and the importance of use as a defining feature not only of access but also of the scope of the legal rights in the invention. That is, use constrains the legal rights; use contains the equitable interests.[20]

The concept of acceptability in the human right to health (trust in use) and the concept of the creation of possession through use (trust in property) resonates with the important relationship between health and development, and between development and notions of autonomy and freedom. By legitimising this relationship of use (as distinct from the mere market-based relationship of access) the fuller human rights framework for health and the goods that form the underlying determinants for health is arguably manifest.

---

17 TRIPS, Article 8.

18 TRIPS, Article 31 (discussed further later in this chapter).

19 In relation to pharmaceuticals see Bass NA (2002) 'Implications of the TRIPS Agreement for Developing Countries: Pharmaceutical Patent Laws in Brazil and South Africa in the 21st Century' 34 *George Washington Law Review* 191. See generally Carvalho NP de (2005) *The TRIPS Regime of Patent Rights*, The Hague: Kluwer Law International, 147–54; and Correa C (1999) *Intellectual Property Rights, the WTO and Developing Countries: The TRIPS Agreement and Policy Options*, London: Zed Books.

20 This relationship to use as the motivating value of equitable interest suggests the importance of the model of innovation itself. Throughout the discussion the problematic nexus between the market and research and development has been considered and this will be revisited in the following chapter.

Compulsory licensing and 'beneficial use'

The flexibilities found within TRIPS towards access to patented products (including medicines) to address domestic emergencies arguably cooperate with this principle of beneficial interests in the invention, as discussed earlier. However, decisions by some governments in developing countries to pursue aggressively the compulsory licensing flexibility in TRIPS, to be examined later in this chapter, exposed the lack of commercial (and indeed political) will towards the full realisation of the flexibility in this provision.

A compulsory licence to a patent is a licence granted by the state to operate a patent with or without the patentee's consent. The TRIPS Agreement sets out specific requirements for the grant of compulsory licences in Article 31. One of the key aspects of this provision is that countries can access compulsory licences to meet needs in the case of national health emergencies or epidemics. These can be concerns not only with cost but also with production capacity (with the usual production of patented medicines being limited by the production capacity of the party licensed to manufacture the drug). In other words, a compulsory licence will be applicable where availability and accessibility is unjustifiably interfered with by the exercise of trade rules (patent rights).

The compulsory licensing provision is a very important flexibility available to all members of TRIPS, but is vulnerable in bilateral agreements where parties may agree to contract out of this provision. The tendencies towards bilateralism and agreement to even stricter standards, sometimes referred to as TRIPS-plus provisions, pose serious threats to access to medicines in developing country partners.

Compulsory licences were first provided in the Paris Convention,[21] Article 5.A:

> 2. Each country of the Union shall have the right to take legislative measures providing for the grant of compulsory licenses to prevent the abuses which might result from the exercise of the exclusive rights conferred by the patent, for example, failure to work.
> 3. Forfeiture of the patent shall not be provided for except in cases where the grant of compulsory licenses would not have been sufficient to prevent the said abuses. No proceedings for the forfeiture or revocation of a patent may be instituted before the expiration of two years from the grant of the first compulsory license.
> 4. A compulsory license may not be applied for on the ground of failure to work or insufficient working before the expiration of a period of four years from the date of filing of the patent application or three years from the date of the grant of the patent, whichever period expires last; it shall be refused if the patentee justifies his inaction by legitimate reasons.

21 Paris Convention for the Protection of Industrial Property of March 20, 1883 (currently 177 contracting parties, as at 1 May 2017).

> Such a compulsory license shall be non–exclusive and shall not be transferable, even in the form of the grant of a sub–license, except with that part of the enterprise or goodwill which exploits such license.[22]

Very importantly, historically the granting of compulsory licences was much broader and was to protect against the potentially anti-competitive monopoly provided by the patent (such as failure to work). The only restriction on the application of a compulsory licence was that such a licence could not be granted for failure to work the invention until four years from the date of filing or three years from the date of grant. Otherwise, there were no restrictions on compulsory licences granted on other grounds,[23] quite unlike the comprehensive qualification of their application in Article 31 of TRIPS. Thus, compared to the wider availability of compulsory licences as originally conceived in the Paris Convention, the TRIPS Agreement compromises, rather drastically, the earlier flexibility provided by the compulsory licence in many jurisdictions.

Under the TRIPS Agreement, a compulsory licence can be issued when certain criteria have been fulfilled, but these may be waived in certain cases, such as a national medical emergency:

> (b) such use may only be permitted if, prior to such use, the proposed user has made efforts to obtain authorization from the right holder on reasonable terms and conditions and such efforts have not been successful within a reasonable period of time. This requirement may be waived by a Member in the case of a national emergency or other circumstances of extreme urgency or in cases of public non-commercial use …[24]

In all cases where the requirement is waived, the patent-holder must be notified as soon as possible that the licence has been authorised. Despite this waiver, the compulsory licence provision is somewhat limited in utility where the production capacity of the country seeking the licence is not able to manufacture the patent:

> (f) any such use shall be authorized predominantly for the supply of the domestic market of the Member authorizing such use;[25]

Paragraph (f) means that a country with no production capacity cannot take advantage of this provision effectively, in that it cannot exploit a compulsory

---

22 Paris Convention for the Protection of Industrial Property: Article 5 (added in 1900 at the Brussels Conference).

23 See UK Patents Act 1949, s 41; also see Johnson P (2012) 'Access to Medicines and the Growth of the Pharmaceutical Industry in Britain' in Dinwoodie G (ed.), *Methods and Perspectives in Intellectual Property*, Cheltenham: Edward Elgar.

24 TRIPS, Article 31(b).

25 TRIPS, Article 31(f).

licence for patented medicines in order to meet a domestic health emergency. Furthermore, this provision means that such a country cannot import medicines produced under compulsory licence from countries that do have production capacity because to do so would mean that production was not 'predominantly for the supply of the domestic market'.

WTO Ministerial Conference, Doha 2001

The importance of flexibilities within trade rules relevant to access to health was expressly addressed in the Fourth WTO Ministerial Conference of 2001, setting the Doha Development Agenda. During this trade round, member states agreed to extend the transitional periods for TRIPS-compliance least-developed countries, extending exemptions from pharmaceutical product patent protection until 2016, and expressly acknowledged the relationship between intellectual property and the right to health in the Ministerial Declaration:

> We stress the importance we attach to implementation and interpretation of the Agreement on Trade-Related Aspects of Intellectual Property Rights (TRIPS Agreement) in a manner supportive of public health, by promoting both access to existing medicines and research and development into new medicines and, in this connection, are adopting a separate declaration.[26]

The Doha Declaration on TRIPS and Public Health[27] was adopted as a separate declaration by the ministerial conference and is significant for reaffirming the importance and relevance of the flexibilities in TRIPS available to member states in the service of public health. Importantly, it affirms that the TRIPS Agreement should be interpreted and applied such that it does not pose an obstacle to a member state's ability to realise the right to health of its citizens. In particular, the declaration establishes that the TRIPS Agreement does not override the sovereignty of member states to undertake appropriate measures to ensure access to essential medicines and health.[28]

The declaration addresses the restriction on the flexibility of the compulsory licence in the context of the human right to health[29] and expressly declares the right of Members to grant compulsory licences:[30]

---

26 WTO Ministerial Declaration, adopted on 14 November 2001. WT/MIN(01)/DEC/1. Paragraph 17. (Doha Declaration).
27 WTO Declaration on the TRIPS Agreement and Public Health, adopted on 14 November 2001. WT/MIN(01)/DEC/2. (Doha Declaration on TRIPS and Public Health).
28 Ibid., paragraphs 4–6.
29 Ibid., paragraph 4.
30 Ibid., paragraph 5.

4. We agree that the TRIPS Agreement does not and should not prevent members from taking measures to protect public health. Accordingly, while reiterating our commitment to the TRIPS Agreement, we affirm that the Agreement can and should be interpreted and implemented in a manner supportive of WTO members' right to protect public health and, in particular, to promote access to medicines for all.

   In this connection, we reaffirm the right of WTO members to use, to the full, the provisions in the TRIPS Agreement, which provide flexibility for this purpose.
5. Accordingly and in the light of paragraph 4 above, while maintaining our commitments in the TRIPS Agreement, we recognize that these flexibilities include:

   In applying the customary rules of interpretation of public international law, each provision of the TRIPS Agreement shall be read in the light of the object and purpose of the Agreement as expressed, in particular, in its objectives and principles.

   Each member has the right to grant compulsory licences and the freedom to determine the grounds upon which such licences are granted.

   Each member has the right to determine what constitutes a national emergency or other circumstances of extreme urgency, it being understood that public health crises, including those relating to HIV/AIDS, tuberculosis, malaria and other epidemics, can represent a national emergency or other circumstances of extreme urgency.

   The effect of the provisions in the TRIPS Agreement that are relevant to the exhaustion of intellectual property rights is to leave each member free to establish its own regime for such exhaustion without challenge, subject to the MFN and national treatment provisions of Articles 3 and 4.[31]

In order to address the different capacities of governments to take advantage of this flexibility, as determined by their production capacity, Paragraph 6 explicitly recognises the difficulties faced by member states with little or no pharmaceutical manufacturing capacity and the limitations of the compulsory licensing provision in these circumstances. In so doing, the Declaration instructs the TRIPS Council to resolve this by the end of 2002.

6. We recognize that WTO members with insufficient or no manufacturing capacities in the pharmaceutical sector could face difficulties in making effective use of compulsory licensing under the TRIPS Agreement. We instruct the Council for TRIPS to find an expeditious solution to this problem and to report to the General Council before the end of 2002.[32]

31 Ibid., paragraphs 4 and 5.
32 Ibid., paragraphs 6.

Responding to this declaration, member states voted in favour of a waiver of this requirement in the case of least-developed and developing countries without manufacturing capacity.[33] This decision introduced what is often referred to as the Paragraph 6 System, waiving the obligations of member states under Article 31(f). Members agreed that this waiver would stand until the relevant TRIPS article was amended, thus allowing for the production of patented medicines under compulsory licence in developed countries for the purposes of export to least-developed and certain developing countries. In the EU, a Regulation was adopted 17 May 2006, giving the provisions of TRIPS Amendment on public health (Article 31*bis*) legal effect within the EU.[34]

The Paragraph 6 System

The decision to implement Paragraph 6 waived the obligations of TRIPS members to manufacture under a compulsory licence for the domestic market only, as provided under Article 31(f). Without this waiver, Article 31(f) posed a significant limit to the amount of generic product that could be exported when manufactured under a compulsory licence. Because of the limitation to the domestic market, this restriction limits the possible supply to countries unable to manufacture under compulsory licence themselves in times of national emergency.

The decision on Paragraph 6 covers both patented products and products made using patented processes. Member states agreed that the waiver would remain in place until of the ratification of Article 31*bis* of the TRIPS Agreement (the public health amendment):

> 2. The obligations of an exporting Member under Article 31(f) of the TRIPS Agreement shall be waived with respect to the grant by it of a compulsory licence to the extent necessary for the purposes of production of a pharmaceutical product(s) and its export to an eligible importing Member(s) in accordance with the terms set out below in this paragraph:
>
> a. the eligible importing Member(s) has made a notification to the Council for TRIPS, that:
>
> i. specifies the names and expected quantities of the product(s) needed;

33 WTO General Council. Implementation of paragraph 6 of the Doha Declaration on the TRIPS Agreement and Public Health. Decision of 30 August 2003 (WT/L/540 and Corr.1).

34 Regulation (EC) No 816/2006 of the European Parliament and of the Council of 17 May 2006 on compulsory licensing of patents relating to the manufacture of pharmaceutical products for export to countries with public health problems.

ii. confirms that the eligible importing Member in question, other than a least developed country Member, has established that it has insufficient or no manufacturing capacities in the pharmaceutical sector for the product(s) in question in one of the ways set out in the Annex to this Decision; and

iii. confirms that, where a pharmaceutical product is patented in its territory, it has granted or intends to grant a compulsory licence in accordance with Article 31 of the TRIPS Agreement and the provisions of this Decision (6);

b. the compulsory licence issued by the exporting Member under this Decision shall contain the following conditions:

i. only the amount necessary to meet the needs of the eligible importing Member(s) may be manufactured under the licence and the entirety of this production shall be exported to the Member(s) which has notified its needs to the Council for TRIPS;

ii. products produced under the licence shall be clearly identified as being produced under the system set out in this Decision through specific labelling or marking. Suppliers should distinguish such products through special packaging and/or special colouring/shaping of the products themselves, provided that such distinction is feasible and does not have a significant impact on price; and

iii. before shipment begins, the licensee shall post on a website (7) the following information:

- the quantities being supplied to each destination as referred to in indent (i) above; and
- the distinguishing features of the product(s) referred to in indent (ii) above;

c. the exporting Member shall notify (8) the Council for TRIPS of the grant of the licence, including the conditions attached to it (9). The information provided shall include the name and address of the licensee, the product(s) for which the licence has been granted, the quantity(ies) for which it has been granted, the country(ies) to which the product(s) is (are) to be supplied and the duration of the licence. The notification shall also indicate the address of the website referred to in subparagraph (b)(iii) above.[35]

The decision thus makes it possible, within the terms set out in the decision itself, for any member country to export generic product made under a compulsory licence. Although technically any member state is entitled to import product under the decision, 23 developed countries are identified as

35 WTO General Council (2003). Implementation of Paragraph 6 of the Doha Declaration on the TRIPS Agreement and Public Health. 30 August 2003. WT/L/540 and Corr.1

announcing voluntarily that they will not use the system to import.[36] Several other countries announced that their use of the system, if any, would be only in circumstances of extreme urgency or emergency.[37]

While these decision of the 23 countries not to use the system is arguably politically prudent, showing good faith on the part of wealthier countries and thus contributing to the progress of the amendment, to an extent this undermines the importance of the amendment as recognition of the beneficial interest. Indeed, recent controversies in the UK regarding approval of drugs on the National Health Service (NHS).[38] Decisions on cost-effectiveness necessarily impact upon delivery of health services to the extent that certain groups are denied access. Recognising this beneficial interest in all citizens would ultimately address the disproportionate pricing alleged in pharmaceuticals, not only in developing countries but also in richer nations, and motivate the availability of medicines at a price that can be paid.

The decision deems least-developed country members as having insufficient or no manufacturing capacities in the pharmaceutical sector, thus entitling them to make direct use of the waiver without first establishing that incapacity. Other eligible importing member states with little or no manufacturing capacity must establish this fact.

The TRIPS amendment on public health

In December 2005, member states agreed and approved a permanent amendment to the TRIPS Agreement[39] in order to transform the interim waiver into a permanent provision. This decision of the General Council was historic in that it was the first time a core WTO Agreement would be amended.

The amendment is in three parts. First, it introduces a new provision in the TRIPS Agreement. Article 31*bis* includes five paragraphs, the first of which provides for pharmaceutical products to be made under compulsory licence and exported to countries with insufficient or no manufacturing capacity:

> 1. The obligations of an exporting Member under Article 31(f) shall not apply with respect to the grant by it of a compulsory licence to the extent necessary for the purposes of production of a pharmaceutical product(s) and its export to an eligible importing Member(s) in accordance with the terms set out in paragraph 2 of the Annex to this Agreement.[40]

---

36 These countries are Australia, Austria, Belgium, Canada, Denmark, Finland, France, Germany, Greece, Iceland, Ireland, Italy, Japan, Luxembourg, Netherlands, New Zealand, Norway, Portugal, Spain, Sweden, Switzerland, United Kingdom and United States of America.

37 These countries are Hong Kong China, Israel, Korea, Kuwait, Macao China, Mexico, Qatar, Singapore, Chinese Taipei, Turkey and United Arab Emirates.

38 See the discussion of pricing in Chapter 9.

39 WTO General Council (2005). Amendment of the TRIPS Agreement. Decision of 6 December 2005. WT/L/641

40 TRIPS, Article 31*bis*.1.

The second part is in a new annex to the TRIPS Agreement, which sets out the terms for using the system. This annex includes definitions, notifications (to inform members of authorisations under compulsory licence), market and other issues: Finally, an appendix to the annex addresses the issue of manufacturing capacity in importing countries.

While it was originally meant to have been ratified by all member states by 1 December 2007, it was nearly a decade later before there were sufficient ratifications for the amendment to come into force, which it finally did, ON 23 January 2017.[41] Critically, most of the developed countries ratified the amendment quickly and it was the developing countries that took time to put the implementing measures in place. In part, this was due to the perceived issues with the first (and still only) notification under the paragraph 6.

First notification under the Paragraph 6 System

Canada was one of the first countries to introduce domestic legislation to implement the decision on Paragraph 6, despite not having yet accepted the protocol amending the TRIPS Agreement. Canada was the first to notify the TRIPS Council of its authorisation to manufacture for export to Rwanda, the first least-developed country to import generic product under the waiver.[42] As a least-developed country, Rwanda is entitled to the transitional period to implement the TRIPS provisions and so is not required to implement the protocol in domestic law.

Rwanda provided official notification to the TRIPS Council in July 2007,[43] as required under Paragraph 2(a) of the Decision, which obliges eligible importing countries to notify with details of the medicines to be imported. As discussed earlier, as a least-developed country, Rwanda is deemed to have insufficient or no manufacturing capacity and therefore not required to fulfil the additional notification obligations regarding eligibility.[44] The notification reported that Rwanda intended to import 260,000 packs of an antiretroviral in the treatment of HIV/AIDS – a fixed-dose combination of Zidovudine, Lamivudine and Nevirapine.

41 Members who have yet ratified the provision may continue to rely on the waiver until 31 December 2017.

42 Importantly, Apotex (the Canadian company) applied to export the drug before Rwanda approached it. Once it had approval it went looking for customers and found Rwanda.

43 Rwanda: Notification under Paragraph 2(a) of the Decision of 30 August 2003 on the implementation of paragraph 6 of the Doha Declaration on the trips agreement and public health. IP/N/9/RWA/1 (19 July 2007).

44 WTO General Council. Implementation of paragraph 6 of the Doha Declaration on the TRIPS Agreement and Public Health. Decision of 30 August 2003 (WT/L/540 and Corr.1): Paragraph 1(b). As a least-developed country with insufficient manufacturing capacity, Paragraph 1(b) does not apply and so Rwanda was not required to notify the desire to be an 'eligible importing member.'

Canada subsequently provided notification in October 2007[45] that it would manufacture and export the generic pharmaceutical product to meet Rwanda's needs, pursuant to Paragraph 2(c), which requires exporting countries to notify the TRIPS Council with relevant information on the compulsory licence. The notification provides information on the conditions of the licence; the details of the medicines themselves including quantities; and the website address of the exporting company (where information on quantities and other details must be published before shipment). Critically, a major delay then came into the system when Rwanda held a public procurement exercise for eight months before announcing in May 2008 the ultimate winner, who then began importing the drug in 2008. Thus, it took three and a half years for Apotex to develop the drug, identify a recipient country and then supply the drug, with most of the delay caused by no country coming forward to request the drug. Then, when Rwanda finally did, its own public procurement laws caused substantial additional delays.

The fact the system has been used only once and the reasons for this have been pondered for some time. A 2012 joint report by the WTO, WIPO and the WHO[46] considered the fact the Paragraph 6 System was not used. The report highlighted that it did not actually cover most procurement scenarios as the more common scenario is that there is no patent in force for the particular drug or the originator will reduce the price following negotiation. It may well be that the Paragraph 6 mechanism has led to the behaviour in pharmaceutical companies changing (e.g., not renewing or extending patent protection or agreeing to cheaper prices) as they wish to avoid generics making their drugs. There have been various other observations made as to why the system is not used, including one repeatedly raised that it is 'too complex and administratively unwieldy for further use',[47] but more likely is that patents blocking drug production is an unusual procurement scenario and the availability of other procurement pathways – including bulk purchasing – and the need for an adequate commercial basis for producers of the drugs needs to be found (as insufficient orders means production is not cost effective).

Compulsory licensing and access to the public sphere

Provision for compulsory licensing, as well as the political and commercial freedom to pursue these mechanisms, will be one of the most significant tools by which to safeguard the beneficial interest in health inventions. While the

45 Canada: Notification under Paragraph 2(a) of the Decision of 30 August 2003 on the implementation of paragraph 6 of the Doha Declaration on the trips agreement and public health. IP/N/10/CAN/1 (8 October 2007).

46 WTO-WIPO-WHO (2012), *Promoting Access to Medical Technologies and Innovation*. Geneva: World Health Organisation.

47 WTO-WIPO-WHO (2012), *Promoting Access to Medical Technologies and Innovation*, 179 (other reasons are also presented on that page).

mechanism developed has barely been utilised, its implementation has had a significant impact on the wider policy debate and also, probably, on the business practices of pharmaceutical companies. Access to the institutions in which these mechanisms are available is necessarily protected, as it were, by civil society activity, as demonstrated in the following discussion.

Civil autonomy in the public sphere – South Africa

Sub-Saharan Africa has the most serious HIV/AIDS epidemic in the world with consequently devastating impacts on development in this region. The 2007 UNAIDS regional data shows that the region of eastern Southern Africa (including South Africa) is particularly affected. This region accounts for 46 per cent of all new HIV global infections in 2015 (notwithstanding the number of new infections has fallen by 14 per cent since 2010) and is affected by national HIV prevalence exceeding 19.2 per cent,[48] with South Africa recorded as having the highest number of HIV infections in the world.[49] According to a World Bank publication, as a result of the huge threat to entire generations and the decimation of the workforce, HIV/AIDS is the main threat to development in this region.[50] Deaths from AIDS break down families and have severe consequences in other areas of local law, such as land rights (e.g., wives have no inheritance rights, therefore losing their home, shelter and food security when their husbands die). As well as access to medicines and healthcare, recent government policy has been fiercely and widely criticised for advocating rejection of Western medicine.

At the 2006 International AIDS Conference in Toronto, there were calls for the dismissal of South African Health Minister Tshabalala-Msimang, for advocating traditional medicines like garlic and beetroot rather than antiretrovirals.[51] These kinds of problems indicate the very real need for not only delivery of affordable medicines, but also working on knowledge transfer, cooperating with local cultural institutions, and building local capacity and infrastructures in health care and management. Since that time South Africa has made huge strides in diagnosis and treatment of HIV/AIDS and now has the biggest treatment programme in the world, which has been almost entirely internally funded.

In the late 1990s, the US placed South Africa on what is known as the Special 301 Watch List.[52] Under Special 301 provisions, the United States

48 UNAIDS (2016) Gap Report. Geneva: United Nations.

49 UNAIDS (2016) Factsheet November 2016 (for Worlds AIDS Day 1 December 2016).

50 Jamison DT et al. (2006) *Disease and Mortality in Sub-Saharan Africa*, 2nd edn, New York: World Bank.

51 Baleta A (2006) '"Dr Beetroot" Sidelined in South Africa' 6(10) *The Lancet* 620; BBC News, 'South Africa Aids Policy Attacked,' 19 August 2006).

52 This is provided by Section 182 of the Trade Act 1974, as amended by the Omnibus Trade and Competitiveness Act of 1988 and the Uruguay Round

Trade Representative (USTR) identifies countries that are not providing adequate and effective protection for intellectual property rights or are denying fair and equitable market access for those relying on intellectual property protection. Placement on the Watch List or Priority Watch List shows that the USTR has identified particular problems in that country in intellectual property protection, enforcement or market access, making such countries the focus for increased bilateral attention.

South African Medicines and Related Substances Control Amendment Act 1997

One of the problems from the perspective of the USTR was the South African Medicines and Related Substances Control Amendment Act 1997, which inserted Section 15C into the Medicines and Related Substances Control Act 1965. This amendment allowed parallel imports of pharmaceuticals[53] and the government could authorise generic substitution of medicines imported and produced under compulsory licences.[54] The act also allowed for the establishment of a pricing committee responsible for instituting a transparent pricing system.[55]

The US objected to the legislation maintaining that it was non-compliant with South Africa's obligations under TRIPS, placing South Africa on the Watch List once more in 1999. However, the TRIPS Agreement specifically does not deal with parallel importation;[56] therefore, at least in this regard, the act could not be a violation of South Africa's obligations. There is nothing in TRIPS that would necessarily prevent South Africa from attempting to import cheaper legitimate products from other parts of the world. In fact, the later competition decision against GSK examined the issue of price-fixing in the region.

In 1998 proceedings against the South African government were commenced by the Pharmaceutical Manufacturer's Association (PhRMA), GSK and other US drug interests.[57] The total of 42 applicants, including 39 pharmaceutical companies, claimed that the act was contrary to South Africa's international obligations under TRIPS. Although there were some efforts at drug donation during this time (e.g., Pfizer instituted a scheme in 2000), these were mostly criticised as mere public relations exercises due to their limited and restrictive application.

Agreements Act (enacted in 1994).

53 Medicines and Related Substances Control Act 1965, Section 15C(a).

54 Medicines and Related Substances Control Act 1965, Section 15C(b).

55 Medicines and Related Substances Control Act 1965, Section 22G.

56 TRIPS, Article 6.

57 Case No 4183/98 18 February 1998. In relation to this legislation see generally Sun H (2003) 'Reshaping the TRIPS Agreement Concerning Public Health' 37 *Journal of World Trade* 163.

Civil society activity

The US-based Treatment Access Group (TAG) was founded in 1992 in New York, its platform being the promotion of research and funding for HIV/AIDS treatment and cure.

TAG and a global coalition of civil society organisations lobbied for the South African case to be dropped and maintained that the act did not violate any international obligations under TRIPS.[58] In early 2001, TAG assembled a coalition of civil society, activists, academics and health workers, joining with the Health GAP Coalition and the Gay Men's Health Crisis (GMHC), to lobby GSK to withdraw the lawsuits in South Africa. 5 March 2001 was announced as a Global Day of Solidarity.

Also during this same period, activism grew in South Africa. On International Human Rights Day, 10 December 1998, the South African AIDS activist organisation, Treatment Action Campaign (TAC) was launched. Founded by Zackie Achmat, an HIV-positive activist, TAC was established on the same issues as US-based groups like TAG and ACT UP, but with important cultural specificity and relevance as a South African organisation, actually having its roots in the anti-apartheid movement. While wealthy white South Africans had access to treatment, black South Africans were denied HIV/AIDS healthcare. The Congress of South African Trade Unions (COSATU) lobbied alongside TAC on these issues of access to medicines.

The High Court, Pretoria, granted TAC the role of *amicus curiae* enabling them to make submissions on behalf of patients' groups and others opposed to the lawsuit. TAC argued on the basis of human rights (human rights to life, dignity, health and the rights of the child). Affidavits disputed the pharmaceutical companies' claims regarding research and development costs, which those companies claimed were reflected in the pricing of the drugs. Evidence was brought to show that the research was mostly conducted by public institutions, including universities and the NIH (US).

Resolution

In April 2001 the lawsuit was withdrawn[59] and the government was allowed to enforce the law as enacted. GSK was one of the first companies to begin the negotiations that ultimately led to the settlement of the dispute. Importantly, pressure from various groups and from international attention on the case had led to reductions of drug prices even before the lawsuit was resolved.

58 Health GAP Coalition / Treatment Action Group (TAG). 'Global Coalition of AIDS Activists Calls on GlaxoSmithKline to Abandon Lawsuits'. Press Release. 3 February 2001.

59 BBC News. 'Drugs Firms Withdraw from AIDS Case' 19 April 2001.

Localisation of TRIPS – Novartis in India

Imatinib (INN) was developed by Novartis in the late 1990s. It received FDA approval to be marketed as Gleevec[60] in May 2001.[61] Novartis obtained exclusive marketing rights (EMR) in India for Glivec. EMR is a temporary monopoly for a period of five years or until the examiner submits a report on the invention when the patent may be granted or the application rejected.[62] Under the amendments to India's patent law in 2005,[63] implemented to make India TRIPS-compliant, every application for EMR is therefore taken as a request for examination towards grant of a patent.[64]

In order to achieve TRIPS compliance, the new law introduced product patents, at the same time providing for a strict test for patentability for the discovery of a new form of a known substance (a 'higher' inventive step being required).[65] The law also allows for any person or group to file a pre-grant opposition.[66]

The dispute

In the case of Glivec, the Cancer Patients Aid Association, together with several generic pharmaceutical companies, filed a pre-grant opposition in the Chennai Patent Office.[67]

The Glivec case became the first major decision on patentability since product patents were introduced in India. It was decided that the application did not constitute an invention, and so the EMR were withdrawn. Glivec was an improved version of an earlier patented drug and, under the new provision,[68] this improvement in efficacy was not enough to demonstrate inventive step and thus warrant patent protection. The opponents contended that the application was merely a new form of a known substance, that the subject matter was anticipated in prior art and that there was no inventive step. They argued that the improvements would be obvious to a person skilled in the art.

In May 2006, Novartis filed two challenges in the Madras High Court, contending non-compliance with TRIPS and the unconstitutionality of Indian patent law, arguing that Section 3(d) would be unconstitutional as an arbitrary standard, thus violating the fundamental right to equality under

---

60 It should be noted that the spelling of the drugs name varies between countries.
61 'FDA Approves Gleevec for Leukemia Treatment' *FDA News* 10 May 2001.
62 Pursuant to Chapter IVA of India's Patents Act 1970; this was repealed by section 21 of the Patents (Amendment) Act 2005.
63 Patents (Amendment) Act 2005, which amended the Patents Act 1970.
64 Patents (Amendment) Act 2005, s. 78.
65 Section 3(d) of the Patents Act 1970, inserted by Patents (Amendment) Act 2005, s.3.
66 Patents Act 1970, s 25, inserted by the Patents (Amendment) Act 2005, s. 23..
67 Basheer S & Reddy TP (2008) 'The "Efficacy" of Indian Patent Law: Ironing out the Creases in Section 3(d)' 5(2) *SCRIPT-ed* 232.
68 Patents Act 1970, Section 3(d).

the Constitution of India.[69]. The High Court rejected these claims and the matter was appealed to the Supreme Court.

Supreme Court

In the *Novartis* judgment,[70] the Supreme Court reviewed the legislative history of the changes noting:

> while fulfilling its commitment under the TRIPS agreement, the Government must not bring in a patent regime where all the gains achieved by the Indian pharmaceutical industry are dissipated and large sections of Indians and people in other parts of the world are left at the mercy of giant multinational pharmaceutical companies[71]

The Court did not expressly rule whether the provisions adopted were compatible with TRIPS, but it acknowledged that the changes made to increase the height of the inventive step relied on the flexibilities in TRIPS.[72] Thus, the Indian law was permitted to have a higher standard of invention for certain types of pharmaceutical inventions.[73] Therefore, one of the flexibilities in Article 27(1), if *Novartis* is right, is to separate the requirement of patentability 'in all fields of technology' from a uniform 'inventive step' standard in all such fields.[74]

Protecting trust – compulsory licences and Thailand

Provisions for compulsory licences are critical in addressing global health equity in access to medicines.[75] At the end of 2006 and into 2007, the Thai government issued three compulsory licenses to produce affordable generic versions of the three patented medicines: efavirenz (antiretroviral marketed as Stocrin by Merck, Sustiva by Bristol-Myers-Squibb);[76] lopinavir and ritonavir (antiretroviral marketed as Kaletra by Abbott Pharmaceuticals);[77]

69 Constitution of India, Article 14.
70 *Novartis v Union of India & Others* (1 April 2013) Civil Appeal No 2706–2727 of 2013.
71 Ibid., paragraph 79.
72 Ibid., paragraphs 101–2.
73 Ibid., paragraph 104.
74 Member states have varying standards for what is an inventive step and so the question is whether the standard must be uniform.
75 WHO (2008). *Improving Access to Medicines in Thailand: The Use of TRIPS Flexibilities.* Report of a WHO Mission to Bangkok, 31 January to 6 February 2008.
76 Director General of the Department of Disease Control, Decree of Department of Disease Control, Ministry of Public Health, on the Public Use of Patent for Pharmaceutical Benefits, 29 November 2006.
77 Director General of the Department of Disease Control, Decree of Department of Disease Control, Ministry of Public Health, Regarding Exploitation of Patent on Drugs & Medical Supplies by the Government on Combination Drug Between Lopinavir & Ritonavir, 29 January 2007.

and clopidogrel (heart medicine, anti-clotting marketed as Plavix by Sanofi-Aventis and Bristol-Myers Squibb).[78]

The compulsory licences were sought in response to two problems: cost and availability.[79] Importantly, factors relevant to access to medicines include not only the cost of the medicine (as determined by the patent-holder marketing the medicine) but also by the availability (as determined by the production capacity and levels of the manufacturer, manufacturing the patent under licence from the patent-holder). The first licence was issued for the HIV/AIDS medicine, efavirenz. The WHO recommends efavirenz on its EML[80] because it has fewer side effects than other treatments on the market as well as being suitable for the treatment of patients co-infected with tuberculosis. For the Thailand government, access to efavirenz/Stocrin faced obstacles of both cost and supply (at times Merck had been unable to supply the drug, apparently due to production capacity). A compulsory licence therefore would address supply issues as well as amount to substantial savings for Thailand's public health budget.

Although it is reported that there were attempts to negotiate a commercial arrangement, during which it is claimed that Merck offered to lower the price, Merck disputes that this occurred before the announcement of the licence. In July 2007, in a letter to the EC Commissioner of Trade, the Thailand Minister of Public Health declared a willingness to negotiate with companies to reach reasonable and agreeable terms.[81] However, ultimately no agreements were reached and the Thai Ministry of Public Health authorised the Government Pharmaceutical Organisation (GPO) to manufacture generic versions of the medicine until 2011, which was later extended until the patent expires.

The controversy

The compulsory licences raise several significant issues. First, the licences are notable for their duration, which are longer relative to the usual conceptualisation

78 Permanent Secretary, Ministry of Public Health, Ministry of Public Health Announcement Regarding Exploitation of Patents on Drugs & Medical Supplies for Clopidogrel, 25 January 2007.

79 See the text of the announcements for compulsory licences. For example, Director General of the Department of Disease Control, Decree of Department of Disease Control, Ministry of Public Health, on the Public Use of Patent for Pharmaceutical Benefits, 29 November 2006.

80 WHO Model List of Essential Medicines List (EML), 15th List, March 2007. Shortly thereafter, in January 2007, additional compulsory licences were authorised for the cardiac medicine clopidogrel (marked by Sanofi-Aventis as Plavis) and the antiretroviral lopinavir/ritonavir (marketed by Abbott as Kaletra). In February, Abbott commenced negotiations towards a lower price rather than the issue of a compulsory licence. However, MSF raised concerns that such negotiations could be problematic and indeed result in the negative outcome of fixing of an anti-competitive price for a number of years.

81 Dr Mongkol N Songhkla, Minister of Public Health. Letter No 0100.3 (July BE 2550 (2007)).

of an 'emergency'. From the perspective of the public interest in preserving access to research benefits, this is an important challenge to the usual scope of what might be understood as a national emergency. Second, as well as communicable diseases (the usual target for compulsory licensing), the licences issued include drugs for heart disease and diabetes. This is also noteworthy as these are diseases usually considered to be Western diseases (with a profitable market) and they are non-infectious diseases, and so not usually considered as within the scope of a national emergency. Finally, the licences introduce significant issues with respect to competition and the market itself, allowing for importation of generic versions from India until production levels in Thailand can be achieved, thus facilitating entry of generic competitors into the Thai market.

This aggressive pursuit of the flexibilities provided to governments in order to meet local public health needs has also been advocated in other countries. In 2008, NGOs applied for a compulsory licence in Colombia for ritonavir and lopinavir for the treatment of HIV/AIDS. The Columbian government rejected the application for a declaration of public interest, but by relying on pricing regulations it cut the price by 55 per cent. These regulations set the price at which a drug may be sold by any person (including a patentee).[82] Abbott finally agreed to comply with the new price. More recently, a second application was made in 2012 for a compulsory licence for Glivec (imatinib). This led to a public interest declaration to lower prices[83] and there was 44 per cent price reduction.

In India, compulsory licences have been sought a few times, In 2012, Natco (an Indian generics manufacturer) obtained a compulsory licence in India for making a generic version of Bayer's cancer drug Nexavar; this was granted on the basis of an inadequate supply in India.[84] This was followed by two unsuccessful applications: one for dastanib, a cancer drug; and another for Saxagliptin, a diabetes drug. In both cases, it was held that the threshold requirements had not been met.

Viral sovereignty – benefit sharing and avian influenza

Indonesia has been the region worst affected by avian influenza, with 112 of the 137 cases being fatal.[85] This represents almost half of the deaths reported worldwide (245) and more than a third of the total reported cases (387).[86] At present there is no vaccine available for avian influenza largely because the way in which the virus will mutate and develop is not clear. Once a strain has been identified, a new influenza vaccine takes at least six months to be developed.

82 See Presidential Decree 126 of 2010.
83 Resolution No 2475 of 2015.
84 Indian Patents Act, s 84.
85 WHO. 'Avian Influenza: Situation in Indonesia'. Update 44. 10 September 2008.
86 WHO. 'Cumulative Number of Confirmed Human Cases of Avian Influenza A/(H5N1) Reported to WHO'. 10 September 2008.

Many states responded by stock-piling anti-viral medicines, particularly Tamiflu (Roche). This means that supplies are in place if a pandemic occurs, whereas relying upon production capacities after the event might mean the inability to supply what is needed. Although this stock-piling has occurred, the effectiveness of the possible treatments against any avian influenza pandemic cannot be known.

Roche donated around 5,000,000 units to the WHO, with 3,000,000 to be stored centrally and 2,000,000 to be stored regionally. Furthermore, Roche has authorised companies in China and India to manufacture Tamiflu, while other firms (including in Thailand) have been manufacturing generic versions. GSK is donating to the WHO 50,000,000 doses of pre-pandemic vaccine.

Global virus-sharing scheme

In 1952, the WHO established the Global Influenza Surveillance Network (GISN) to promote the sharing of virus samples towards preventing pandemics of the scale of 1918. The network is made up of four WHO collaborating centres (CCs) and 122 national influenza centres (NICs) in 94 countries. The NICs are responsible for collecting virus samples and preliminary tests before delivering those strains to CCs for further work towards vaccines.

The history of the virus-sharing system is based in the seasonal influenza vaccine where there is a markedly greater market in industrialised countries. However, the crisis in avian influenza is prevalent in developing countries (particularly southeast Asia). Therefore, there were concerns that the scheme should be revised to account for the interests of developing country donors.

In 2004, the WHO H5 Reference Laboratory Network was established as an ad hoc component of the WHO GISN, its terms of reference including the transfer of knowledge and capacity to local human resources. The system was adapted to provide for greater transparency, including the obligation to provide information on the process to developing countries providing samples, and for benefit-sharing, ensuring that developing countries participate in and have access to the benefits of the research.

Donation of samples and access and benefit-sharing

In December 2006, Indonesia announced that it would not continue sharing H5N1 samples until some provision for the sharing of benefits with the original donors was established and in January 2007 the government stopped sending samples to the WHO. The Indonesian government raised concerns that the donation of the virus sample was the donation of an Indonesian genetic resource, subsequently used by foreign researchers to design vaccines which would ultimately be made the subject of private patent rights and sold back to the Indonesians. Thailand health officials described this as intellectual property piracy on the one hand and biopiracy on the other.[87] Further, concerns for actual capacity for global production are also related, with current production capacity being below potential need. The lack of autonomy and influence with respect to subsequent use of samples and participation in research eroded the trust in the international system and led to the breakdown of the donor relationship.[88]

In February, the Indonesian government signed a memorandum of understanding (MOU) with Baxter Healthcare to develop a vaccine for the H5N1 strain.[89] The MOU provided for cooperation between Baxter and Indonesia, whereby Indonesia would send Baxter samples in return for its expertise in research and development. However, this private bilateral arrangement was widely criticised as a possible threat to an organised global response and access to vaccines.[90] In particular, one of the main activities of the WHO system is to monitor the virus and mutations, which would be compromised by private arrangements. But Indonesia responded by maintaining that other organisations would be granted access provided the samples were not used for commercial purposes (that is, that access to subsequent products developed from the sample would not be limited by intellectual property protection).

In late March 2007, WHO officials met with the Indonesian government in Jakarta. Ahead of this meeting, the Indonesian government had requested guarantees that subsequent benefits would be accessible and shared, and that those guarantees be legally binding on the WHO and pharmaceutical companies. At the end of the two-day meeting, the Minister of Health for Indonesia announced that sharing of the H5N1 virus samples would resume immediately. The meeting established that the WHO CCs would continue risk assessment and development of the H5N1 samples towards vaccine production, but that the process would be documented in a revised terms of reference for the WHO laboratories. The revised terms of reference would determine precisely what CCs could do with samples provided through the surveillance scheme.

---

87 Suwit Wibulpolprasert, senior advisor on health economics at Thailand's Ministry of Public Health, reported in Gerhardsen TIS (2007) 'Health Assembly Tackles Proposals on Avian Flu Virus Sharing' *Intellectual Property Watch* 16 May.

88 See further the discussion in Sedyaningsih ER et al. (2008) 'Towards Mutual Trust, Transparency and Equity in Virus Sharing Mechanism: The Avian Influenza Case of Indonesia' 37 *Annals of Academic Medicine Singapore* 482; and Chan CK & De Wildt G (2007) 'Developing Countries, Donor Leverage, and Access to Bird Flu Vaccines'. DESA Working Paper No 41. ST/ESA/2007/DWP/41.

89 'Baxter Continues Collaborations with Global Health Authorities to Advance Pandemic Preparedness: Company Clarifies Memorandum of Understanding with Indonesia' Baxter press release, 7 February 2007.

90 Garrett L & Fidler DP (2007) 'Sharing H5N1 Viruses to Stop a Global Influenza Pandemic' 4(11) *PLoS Medicine* e330; Holbrooke R & Garrett L 'Sovereignty that Risks Global Health' *Washington Post* 10 August 2008; and 'Experts Say Indonesian Deal on H5N1 Virus Jeopardizes Race for Pandemic Vaccine' *International Herald Tribune* 7 February 2007.

In March 2007 an agreement between the Indonesian government and the WHO was reached to improve access to current and potential pandemic influenza vaccines.[91] These subsequent benefits would be protected through the use of material transfer agreements (MTAs). The Indonesian Health Minister, Siti Fadillah Supari, explained that the MTA would require pharmaceutical companies to obtain prior informed consent from the Indonesian government before proceeding to develop a vaccine from the donated virus sample.

Pandemic influenza preparedness (PIP)

At the 60th World Health Assembly in 2007, Resolution WHA60.28[92] was adopted, safeguarding the virus-sharing system and recognises the need for access and benefit-sharing. On this issue the text also recognises Indonesia's requests for prior informed consent. The resolution led to the establishment of a working group. And the report of the working group led to the adoption of the Pandemic Influenza Preparedness Framework by the WHO.

A working paper on patent issues, presented early in the process,[93] while not dealing directly with alternative ownership and benefit-sharing schemes, identifies the intersecting rights in genetic material that may be at stake in the development process:

> There may be a wide range of different rights, entitlements and obligations over genetic materials, such as physical property rights, custodial rights and obligations, and entitlements concerning prior informed consent and equitable benefit sharing. How do the entitlement to apply for and to hold a patent, and the rights granted under a patent, overlap or otherwise interact with these other rights over genetic materials used in the patented invention?[94]

The paper also raises for discussion the important points regarding the provision of essential starting-material. The provision of vital and crucial samples confers a sense of authority over subsequent inventions and an entitlement to fair and equitable sharing in the benefits of those inventions. This sense of custodianship has thus contributed to Indonesia's assertion of sovereignty with respect to virus samples as national genetic resources. The relevance of MTAs in this context is identified in the background paper:

91 WHO. 'Indonesia to Resume Sharing H5N1 Avian Influenza Virus Samples Following a WHO Meeting in Jakarta'. News Release. 27 March 2007.

92 WHA. Resolution WHA 60.28. Pandemic influenza preparedness: sharing of influenza viruses and access to vaccines and other benefits. 23 May 2008.

93 WIPO Life Sciences Program (2007). 'Patent Issues Related to Influenza Viruses and their Genes: An Overview'. Background paper to A/PIP/IGM/3.

94 Ibid., 16.

Observation: inventorship, ownership and entitlement to apply

> If two research teams within a research partnership contribute inventively to the one patentable, and one team seeks a patent without recognition of the other, then various legal remedies are available. While the entitlement to apply for and to hold a patent must be derived from the genuine inventor(s), ownership of patents can also be transferred on the basis of contracts relating to non-inventive inputs to the invention – such as research contracts for paid research, or material transfer agreements providing genetic materials.[95]

The principles adopted in the framework acknowledge sovereign rights of states with the Eleventh Principle being to:

> recognize the sovereign right of States over their biological resources and the importance of collective action to mitigate public health risks.[96]

The standard transfer agreement for exchanges of biological material under the system places a particular restriction on obtaining intellectual property rights related to viruses:[97]

> **Article 6. Intellectual property rights**
>
> 6.1 Neither the Provider nor the Recipient should seek to obtain any intellectual property rights (IPRs) on the Materials.
> 6.2 The Provider and the Recipient acknowledge that any IPRs on the Materials obtained before the date of adoption of the Framework by the World Health Assembly will not be affected by SMTA 1.
> 6.3 The Provider under SMTA 1 may have used technology protected by IPRs for the generation and/or modification of the Materials. Any recipient of such Materials acknowledges that such IPRs shall be respected.

However, in many cases, the material (e.g., the virus) obtained is not going to be protected by intellectual property rights (as it is a product of nature). The standard agreement does not preclude the patenting of vaccines or other medicines derived from working on the material. But it does suggest that such a patent *may* be licensed royalty free to a local pharmaceutical company in the donating country.[98] It is not clear how close to *must* this *may* turns out to be or whether it is a mere statement of what is a desirable outcome.

---

95 Ibid., 26–27.
96 WHO (2011) Pandemic influenza preparedness Framework for the sharing of influenza viruses and access to vaccines and other benefits, 4.
97 Ibid., 31.
98 Ibid., paragraph 6.13.4.

These case studies are crucial, but by no means comprehensive, in representing the interplay between state coercion, market-based ethics and user autonomy through civil society access to the public sphere. A critical feature of these examples is the way in which beneficial interests in inventions may be threatened and protected within the current intellectual property system, largely on the basis of localisation of intellectual property laws such that they are acceptable to regional health and development needs. This process of localisation is a critical feature of the usefulness of the system in addressing fundamental rights to health and research benefits. This usefulness is the overriding criterion for the delivery of the right to health. Indeed, the interrogation of the value of 'use' has informed the discussion throughout, but is of particular significance when examining use of products and, as the following discussion will consider, the usefulness of the model of innovation.

9 Use

> That's the whole thing about Western democracy is that everything's based on property rights. And that's not what Maori society was ever based on – property rights. It was all about the communal good, the collective good for the community.[1]

Introduction

Recalling the discussion of private property as the basis for the articulation for the Western model of democracy, the characterisation of access must therefore account for the presumption of ethical priority attached to market freedom as the basis for individual will and democratic freedom. Indicated throughout is the potential quandary of access as distinct from use. Arguably, the intellectual property system does not regulate nor does it limit access as such. Indeed, one of the critical principles of the patent system is to introduce a means by which to exclude use while at the same time providing access to knowledge (through the published patent application) that might otherwise remain secret (through reliance upon trade secrets). Therefore, access in terms of the intellectual property system is something which it by definition provides. The important value at stake, arguably, is the ability to use the knowledge.

Law's colonisation of place

Access, in the sense of physical property, implies the value to which the property-holder has the opportunity to deny to others. However, this conceptualisation is limiting in the context of products in which intellectual property rights subsist. Access must be much more meaningful in the sense that it is the opportunity not merely to cross the path but to work the land. Indeed, the contemporary knowledge economy and the trend towards international harmonisation of intellectual property rights within that economy arguably render 'place', as it were, irrelevant.

1 Angeline Ngahina Greensill (Tainui/Ngati Porou), lawyer, interviewed in *The Leech and the Earthworm* (2003) Silver M & Pugh M (dir & scr) Harry D (prod)..

The incapacity and irrelevance of the intellectual property system with respect to traditional knowledge and cultural expressions makes this colonising effect of these legal rights all too clear. The 'colonising' effect of the law internationalises the knowledge economy and, despite the territorial nature of intellectual property law, overrides boundaries through international trade and through free trade agreements. Thus, the modern knowledge economy does not rely on competitive concepts of place and exclusion from access; the possessory power resides instead in knowledge and the regulation of its use. Thus, the opportunity not merely for access but for use is the critical value at stake in the knowledge economy.

The concept of access and the human right to health

> They conveyed their full estates of their lands, in their good health to friends in trust properly called feoffees in trust, and then they would, by their wills, declare how their friends should dispose of their lands; and if those friends would not perform it, the Court of Chancery was to compel them by reason of the trust; and *this trust was called the use of the land ... for the use was to the estate like a shadow following the body.*[2]

When examining access to medicines and access to knowledge, this necessarily introduces a broader and fuller concept of access. The definition of 'access' in this sense is enhanced by the four principles of the right to health: availability; accessibility; acceptability; and quality.[3] These four elements constitute the broader possessory concept of 'use' of which access is a component.

Therefore if private property rights suggest the participation in the public sphere (the democratisation of the public sphere) then it is only when genuine accessibility is achieved that the right to health can be understood to be fully realised. And as a component of the right to cultural life, this accessibility to the services, goods and information necessary to health is not merely a personal interest but an important aspect of the broader social benefit:

> Only the rights of political participation ground the citizen's reflexive, self-referential legal standing. Negative liberties and social entitlements, on the contrary, can be paternalistically bestowed ... Historically speaking, liberal rights crystallized around the social position of the private property owner.[4]

2 Bacon F (1857) *The Works of Francis Bacon, Lord Chancellor of England. With a Life of the Author by Basil Montagu, Esquire.* Philadelphia, PA: Parry & McMilland, 262–3 (emphasis added).

3 CESCR. General Comment No 14 (2000). The right to the highest attainable standard of health (article 12 of the International Covenant on Economic, Social and Cultural Rights. 22nd Session. E/C.12/2000/4. 11 August 2000. Paragraph 12.

4 Habermas J (1997/[1992]) *Between Facts and Norms: Contributions to a Discourse Theory of Law and Democracy*, Rehg W (trans), Cambridge: Polity Press, 78.

Use, in this context, generates the relationship of possession in the sense of historical relationships to land, *like a shadow following the body*. During the period of feudal law, land could not be devised by will.[5] Rather, it was held in strict feudal incidents of tenure whereby relationships to land were constructed in a hierarchy of obligations between vassals and lords. The 'use' was developed in order to overcome the rule as to divestiture by will. In this way, use constitutes 'ownership' and authority with respect to the land. This is of particular interest in the context of the contemporary model of Western democracy modelled on private property rights. That is, use, in the fuller sense, appropriates this proprietary language and is part of the underlying mechanism for realisation of the right to cultural life. The right to cultural life incorporates participation through use.

Access and the right to cultural life

Recalling the earlier discussion of health and human rights, the right to health is importantly and meaningfully an element of the full realisation of the right to cultural participation – not only in terms of the access to the benefits of scientific research[6] but also in the broader sense of the right to cultural life.[7] Incorporating both physical and mental well-being, the definition of health not only includes cultural identity but also relies upon attention to cultural diversity in its very interpretation and realisation, as explained in the Committee on Economic, Social and Cultural Rights General Comment and the element of 'acceptability'.[8]

Therefore, the full realisation of the right to health derives from more than mere entitlement to access. It necessarily comprises the four principles of the right, which arguably constitute the fuller concept of 'use.' Importantly, participating in this public sphere and within this logic of the proprietary model of democracy and freedom, fulfilling use also fulfils the basis for 'possession' in a sense of meaningful and accessible use and benefit. That is, the opportunity to use accounts for differences in life chances and addresses the genuine value upon which the Western model of democracy is articulated. Use thus fulfils 'ownership,' that is, the political participation of individuals regardless of individual life chances.

A human rights concept of use

The word use itself thus derives its meaning in law from use as benefit and possession (the act of possessing for benefit)[9] and more generally perhaps use

5 See further the discussion in Gray K & Gray SF (2009) *Elements of Land Law*, 5th edn, Oxford: Oxford University Press, paragraph 1.4.25 et seq (p 79 et seq). For greater detail see Simpson AWB (1986) *A History of The Land Law*, 2nd edn, Oxford: Oxford University Press.
6 ICESCR Article 15.1(b).
7 ICESCR Article 15.1(a).
8 CESCR. General Comment No 14, paragraph 12.
9 *The Oxford English Dictionary* 2nd edition.

as need (to have use for).[10] Drawing upon the four elements of the human right to health, access is understood as an element of the fuller concept of use. From the General Comment on Article 12, previously discussed in Chapter 3:

> The right to health in all its forms and at all levels contains the following interrelated and essential elements, the precise application of which will depend on the conditions prevailing in a particular State party:
>
> a. *Availability*. Functioning public health and health-care facilities, goods and services, as well as programmes, have to be in sufficient quantity within the State party …
> b. *Accessibility*. Health facilities, goods and services have to be accessible to everyone without discrimination, within the jurisdiction of the State party. Accessibility has four overlapping dimensions:
>   i. Non-discrimination …
>   ii. Physical accessibility …
>   iii. Economic accessibility (affordability) …
>   iv. Information accessibility …
> e. *Acceptability*. All health facilities, goods and services must be respectful of medical ethics and culturally appropriate …
> f. *Quality*.[11]

As discussed earlier, these four principles are critical to the meaningful realisation of the inclusive right to health. Therefore, these principles also underpin the interpretation of the context in which individuals may access their beneficial interests in the products of scientific research. It is thus useful to consider the interpretation of the intellectual property and related frameworks relevant to health and medicines through these essential elements. With respect to availability, important issues are raised by market-driven research and development agenda and the way in which the market will influence where these research resources are directed. Furthermore, patent rights will control the production capacity as this capacity and subsequent supply to the market is limited to the capacity of the manufacturer. The principle of accessibility is also supported by the principles of acceptability, including not only access to health facilities and goods, but also the opportunity take advantage of that access (regardless of life chances and cultural differences), raising issues regarding the contribution of the intellectual property system to an environment in which the benefits of scientific research can be enjoyed by all. Finally, the intellectual property system, and patents in particular, imply a certain oversight with respect to quality (at least in terms of the inventive contribution to the art). This is supported by regulatory systems concerned

10 Ibid..
11 CESCR. General Comment No 14, paragraph 12.

with the safety and efficacy of new products. Therefore, the way in which the system cooperates with the realisation of this essential element of quality in facilities and goods must also be addressed in the overall context of 'access.'

What is reaffirmed in this human rights approach to the interpretation of the efficacy of the patent system is the broader meaning of 'access.' Again, arguably use is the critical value for which access is an essential and determining element, but an element which does not constitute the full entitlement of individuals to the benefits of scientific research and progress.

Market use

Regulatory laws concerned with the control of medicinal products in the interests of safety and efficacy, licensing, patient information and labelling, safe use and marketing are all of crucial importance to the infrastructure in place to deliver and medicines in the market. Indeed, such laws will influence not only the immediate availability of the medicine, but also the pricing (for instance, through support to the market-based model and supporting laws for extensions or restoration of monopolies to account for regulatory delays). Furthermore, such regulatory frameworks are of critical relevance to the environment for innovation in that they may impact upon the accessibility of information, products and research freedom.

Earlier discussions of data exclusivity[12] examined the way in which the dynamics of the market are translated into the circumstances for regulating the use not only of the invention (the patent system) but also of the data (data exclusivity). That is, the monopoly is motivated by proposed incentives to innovation (the patent) as well as by the preservation of the market itself (data exclusivity). As well as critical manipulation of access and use of the benefits of scientific research, related regulatory processes introduce other support as well as tensions for the availability and accessibility of medicines on the market.

Availability on the market

In Europe, the key legislation is the Medicinal Products for Human Use Directive.[13] The directive gives authority for the assessment and management of applications for approval to market drugs to the public. Such authorisation for marketing is granted to the competent and independent national authority,[14]

12 See the discussion in Chapter 5.

13 Directive 2001/83/EC of the European Parliament and of the Council of 6 November 2001 on the Community code relating to medicinal products for human use as amended by numerous subsequent directives.

14 In the UK, the relevant regulatory framework is introduced by the Medicines Act 1968 and various European medicines legislation. The Medicines Act established what is now called the Medicines and Healthcare Products Regulatory Agency (MHRA). The Medicines Act gives the UK agency powers to enforce and prosecute breaches of the law.

which will also have the duty to monitor the safety of medicines after they have been approved for marketing.[15] In addition to the national bodies there is a central administrative agency, the European Medicines Evaluation Agency (EMEA), which operates as a pharmaco-vigilance network, responsible for all applications for marketing authorisation within the EU and the monitoring of safety after approval.

Accessibility on the market

While regulatory authorities determine the actual legality of the drug with respect to the market, the infrastructure for pricing impacts directly upon accessibility in both developing and developed countries. The opportunity to define markets through the monopoly granted by patents raises issues of accessibility not only in developing countries and neglected markets, but also in providing national health services in developed countries.

In the UK, profits on branded pharmaceuticals sold to the National Health Service (NHS) are capped by the Pharmaceutical Price Regulation Scheme (PPRS). In 2007, the UK Office of Fair Trading (OFT)[16] undertook a market study into the PPRS and the pricing of pharmaceuticals.[17] The market study advocates value-based pricing determined by therapeutic benefits to patients. Specifically, the study explains the advantages of over current profit-cap and price-cut schemes such that there is a relationship between the price and the benefit, as distinct from a discounting scheme which nevertheless affirms the original price and does not really interrogate the rationale for price decisions:

> [W]hile such measures may bring small improvements, they would not address the fundamental concerns we have with existing arrangements. To ensure value for money from NHS expenditure and give good, stable investment incentives to companies in the long run, there is a compelling case for reform of the scheme towards a value-based pricing system that would relate the prices of products to their clinical value relative to existing treatments.[18]

The report advocates both ex-post value-based pricing (which maintains freedom to set prices but introduces *ex-post* review of cost effectiveness to replace PPRS profit and price controls) and *ex-ante* value-based pricing (which would replace PPRS controls, but would also include a fast track ex-ante assessment of cost-effectiveness commencing during the licensing process.[19] These proposals are significant in that they operate not to interfere

15 Directive 2001/83/EC: Title IX (Articles 101–108).
16 Subsequently replaced by the Competition and Markets Authority.
17 Office of Fair Trading (2007). The Pharmaceutical Price Regulation Scheme. Market Study.
18 Ibid., page 5.
19 Ibid., pages 5–7.

with the legal rights to the invention, but to safeguard the beneficial interest in the invention which may be compromised by pricing protection afforded by those legal rights. While initiatives such as tiered or differential pricing directly deal with costs in specific markets, these initiatives do not deal directly with the ideology underpinning the pricing of medicines, as identified in the OFT study. Indeed, they do more to sustain the market-based approach to innovation 'futures' (that is, that innovation in the future depends upon market advantages in the present) than to preserve the simultaneous interests in the legal rights and the beneficial interests in the inventions.

Differential pricing

The concept of differential pricing is often advocated as an answer to problems in particular markets, especially those in developing countries. Many governments consider differential pricing (also called tiered pricing) to be a much more desirable approach to negotiating access in various cases, rather than proceeding to compulsory licences.[20] Differential pricing works by creating different markets for a drug in different countries (rather than presuming the same price in a global market). This means that different classes of buyers are charged different prices for the same medicinal product. It is applied commonly in the context of vaccines in order to achieve greater coverage in low-income countries, where the price will be lower, while maintaining the market in richer countries, where higher prices and greater profits will be possible.

The lower price is achieved through bulk purchase of product, through procurement systems. As well as facilitating availability of product in low-income countries, differential pricing systems increase coverage of product and create markets in those regions. An important example of a procurement system is the Expanded Programme on Immunisation (EPI) established in 1974 by the United Nations Children's Fund (UNICEF) and the Pan-American Health Organization (PAHO).

The success of such systems also relies upon the separation of such markets and the prohibition of parallel imports of the cheaper medicines into the more profitable markets. If the patent owner has authorised the sale of a patented medicine through a bulk procurement system in a developing country, the patent owner can prevent the resale of those goods within another country, because the rights may not be exhausted in that second jurisdiction.[21] For example, the patent rights, in effect, will protect the rationale of the bulk procurement system because it will not be possible for a party to buy

---

20 For instance, see European Commission 'Access to Medicines: EU Clears Plan to Ensure Delivery of Cheap Medicines to Developing Countries', Press Release. 26 May 2003 (IP/03/748). See further the discussion in Raghavan C (2001) 'EU for "Differential Pricing" over Compulsory Licensing" *South-North Development Monitor* 31 May.

21 On this subject generally see Stothers C (2007) *Parallel Trade in Europe* Oxford: Hart Publishing.

discounted drugs for distribution in Rwanda and then try to sell them at a huge profit in the United Kingdom. However, patent rights will be no protection against inappropriate dealings with the goods within the intended region of supply. Therefore, if the infrastructure is not in place to guarantee the distribution of the drugs to those individuals in need, but rather allows them to be diverted to more profitable markets in the country, then the system may fail. The success of differential or tiered pricing therefore relies upon the local economic and political infrastructure. This infrastructure is critical to the success of the system so that drugs are supplied to the intended beneficiaries and not diverted elsewhere.

Accessibility for innovation and development

In the United States, the key regulatory authority is the Food and Drug Administration (FDA). Two major pieces of US federal legislation, outside the central intellectual property framework and relevant to this discussion of the supporting regulatory framework, deal with intellectual property and competition and are of particular importance in safeguarding access to medicines for both therapeutic and research purposes.

The first of these is more commonly known as the Bayh–Dole Act.[22] The importance of this legislation for medicines and intellectual property is that it provides for compulsory licensing by the government where universities and other institutions developing research from external funding fail to work the invention or to take reasonable steps to commercialise the subsequent invention. The act affirms the rights of universities and other public-sector researchers over research resulting from external federal funding. This means that such research becomes more convincingly the subject matter of private rights rather than the interests in any invention arising from that research vesting in the government.

However, the act also creates a march-in right for the government, which can petition to exercise that strictly limited right on its own initiative or at the request of a third party provided certain criteria are met. These criteria include the failure to take reasonable steps to commercialise certain technologies, which may lead to the request to license. The right is very rarely used, except in the case of petitions to the National Institutes of Health. The result is that it has become part of the business model of pharmaceutical companies undertaking contracts for drugs licensed under Bayh–Dole to consider the risk of a petition for march-in rights.

The second important piece of US federal legislation is the Drug Price Competition and Patent Term Restoration Act, more usually known as the Hatch–Waxman Act. The Hatch–Waxman Act came into force in 1984 and establishes the current system for generic medicines in the US. The act

22 Also known as the University and Small Business Patent Procedures Act. This act was adopted in 1980, codified in 35 U.S.C. 200–212 and implemented by 37 CFR 401.

amends the Federal Food, Drug and Cosmetic Act, providing for restoration of patent term (to account for regulatory delays) and abbreviated new drug applications (ANDA) for generic medicines.[23] This system is clearly comparable to the system for supplementary protection certificates considered earlier.[24]

The provision for patent term restoration is based upon the rationale that regulatory delays undermine the opportunity for the patent holder to realise the full potential of the patent monopoly.[25] The period by which the patent term may be restored is calculated from the date of commencement of the clinical trial for the new product to the date of application for approval. The extra period is calculated as half this time plus the whole amount of time expended in regulatory review. In all cases, patent term restoration is capped at five years and market exclusivity can be no more than fourteen years.[26]

The Hatch–Waxman Act also provides for abbreviated approval of generic products.[27] This is possible by permitting application for the approval of generic products to rely upon the approval of the originator's product together with the accompanying clinical data.

The act also introduces the research exception in the US, sometimes referred to as the Bolar exception after the decision in *Roche Products v Bolar Pharmaceutical.*[28] This exception provides for the experimental use of a patented producted (i.e., non-commercial use) for the purposes of obtaining FDA approval for generic versions.

As may be recalled from earlier discussions, where diseases are rare or where the market for suitable medicines and treatments is small, the medicines are unlikely to be marketed or research and development may be limited. These 'orphan drugs' and their development and improvement is a key concern for the WHO (as many 'orphan diseases' are tropical and sub-tropical diseases of developing countries). The US Orphan Drug Act was introduced in 1983 to address research and development in rare or 'orphan' diseases. Orphan drug status entitles the company undertaking the research to tax advantages and extended marketing exclusivity.[29]

Other provisions relevant to directing incentives towards research in orphan diseases include an administrative system known of priority review vouchers.[30] The original system of priority review vouchers related to for

23 21 USC 355 (j).
24 In Chapter 5, this volume.
25 35 USC 156.
26 35 USC 156 (c).
27 In particular, those listed in the *Approved Drug Products with Therapeutic Equivalence Evaluations* (Orange Book) regularly published by the Food and Drug Administration (FDA).
28 *Roche Products Inc. v. Bolar Pharmaceutical Co.*, 733 F.2d 858 (Fed. Cir. 1984).
29 Seven years.
30 The administrative system was created by amendments to the Food, Drug and Cosmetic Act, 21 USC 351 by the Food and Drug Administration Amendments Act. The system was first proposed in the article, Ridley DB et al (2006) 'Developing Drugs for Developing Countries' 25(2) *Health Affairs* 313.

companies seeking to register drugs and vaccines for neglected tropical diseases. It was extended in 2012 so that vouchers can also be granted for rare paediatric diseases,[31] that is a disease which primarily affects under-18s and affects fewer than 200,000 persons in the United States. It was extended again in 2016 to cover medical countermeasures.[32]

Priority review vouchers provide new incentives for research into neglected tropical diseases. The effect of the voucher is to gain fast-track approval for other (potentially more profitable) drugs that company may seek to register in the future, potentially reducing registration times by almost a year. However, the vouchers themselves are valuable commodities to facilitate partnerships and to sell onto other companies, thus providing alternative means of financing clinical trials and creating partnerships researching in relation to neglected and rare diseases.

So far four priority review vouchers have been awarded for tropical diseases and nine for rare paediatric diseases. Seven of the thirteen vouchers are yet to be used. Only one has been used by the company who was granted the voucher in the first place. The remaining vouchers have been sold for between $67 million and $350 million (some of which have been subsequently used).[33]

Economic accessibility and the pricing of medicines

As introduced earlier, patent rights preserve a monopoly upon which markets and pricing may be define irrespective of any meaningful calculation of 'quality' or 'benefit' in the product. That is, pricing is directed by a purely profit-driven approach as distinct from identifying a relationship between (therapeutic) value and the consumer. These are issues not only for poorer, developing countries but also for national programmes to deliver health care and national services in developed countries, as the earlier consideration of the PPRS indicates. For instance, the UK National Institute for Health and Clinical Excellence (NICE), which advises the NHS, is routinely criticised for its refusal to supply certain medicines on the NHS for reasons of cost-effectiveness in particular in relation to cancer treatments. This is demonstrated by NICE having refused to include Avastin (bevacizumab), owned by Roche, on the approved list for six different cancers on the grounds that the cost is too high for the minimal benefit.[34] Ironically, there have been fights to make

---

31 Under the Food and Drug Administration Safety and Innovation Act.

32 Under the 21st Century Cures Act.

33 Gaffney, A et al 'Regulatory Explainer: Everything You Need to Known About FDA's Priority Review Vouchers' (posted 3 November 2016, updated 21 February 2017) on http://www.raps.org/Regulatory-Focus/News/2015/07/02/21722/Regulatory-Explainer-Everything-You-Need-to-Know-About-FDA's-Priority-Review-Vouchers

34 PharmaTimes 'Final NICE No for Avastin in Ovarian Cancer' (22 May 2013): http://www.pharmatimes.com/news/final_nice_no_for_avastin_in_ovarian_cancer_1005060.

Avastin available for diabetic macular oedema patients on the grounds it is cheaper and more effective than other medicines.[35]

The fight in 2008 is exemplary of how such cost/benefit decisions are received. The decision was widely criticised as these pharmaceuticals presented the very few current options for patients with this advanced renal cancer. Charities and patient groups, including Cancer Research UK, condemned the decision and launched public web logs to discuss the proposal.[36] These civil society groups were also joined by practitioners raising concerns regarding the effectiveness of the alternative treatment, interferon.[37] However, Professor Peter Littlejohns, Clinical and Public Health Director at NICE, defended the decision in the press,[38] maintaining that providing these treatments would mean forgoing treatments for other patients in other areas.

The controversy continued when the Chair of NICE, Professor Sir Michael Rawlins, directed the blame at disproportionate over-pricing by the industry rather than the decisions on cost-effectiveness imposed upon and by governments.[39] In his comments on the structure of the industry and the business model of the pharmaceutical company, the Chair's comments imply objectives of profits and share prices as distinct from needs-based research agenda. Furthermore, marketing costs are included in drug prices, despite the prohibition of such advertising in the UK, as distinct from the US:

> Traditionally the pharmaceutical industry will admit that they actually charged what they think the market will bear. The wiser ones are recognising that that model is no longer available.[40]

These comments are supported by the 2007 market study of the OFT.[41]

As considered elsewhere in this discussion, the importance of civil society (including patient groups) to the motivation of normative changes is significant, particularly in protecting the relationship between benefits and price. For example, when Abbott Laboratories raised the price of the HIV/

---

35 Wanna O 'Avastin Packs "Most Cost-Effective" Punch" www.aop.org.uk/ot/science-and-vision/research/2016/06/10/avastin-packs-most-cost-effective-punch.

36 Cancer Research UK (2008).' Cancer Research UK Expresses "Deep Concern" on Kidney Cancer Drug Decision". Press Release. 7 August.

37 For instance, *The Independent* reported Professor John Wagstaff of the South Wales Cancer Institute as stating there would be no point in referring patients as around 75 per cent gain no real benefit from interferon: Kirby J (2008) '"Devastating blow" to Kidney Cancer Sufferers." *The Independent*, 7 August 2008.

38 BBC News. 'Row over NHS Kidney Drug Decision.' 7 August 2008.

39 Hinsliff G (2008). 'Health Chief Attacks Drug Giants over Huge Profits', *The Observer*, 17 August 2008.

40 Professor Sir Michael Rawlins quoted in Hinsliff, "Health Chief Attacks Drug Giants".

41 Office of Fair Trading (2007). The Pharmaceutical Price Regulation Scheme. Market Study.

AIDS drug, Norvir (ritonavir), by just over 400% in 2003,[42] civil society oversight was the effective mechanism by which to address this obstruction to the beneficial interest.

Norvir, which received FDA approval in 1996, is a protease inhibitor (PI) and is an essential component in highly active anti-retroviral treatment (HAART) used to treat HIV/AIDS. Although initially marketed as a standalone PI, Norvir subsequently became more commonly used in low doses as a booster in HAART. Abbott then introduced Kaletra around four years later as a fixed-dosed combination product and the only such product to include Norvir/ritonavir. The wholesale price of Norvir was then raised in 2003, but not that of Kaletra (despite containing ritonavir). Raising the price of Norvir effectively raised the price required to access the eight out of nine competitors' drugs that rely upon Norvir as the booster in HAART. Kaletra thus became a cheaper alternative, but not necessarily a medically appropriate one for all candidates. The Kaletra patent expired in 2016.

In May 2004, the US-based civil society coalition, Prescription Access Litigation (PAL) filed a class action anti-trust claim in Illinois state court against Abbott and in October 2004 filed a federal class action suit in the US District Court in California.[43] In August 2008 Abbott agreed to settle and this was approved by the District Court and faced an unsuccessful attempt to quash the settlement.[44]

Pricing and essential medicines

Essential medicines are those medicines identified as necessary for priority health requirements of a particular population. The WHO has published the Essential Medicines List (EML) every two years since 1977, with updates to the list undertaken by a committee of independent experts. The list was introduced to assist governments in the selection of medicines for local public health requirements. The EML also acts as an important resource for the production of national medicines lists.

The production of national lists was recommended in 1978 when the WHA passed a resolution on the importance of generic names in national drug formularies.[45] Of the 194 member states of the WHO, 156 have produced official essential medicines lists. In some member states, regional lists have also been produced. Medicines are selected for inclusion in the list through an evidence-based process, taking account of various issues including public

42 From USD205.74 to USD 1028.71 for 120 capsules.

43 *In re Abbott Laboratories Norvir Anti-Trust Litigation*, 562 F.Supp.2d 1080 (ND Cal 2008). See *Meijer v Abbott Laboratories* (ND Cal, 11 August 2011).

44 John Doe v. Abbott Laboratories, 571 F. 3d 930 (9th Cir 2009).

45 Resolution on the importance of using non-proprietary names in establishing national drug formularies WHA31.32. The INN system is considered further later in this section.

health relevance; quality; safety; efficacy; cost-effectiveness; and availability (including quantity and dosage forms).

The list includes medicines addressing priority diseases like malaria, tuberculosis and reproductive health, as well as chronic diseases like diabetes and cancer. Antiretroviral medicines (ARVs) were introduced in 2002.

Information accessibility and the politics of names

In the area of pharmaceuticals, the system of International Non-proprietary Names (INN)[46] for pharmaceuticals shares similar principles of denying registration of information that is necessary to all competitors in the field and is necessary for all customers to make their decisions. Indeed, without this protection of the critical identification of the invention, as distinct from the patent, is compromised. In fact without protection for the non-proprietary name, the patent would become identical with the invention, thus compromising the beneficial interests to the advantage of the legal rights in the invention. Therefore, the system of INNs is crucial to the realisation of access to the benefits of research and progress in medicines.[47] All INNs, also known as 'generic names,' are unique, non-proprietary and universally-recognised. Thus, INNs maintain medicinal knowledge as a public good. In other words, it maintains the medicine as a 'kind' as distinct from an individual product as a good.

The INN system is concerned with consumer information and safety and ensuring against confusion. The INN system means that each pharmaceutical substance is identified by a unique and universally available name. Each name must be genuinely unique, distinctive in sound and spelling and not likely to be confused with any other names in common use.[48] INNs for pharmacologically related substances also indicate that relationship by using a common 'stem.' Pharmaceutical products sharing a common stem[49] can then be recognised by pharmacists, medical practitioners and others as belonging to a group of substances with similar pharmacological activity.

46 The modern INN system was established in 1950 by a World Health Assembly resolution WHA3.11. In 1953 it began operations and the first list of INNs for pharmaceutical substances was published. The cumulative list of INN now includes around 7000 names designated since that time. The list of names grows by around 120–150 new INNs every year indicating also an increase in the utilisation of the system. INNs are not given for herbal or homeopathic products, nor for products with a long history of used under a well-established name (for instance, morphine) or trivial chemic names. Some of the radicals and groups are given a shorter non-proprietary name which, when used with an INN, is referred to as an International Nonproprietary Name (Modified) or INNM.

47 See generally WHO (1997) Guidelines on the Use of International Nonproprietary Names (INNs) for Pharmaceutical Substances (WHO/PHARM S/NOM 1570).

48 Ibid., Part 1.1.

49 Ibid., Part 3.2.

As an international nomenclature for pharmaceutical substances, the INN system makes it possible to prescribe and dispense medicines safely no matter which branded product is used. This also assists in the clear identification of generics which enter the market and compete after the expiration of the patent on the original product. Importantly, as an international system it assists with the delivery of safe and effective information worldwide.

To facilitate international availability, the names are designated as non-proprietary. That is, the names are genuinely in the public domain to be accessed as universally available public property.[50] To achieve this objective, the WHO formally places the names in the public domain to be used without any restriction whatsoever to identify pharmaceutical substances in pharmacopoeias, product labelling and information, drug regulation, scientific literature, advertising and of course for generics.

The relationship between the INN and the trade mark on product labelling is very important. The distinction between trademarks and INNs or generic names must be preserved in order to maintain the utility of the INN.[51] Measures in various jurisdictions have included mandating a minimum size for the INN which must be printed under the trademark labelling and advertising; requiring the INN to be at least half the size of the proprietary name on the labelling; and requiring the INN to be larger than the proprietary name. Most importantly, in all cases the trademark cannot be derived from the INN and must not include their common stems. This is critical to guarding against confusion and to protecting the safety of consumers. In Europe the relevant legislation can be found in the Medicinal Products for Human Use Directive.[52]

The WHO is responsible for determining INNs in consultation with experts from the WHO Expert Advisory Panel on the International Pharmacopoeia and Pharmaceutical Preparations. For a new INN a request or application is made by the manufacturer or inventor. The request is reviewed according to a strict procedure examining for similarities with published INN[53] and trademarks and then forwarded to the INN experts for comment.[54] Once a name is agreed this applicant is informed and a proposed INN is then published in WHO Drug Information for comment or objection for an objection period of four months.[55] In case the name has to be reviewed or modified after this period, the proposed name is not to be used until it is given the status of a recommended INN. When selecting new INNs, the rights of existing trademark owners are given due regard and interested persons are entitled to file formal objections during the selection process of a new INN if

50 Ibid., Part 4.
51 Ibid., Part 4 and Annex 6 (Article 8.b).
52 Directive 2001/83/EC of the European Parliament and of the Council of 6 November 2001 on the Community code relating to medicinal products for human use as amended (Medicinal Products for Human Use Directive).
53 Ibid., Annex 6 (Article 3).
54 Ibid., Part 5.2 and Annex 6 (Article 3).
55 Ibid., Annex 6 (Article 5).

they believe the proposed INN will be in conflict with an existing trademark. WHO will not recommend an INN in the face of such an objection and will try to resolve the objection or reconsider the name. If at the end of that period no objection has been made, the name will be published with the status of a recommended INN and is unlikely to be modified further. Therefore, once published as a recommended INN it is immediately available for use in labelling, publications and drug information in order to provide universal identification of the active pharmaceutical substance.

The WHO sends list of proposed and recommended INNs to all 194 member states as well as national pharmacopoeia commissions and other bodies designated by members, together with a note from the Director-General requesting members to take the necessary steps to prevent the creation of private proprietary rights in these names.[56] This of course includes the prohibition of registration of the names as trademarks. The US, UK and Japan all have organisations to oversee non-proprietary drug nomenclature, each of which publishes national names (for example, British Adopted Names (BAN)). However, these national publications are becoming less relevant and the majority of pharmaceuticals are usually identified by an INN, thus avoiding the problem of different generic names in different countries. There has been adoption of INNs across the EU. As explained earlier, the law in Europe is harmonised by the Medicinal Products for Human Use Directive, which means that even those countries with their own national organisations, including UK and the BAN, will generally adopt INNs as published by the WHO.

Commercial will and the right to health

Mechanisms to promote access within the current commercial and legal framework necessarily rely upon commercial will to innovate upon traditional models. Nevertheless, the attraction of cooperation in patent pooling is the advantage of protecting the basic architecture of the patent system while perhaps shifting the perspective to account for beneficial interests to the invention.

Patent pooling

A patent pool is a consortium of at least two companies agreeing to cross-license patents relating to a particular technology, often introduced as a measure between competitors to avoid infringement and litigation. Therefore, a patent pool can also create a monopoly over certain technology if competitors cooperate in such a way (and cross-license rather than sue for infringement or revocation of weak patents). As a result, competition issues can become very important when a large consortium or 'cartel' is formed.

As a business model, patent pools are not new but have been relevant throughout the modern patent system. One of the first patent pools was

56 In the European Union, see ibid. Annex 6 (Article 8).

formed in 1856 by sewing-machine manufacturers Grover, Baker, Singer, Wheeler, and Wilson.[57] As described above, this patent pool was motivated by accusations of patent infringement and invalidity. Rather than engaging in costly lawsuits, possibly leading to the revocation not only of a competitor's patent but also perhaps one's own, it is often more prudent to seek cross-licensing. This is indeed what happened in this case and the parties agreed to cross-license rather than decimate their profits through the pursuit of expensive and high-risk litigation. Patent pools remain very relevant to the business models of modern patent industries as they reduce coordination costs and the risks of litigation (not only the loss of the lawsuit but also the vulnerability of one's own patent to a counter-suit for revocation by the allegedly infringing patent).[58]

The most established example of patent pools is the Medicines Patent Pool (MPP) which is a United Nations-backed public health organisation. It aims to increase access drugs for HIV/AIDS, viral hepatitis C and tuberculosis in low- and middle-income countries. To date it has agreements with nine patent-holding companies for twelve HIV medicines, two hepatitis C medicines, one tuberculosis treatment and an HIV treatment platform. This has enabled sixteen generic manufacturers to be licensed to sell the drugs to relevant country.

Importantly the MPP is characterised by its voluntary nature as well as the autonomy of participating patent-holders to provide limited licences so as to restrict the field of use and countries to which the licence will apply.

'Norm cascades' in the right to health

As emphasised throughout this work, cooperation with civil society is a crucial factor in the legitimacy of developments in health and access to research. Civil society participation embodies communication with and constitutes access to the public sphere, thus motivating legitimacy in the development and application of the law. Thus, civil society participation is an element of both the formal rights agenda pursued in institutional settings and the acceptability of the way in which entitlements and freedoms are realised within that institution. This relationship to use as the motivating value of equitable interest suggests the importance of the model of innovation itself.

This promotion of communication between spheres and cooperation with the user in the realisation of access to benefits is meaningfully incorporated in the role of civil society in institutional change. Thus, it is through genuine

57 Hounshell DA (1984) *From the American System to Mass Production 1800–1932: The Development of Manufacturing Technology in the United States*, Baltimore, MD: Johns Hopkins University Press, 67–68. See also Calder L (2001) *Financing the American Dream*, Princeton, NJ: Princeton University Pres, 162.

58 There are, however, competition law issues associated with patent pools: see Roughton, Johnson and Cook (2014) *The Modern Law of Patents*, 3rd edn, Lexisnexis, paragraph 21.214 to 21.227.

communication and participation in the public sphere, as materialised by civil society organisations, that the user achieves self-determination and meaningful use of research benefits in the context of health (as distinct from mere market access):

> An autonomous basis in *civil society*, a basis independent of public administration and private market relations, is a precondition for civil self-determination. This basis preserves political communication from being swallowed up by the state apparatus or assimilated to market structures.[59]

This final section therefore represents that achievement in the public sphere, through direct interrogations to the dominant model of innovation itself. These proposals do not simply address access after the event of the product, but introduce initiatives for research and development agenda. Of particular note, the Medical Research and Development Treaty (MRDT)[60] identifies processes of innovation outside the market-based framework and introduces prize funds as incentives in order to maintain this separation. Such prizes are related directly to clinical evidence of benefits, not unlike the pricing proposals advocated by the OFT, discussed in the previous chapter. At this level of activity civil society organisations area not merely implementing policy by mediating but are genuinely intervening as users in the public sphere, embodying the fuller concept of use and addressing the necessary conditions for the realisation of the right to health.

Prize-fighting

Motivated by the early proposals in the MRDT, scholars have examined the use of prizes to stimulate innovation in the context of medical research and development.[61] The use of prizes as distinct from private intellectual property rights might be limited in application.[62] For instance, a prize may not be effective as an incentive for more valuable drugs with much more profitable markets. Nevertheless, various schemes proposed may be very relevant in the promotion of innovation and new medical knowledge and should be examined.

59 Habermas, *Between Facts and Norms*, 269.

60 Developed by Tim Hubbard (Sanger Institute) and James Love (KEI) (original emphasis).

61 Most notable perhaps in this regard is the Nobel Prize-winning economist, Joseph Stiglitz. For example, see his comment in Stiglitz J (2006) 'Give Prizes Not Patents', *New Scientist* 16 September: 21. See further Stiglitz J (2006) 'Scrooge and Intellectual Property Rights', 333 *British Medical Journal* 1279. There has also been work examining the use of prizes historically: see in particular, Burrell R. and Kelly C. (2014) 'Public Rewards and Innovation Policy: Lessons from the Eighteenth and Nineteenth Centuries' 77 *Modern Law Review* 858.

62 There is a strong historical precedent for such prizes, the most famous of which is the prize for determining longitude while at sea. See the Discovery of the Longitude at Sea Act 1713 (and the subsequent acts increasing the prize).

The 60th World Health Assembly, in May 2008, adopted a resolution[63] requesting the WHO Director-General to facilitate progress of the development of a global strategy and plan of action, including:

> to encourage the development of proposals for health-needs drive research and development for discussion at the Intergovernmental Working Group that covers a range of incentive mechanisms and includes also addressing the linkage between the cost of research and development and the price of medicines, vaccines, diagnostic kits and other health-care products and a method for tailoring the optimal mix of incentives to a particular condition or product, with the object of addressing diseases that disproportionately affect developing countries.[64]

In June 2007, US Democrat senator, John Edwards, issued a statement on medical innovation prizes. In his campaign policies for the Democrat presidential candidacy, Edwards included proposals for prizes to stimulate innovation, rather than relying on patents alone.[65] Importantly, prizes would supplement rather than replace patents (abolishing the patent system for some areas of technology would be contrary to obligations under TRIPS).[66]

In October 2007, US senator Bernie Sanders introduced the Medical Innovation Prize Fund Bill in the US Senate for the first time.[67] He has introduced similar bills in subsequent sessions with the most recent version being introduced in 2017.[68]

The Sanders bill would introduce large financial rewards or 'prizes' for developers of new products, but would eliminate market exclusivity for new drugs. The objective is to eliminate patent monopolies and allow for generic competition in the market, with a view to reducing prices. The bill contains certain congressional findings,[69] including the link between high prices and conventional market-based incentives for research and development, with reference to market exclusivity in particular. Similarly, these market-based approaches are identified as resulting in research gaps for certain diseases, particularly in resource-poor regions of the world, ultimately leaving US citizens vulnerable in a globalised environment. Prize funds are thus advocated in the findings as a way to 'de-couple the

63 WHA. Resolution WHA60.30, Public Health, Innovation and Intellectual Property. 24 May 2007.
64 Ibid., paragraph 3.
65 Edwards J (2007) "Making Health Care Affordable, Accountable and Universal" Press Release, 14 June.
66 In particular, TRIPS Article 27.1.
67 S. 2210. An earlier bill, HR 417, 109th Congress (proposed by Rep Sanders when in the House of Representatives), included similar proposals for prize funding. Section 4 of the earlier bill included provisions very similar to Section 5 of S 2210.
68 S. 495.
69 Section 2: Findings.

reward for product research development from the price of the product' and to address these questions framed as issues of national interest and security.

The bill is not an abolition of the patent system as such, but the monopoly rights to control manufacture and sale of products would no longer be in place. The patent grant would establish instead entitlement to the cash reward for a new invention. Concerns have repeatedly been raised that it would render the US non-compliant with TRIPS, particularly with respect to the minimum exclusive rights of the patentee set out under Article 28. However, some have argued that the bill would be compatible by virtue of Article 30, which allows for limited exceptions,[70] but it is unclear whether Article 30 would allow such a broad exception to basic patent rights. In particular, Section 5 of the proposed bill seeks to eliminate market exclusivity, and Section 5(a) specifically provides for direct curtailment of the basic rights conferred by TRIPS under Article 28. On a related question, the WTO issued a panel decision in 2000 in relation to certain exceptions under Canadian law pertaining to pharmaceutical products.[71] This decision indicates that the scope for exceptions permitted under Article 30 is narrow and would not necessarily accommodate what may be interpreted as an effective exclusion of a specific industry or technology from the rights as defined under Article 28. While the bill has been repeatedly introduced, it has yet to progress beyond being referred to committee in the Senate (the first stage of the process).

In the United Kingdom, there was a simpler approach adopted. The Health Act 2009 empowers the minister to make payments for prizes for innovation in the provision of health services in England.[72] The power to grant such awards could be conferred upon a committee. Despite being little more than a power to make an award (and no duty to do so), the provision has yet to be brought into force and now it appears unlikely it will ever happen.

Throughout this discussion has been a preoccupation with the problematic conversion of public goods (health and knowledge) into commercial commodities, and with that the conversion of fundamental human rights to health, to cultural life and to the benefits of scientific progress and its applications, into simply derogable standards and the individual users into simple bystanders. Civil society intervention and participation challenges that paradigm and persists as the important mechanism to communicate with

---

70 For instance, see the discussion in Love J (2007) "Measures to Enhance Access to Medical Technologies, and New Methods of Stimulating Medical R & D" 40 *UC Davis Law Review* 681.

71 Report of the WTO Panel, "Canada: Patent Protection of Pharmaceutical Products," 17 March 2000, WT/DS114/R. The WTO decision allowed the Bolar exception under Canadian law, but would not condone stockpiling for sales after the expiration of the patent period.

72 Health Act 2009, s 14.

the public institutions of health and intellectual property and to assert the intentional use and custodial relationship over knowledge. Mere legal rights to inventions (defined in the patent) should not undermine or interfere with the beneficial rights to the invention (safeguarded as a public good). Indeed, we take scientific progress on trust.

Conclusion

> It would certainly, for example, be very desirable, in order to the firm and clear establishment of a miracle, that it should be performed in the presence of the Academy of Sciences of Paris, or the Royal Society of London, and the Faculty of Medicine, assisted by a detachment of guards to keep in due order and distance the populace, who might by their rudeness or indiscretion prevent the operation of a miracle.[1]

Towards achieving global health equity, the guards surrounding the institutions of health and intellectual property must be challenged. The impudence of access to the public sphere is only suggested by the institutions that safeguard the dominant relationships to innovation, property and profit. But the charge of rudeness cannot be maintained in the face of inequities in access to health. And the conventional separation of the state and the user is not only untenable but also unrealistic when it comes to addressing critical issues of access to medicines and participation in scientific progress.

Access to the public sphere is fundamental to innovation and scientific progress and to the usefulness of those developments to the users themselves. Where trust is undermined in the institutions charged with delivering that progress, the possibility of accessing benefits and participating in that progress is similarly compromised. The opportunity for miracles is no longer taken on faith as the motives and standing of the institutions responsible for their pursuit and their delivery are disarmed.

Progress must be measured not in profits, but in use. A persistence of the market as the designator of progress, arbiter of innovation and measure of value will not establish miracles, it will surely prevent them.

---

1 Voltaire M de(1843) *A Philosophical Dictionary*, London: W Dugdale, 222.

… and conclusion

> 'Everyone strives to reach the Law', says the man, 'so how does it happen that for all these many years no one but myself has ever begged for admittance?'
>
> The doorkeeper recognizes that the man has reached his end, and, to let his failing senses catch the words, roars in his ear: 'No one else could ever be admitted here, since this gate was made only for you. I am now going to shut it.'[1]

In the intervening years between this and the first edition, an enormous amount has been achieved towards the goal of global health equity. While this has included many transformative moments in intellectual property law, possibly one of the greatest achievements in relation to intellectual property and health is the understanding that this is not an easy question of intellectual property policy. Indeed, it is often not a question of intellectual property at all. Arguably, in these past years, the major achievements have been made through recognising and confronting the broader, wider, and more complex issues of innovation, development, health policy and equity.

The guards surrounding the institutions of intellectual property have perhaps stood firm, but the agitation at the gates has opened onto a much larger domain of increasing complexity. What has been achieved is the motivation of genuine change beyond the law, beyond the product, and to behaviour. Pharmaceutical companies, legislators, and policy-makers are 'learning' change.

In a way, it is a solution before the law.

1 Kafka F, (1992 [1915]) 'Before the Law', in *Kafka: The Complete Short Stories.* W and E Muir trans. London: Minerva.

Selected bibliography

Annas GJ (2004) 'Mapping the Human Genome and the Meaning of "Monster Mythology,"' in Burley J and Harris J (eds) *A Companion to Genethics*, Malden, MA: Blackwell.

Arnason E and Wells F (2006) 'deCODE and Iceland: A Critique', in Clarke A and Ticehurst F (eds) *Living with the Genome: Ethical and Social Aspects of Genetics*, Basingstoke: Palgrave Macmillan.

Bacon F (1857) *The Works of Francis Bacon, Lord Chancellor of England. With a Life of the Author by Basil Montagu, Esquire*, Philadelphia, PA: Parry and McMilland.

Baker BK (2005) 'India's 2005 Patent Act: Death by Patent or Universal Access to Second- and Future-Generation ARVs.' Background Paper. Health Gap: Global Access Project. 19 September.

Baleta A (2006) '"Dr Beetroot" Sidelined in South Africa', 6(10) *The Lancet* 620.

Basheer S and Reddy TP (2008) 'The "Efficacy" of Indian Patent Law: Ironing out the Creases in Section 3(d)', 5(2) *SCRIPT-ed* 232–266.

Basheer S (2005) 'India's Tryst with TRIPS: The Patents (Amendment) Act 2005' 1 *Indian Journal of Law and Technology* 15–46.

Bass NA (2002) 'Implications of the TRIPS Agreement for Developing Countries: Pharmaceutical Patent Laws in Brazil and South Africa in the 21st Century', 34 *George Washington Law Review* 191.

Baxter (2007) 'Baxter Continues Collaborations with Global Health Authorities to Advance Pandemic Preparedness: Company Clarifies Memorandum of Understanding with Indonesia', News Release, 7 February.

BBC News (2001) 'Drugs firms withdraw from AIDS case', 19 April.

BBC News (2006) 'South Africa Aids policy attacked', 19 August.

BBC News (2008) 'Row over NHS Kidney Drug Decision', 7 August.

Beck U (1992/ [1986]) *Risk Society: Towards a New Modernity*, London: SAGE.

Bently L and Sherman B (2014) *Intellectual Property Law*, 4th edn, Oxford: Oxford University Press.

Beyleveld D and Brownsword R (1998) 'Human Dignity, Human Rights and Human Genetics' in Brownsword R, Cornish W and Llewelyn M (eds) *Law and Human Genetics: Regulating a Revolution*, Oxford: Hart.

Beyleveld D, Brownsword R and Llewelyn M (2000) 'The Morality Clauses of the Directive on Legal Protection of Biotechological Inventions: Conflict, Compromise and the Patent Community', in Goldberg R and Lonbay J (eds) *Pharmaceutical Medicine, Biotechnology and European Law*, Cambridge: Cambridge University Press.

Borges JL (1975) *A Universal History of Infamy*, NT di Giovanni (trans), London: Penguin.

Burrell R and Kelly C (2014) 'Public Rewards and Innovation Policy: Lessons from the Eighteenth and Nineteenth Centuries', 77 *Modern Law Review* 858.

Calder L (2001) *Financing the American Dream*, Princeton, NJ: Princeton University Press.

Canguilhem G (1991/ [1966]) *The Normal and the Pathological*, New York: Zone.

Canguilhem G (1994) *A Vital Rationalist: Selected Writings from Georges Canguilhem*, Delaporte F (ed), Goldhammer A (trans), New York: Zone.

Cape Times (2008) 'Medicine's Two-Tier System Rejected', Editorial, 4 September.

Carmichael, M (2010) 'Can DeCode, A BioTech Star Gone Bust, Come Back': *Newsweek*, 11 February.

Carvalho NP de (2005) *The TRIPS Regime of Patent Rights*, The Hague: Kluwer Law International.

Chan CK and De Wildt G (2007) 'Developing Countries, Donor Leverage, and Access to Bird Flu Vaccines', DESA Working Paper No 41. ST/ESA/2007/ DWP/41. New York: DESA.

Chan M (2008) 'Return to Alma-Ata', 372(9642) *The Lancet*, 13 September, 865–866.

Chokshi DA, Parker M and Kwiatkowski D (2006) 'Data Sharing and Intellectual Property in a Genomic Epidemiology Network: Policies for Large-Scale Research Collaboration', 84(5) *Bulletin of the World Health Organization*, May, 382–387.

Chunsuttiwat S (2008) 'Response to Avian Influenza and Preparedness for Pandemic Influenza: Thailand's Experience', 13(s1) *Respirology* s36.

Cockerham WC (2005) 'Medical Sociology and Sociological Theory', in Cockherham WC (ed) *The Blackwell Companion to Medical Sociology*, Malden, MA: Blackwell.

Cook T (2006) 'Patenting Genes', in Pugatch M (ed) *The Intellectual Property Debate: Perspectives from Law, Economics and Political Economy*, Cheltenham: Edward Elgar.

Correa C (1999) *Intellectual Property Rights, the WTO and Developing Countries: The TRIPS Agreement and Policy Options*, London: Zed Books.

Crespi SR (2006) 'The Human Embryo and Patent Law: A Major Challenge Ahead?' 28(11) *European Intellectual Property Review* 569–575.

Davies M and Naffine N (2001) *Are Persons Property? Legal Debates About Property and Personality*, Aldershot: Ashgate.

Dickenson D (2007) *Property in the Body*, Cambridge: Cambridge University Press.

Drews J (2005) 'Drug Research: Between Ethical Demands and Economic Constraints', in Santoro MA and Gorrie TM (eds) *Ethics and the Pharmaceutical Industry*, Cambridge: Cambridge University Press.

Dutfield G (2003) *Intellectual Property and the Life Science Industries: A Twentieth Century History*, Aldershot: Ashgate.

Economist (2008) 'The Bitterest Pill', Editorial, 26 January.

Economist (2008) 'All Together Now', Editorial, 24 July.

Farmer P (2005) *Pathologies of Power: Health, Human Rights, and the New War on the Poor*, Berkeley, CA: University of California Press.

Fiedman DA, Landes W and Posner R (1991) 'Some Economics of Trade Secrets Law', 5(1) *Journal of Economic Perspectives* 61–72.

Forbes' (2007) 'Swiss Government Not to Take Novartis Case to WTO', Editorial, 8 August.

Garrett L and Fidler DP (2007) 'Sharing H5N1 Viruses to Stop a Global Influenza Pandemic', 4(11) *PLoS Medicine* e330.

Gerhardsen TIS (2007) 'Health Assembly Tackles Proposals on Avian Flu Virus Sharing', *Intellectual Property Watch*, 16 May.

Gershon D (1994) 'US and British Researchers Agree not to Seek Gene Fragment Patents', 367 *Nature* 583.

Gervais D (2003) *The TRIPS Agreement: Drafting History and Analysis*, 2nd edn, London: Sweet and Maxwell.

Gibson J (2005) *Community Resources: Intellectual Property, International Trade and Protection of Traditional Knowledge*, Aldershot: Ashgate.

Gibson J (2006) *Creating Selves: Intellectual Property and the Narration of Culture*, Aldershot: Ashgate.

Gibson J (2007) 'Audiences in Tradition: Traditional Knowledge and the Public Domain', in Waelde C and MacQueen Q (eds), *Intellectual Property: The Many Faces of the Public Domain*, Cheltenham: Edward Elgar.

Gibson J (2007) 'The Discovery of Invention: Gene Patents and the Question of Patentability', 12 *Journal of Intellectual Property Rights* 38–45.

Gilliam S (2008) 'Is the Declaration of Alma-Ata Still Relevant to Primary Health Care?' 336 *British Medical Journal*, 6 March, 536–538.

Global Forum for Health Research (1999) *The 10/90 Report on Health Research, 1999*. Geneva: GFHR.

Goldstein K (1995/ [1934]) *The Organism: A Holistic Approach to Biology Derived from Pathological Data in Man*, New York: Zone.

Gray K and Gray SF (2005) *Elements of Land Law*, Oxford: Oxford University Press.

Greenpeace (1997) 'Greenpeace Condemns Commercialization of Life', Press Release, 27 November.

Greenpeace (1998). 'Biopiracy Urged by EU Biotechnology Patent Directive', Press Release, 12 May.

Grubb P (2004) *Patents for Chemicals, Pharmaceuticals and Biotechnology: Fundamentals of Global Law, Practice and Strategy*, 4th edn, Oxford: Oxford University Press.

Habermas J (1975/ [1973]) *Legitimation Crisis*, McCarthy T (trans), Boston, MA: Beacon Press.

Habermas J (1987/ [1981]) *The Theory of Communicative Action: Volume 2 Lifeworld and System: A Critique of Functionalist Reason*, McCarthy T (trans), Cambridge: Polity Press.

Habermas J (1994/ [1991]) *The Past as Future*, Pensky M (trans), Cambridge: Polity Press.

Habermas J (1997/ [1992]) *Between Facts and Norms: Contributions to a Discourse Theory of Law and Democracy*, Rehg W (trans), Cambridge: Polity Press.

Habermas J (1998/ [1996]) *The Inclusion of the Other: Studies in Political Theory*, Cronin C and de Greiff P (trans), Cambridge: Polity Press.

Habermas J (2001/ [1998]) *The Postnational Constellation: Political Essays*, Pensky M (trans and ed), Cambridge: Polity Press.

Hamlyn M (2008) 'Health Minister Snubbed in Bill', *News 24 South Africa*, 3 September.

Hammond E (2008) 'WHO-linked Centre Lays Patent Claim Related to Bird Flu Virus', *South-North Development Monitor*, 19 August.

Health24 (2008) 'Health Minister Not Qualified: TAC', 5 August.

Hestermeyer H (2007) *Human Rights and the WTO: The Case of Patents and Access to Medicines*, Oxford: Oxford University Press.
Hinsliff G (2008) 'Health Chief Attacks Drug Giants over Huge Profits', *The Observer*, 17 August.
Hogerzeil HV, Samson M, Casanovas J and Ocora L (2006) 'Is Access to Essential Medicines as Part of the Fulfilment of the Right to Health Enforceable through the Courts?' 368(9532) *The Lancet* 22 July, 305–311.
Holbrooke R and Garrett L (2008) 'Sovereignty that Risks Global Health', *Washington Post*, 10 August.
Hollis A and Pogge T (2008) *The Health Impact Fund: Making New Medicines Accessible for All*, New Haven, CT: Incentives for Global Health.
Holtug N (2001) 'Creating and Patenting New Life Forms', in Kuhse H and Singer P (eds) *A Companion to Bioethics*, Malden, MA: Blackwell.
Hounshell DA (1984) *From the American System to Mass Production 1800–1932: The Development of Manufacturing Technology in the United States*, Baltimore, MD: Johns Hopkins University Press.
Husserl E (1970/ [1936]) *The Crisis of European Sciences and Transcendental Phenomenology: An Introduction to Phenomenological Philosophy*, Carr D (trans), Chicago, IL: Northwestern University Press.
International Centre for Trade and Sustainable Development (ICTSD) (2006) 'IP Standards In US–Peru FTA To Affect Talks with Colombia and Ecuador?' 10(2) *Bridges Weekly Trade New Digest*, 25 January.
International Commission of Jurists (2008) 'Day of General Discussion on the Right to Take Part in Cultural Life (Article 15(1)(a) of the Covenant)', Background Paper, E/C.12/40/9. 9 May.
International Herald Tribune (2007) 'Experts Say Indonesian Deal on H5N1 Virus Jeopardizes Race for pandemic vaccine', Editorial, 7 February.
Jamison DT et al. (2006) *Disease and Mortality in Sub-Saharan Africa*, 2nd edn, New York: World Bank.
Johnston E (2008) 'NHS Denies "Effective" Cancer Drugs due to Cost', *The Independent*, 8 August.
Johnson, P (2017) 'The Parker Committee 1916', 7 *Queen Mary Journal of Intellectual Property* 156–190.
Johnson, P (2012) 'Access to Medicines and the Growth of the Pharmaceutical Industry in Britain', in Dinwoodie G (ed.) *Methods and Perceptions of Intellectual Property*, Cheltenham: Edward Elgar.
Johnson P (2017) *Privatised Law Reform: A History of Patent Law through Private Legislation, 1620–1907*, Abingdon: Routledge, 104–6.
Kahn T (2008) 'AIDS Session Gets a Miss from Minister', *Business Day* (Johannesburg), 1 August.
Karimova T (2016) *Human Rights and Development in International Law*, London: Routledge
Kesby M (2004) 'Participatory Diagraming and the Ethical and Practical Challenges of Helping Africans *Themselves* to Move HIV Work "Beyond Epidemiology,"' in Kalipeni E et al. (eds) *HIV and AIDS in Africa: Beyond Epidemiology*, Malden, MA: Blackwell.
Kirby J (2008) '"Devastating Blow" to Kidney Cancer Sufferers', *The Independent*, 7 August.

Kirsch S (2002) 'Property Limits: Debates on the Body, Nature and Culture', in Hirsch E and Strathern M (eds) *Transactions and Creations: Property Debates and the Stimulus of Melanesia*, Oxford: Berghahn.

Kumagal K (1999) *History of Japanese Industrial Property System*, Tokyo: JPO.

Lafranière S (2007) 'Mbeki Fires Aide Who Reshaped HIV policy', *International Herald Tribune*, 9 August.

Lash S (2000) 'Risk Culture', in Adam B, Beck U and Van Loon J (eds) *The Risk Society and Beyond: Critical Issues for Social Theory*, London: SAGE.

Lehrman S (1996) 'US Drops Patent Claim to Hagahai Cell Line', 384(6609) *Nature*, December, 500.

Lievens A, Petrillo M, Querci, M and Patak A (2015) 'Genetically Modified Animals: Options and Issues for Traceability and Enforcement', 44 *Trends in Food Science and Technology* 159–176.

Locatelli F and Roger S (2006) 'Comparative Testing and Pharmacovigilance of Biosimilars', 21 (Supplement 5) *Nephrology Dialysis Transplantation* 13–16.

Love J (2007) 'Measures to Enhance Access to Medical Technologies, and New Methods of Stimulating Medical R and D', 40 *UC Davis Law Review* 679–717.

Low M (2008) 'Medicines Bill Under Fire', *News 24 South Africa*, 12 June.

Lupton D (2003) *Medicine as Culture*, 2nd edn, London: SAGE.

Lwanda JL (2002) 'Politics, Cutlure, and Medicine: An Unholy Trinity? Historical Continuities and Ruptures in the HIV/AIDS Story in Malawi', in Kalipeni E, Craddock S, Oppong JR and Ghosh J (eds) *HIV and AIDS in Africa: Beyond Epidemiology*, Malden, MA: Blackwell.

MacDonald TH (2006) *Health, Trade and Human Rights*, Oxford: Radcliffe.

Maser C (1999) *Ecological Diversity in Sustainable Development: The Vital and Forgotten Dimension*, London: CRC Press.

Mellstedt H, Niederwieser D and Ludwig H (2007) 'The Challenge of Biosimilars', 19(3) *Annals of Oncology* 411–419.

Merz JF (2007) 'Are Human Gene Banks Worth It?' in Steinberg D (ed) *Biomedical Ethics: A Multidisciplinary Approach to Moral Issues in Medicine and Biology*, Hanover, NH: University Press of New England.

Mgbeoji I (2006) *Global Biopiracy: Patents, Plants, and Indigenous Knowledge*, Vancouver: UBC Press.

Mills O (2005) *Biotechnological Inventions: Moral Restraints and Patent Law*, Aldershot: Ashgate.

Nowicki M (2007) 'Basic Facts About Biosimilars', 30 *Kidney and Blood Pressure Research* 267–272.

Nwabueze RN (2007) *Biotechnology and the Challenge of Property: Property Rights in Dead Bodies, Body Parts, and Genetic Information*, Aldershot: Ashgate.

Nyan O (2008) 'Case Study 2: Ethnicity', Presentation to the Genome-Wide Association Studies and Ethics Meeting, The Wellcome Trust, 24 July.

O'Hearn D and McCloskey S (2008) 'Globalisation and Pharmaceuticals: Where is the Power? Where to Resist?' in O'Donovan O and Glavanis-Grantham K (eds) *Power, Politics and Pharmaceuticals*, Cork: Cork University Press.

Peel M (2008) 'Woman Faces £16000 Penalty after Sharing Computer Game', *Financial Times,* 19 August.

PharmaTimes (2013) 'Final NICE No for Avastin in Ovarian Cancer', 22 May.

Pila J (2001) 'Methods of Medical Treatment Within Australian and United Kingdom Patents Law', 24(2) *UNSW Law Journal* 420–459.

Plant A (1934) 'The Economic Theory Concerning Patents for Invention', 1 *Economica* 30–51.

Politi J (2008) 'Top US Official Sees 'No Alternative' to Doha', *Financial Times*, 6 August.

Pottage A, Cornish W and Llewelyn M (1998) 'The Inscription of Life in Law: Genes, Patents and Bio-politics', in Brownsword R et al. (eds) *Law and Human Genetics: Regulating a Revolution*, Oxford: Hart Publishing.

Raghavan C (2001) 'EU for "Differential Pricing" over Compulsory Licensing', *South–North Development Monitor*, 31 May.

Ravvin M (2008) 'Incentivizing Access and Innovation for Essential Mechanisms: A Survey of the Problems and Proposed Solutions', 1(2) *Public Health Ethics* 110–123.

Rehbinder E et al. (2009) *Pharming: Promises and Risks of Biopharmaceuticals Derived from Genetically Modified Plants and Animals*, New York: Springer.

Reilly PR (2006) 'Informed Consent in Human Genetic Research', in Clarke A and Ticehurst F (eds) *Living with the Genome: Ethical and Social Aspects of Human Genetics*, Basingstoke: Palgrave Macmillan.

Resnik DB (2004) *Owning the Genome: A Moral Analysis of DNA Patenting*, New York: SUNY Press.

Ridley DB, Grabowsku HG and Moe JL (2006) 'Developing Drugs for Developing Countries', 25(2) *Health Affairs* 313–324.

Robie D (1997) 'Cell Lines and Commodities: The Hagahai Patent Affair', 4(1) *Pacific Journalism Review* 78–91.

Rodriguez Cervantes S (2006) 'FTAs: Trading Away Traditional Knowledge', GRAIN Briefing Paper, March.

Ropp A von der and Taubman T (2006) 'Bioethics and Patent Law: The Cases of Moore and the Hagahai People', 5 *WIPO Magazine*, October, 16–17.

Rössler B (2004) 'Gender and Privacy: A Critique of the Liberal Tradition', in Rössler B (ed) *Privacies: Philosophical Evaluations*, Stanford, NJ: Stanford University Press.

Roughton A, Johnson P and Cook T (2014) *The Modern Law of Patents*, 3rd edn, London: LexisNexis.

Salazar S (2003) 'The World of Biotechnology Patents', in Bellmann C, Dutfield G nad Melendez-Ortiz R (eds) *Trading in Knowledge: Development Perspectives on TRIPS, Trade and Sustainability*, London: Earthscan.

Scherer FM (2002) 'The Economics of Human Gene Patents', 77(12) *Academic Medicine* 1348–1367.

Sedyaningsih ER, Isfandari S, Soendoro T and Supar SF (2008) 'Towards Mutual Trust, Transparency and Equity in Virus Sharing Mechanism: The Avian Influenza Case of Indonesia', 37 *Annals of Academic Medicine Singapore* 482–488.

Shashikant S (2008) 'WHO: Concerns over Chair's Text on Sharing of Flu Viruses and Benefits', *South–North Development Monitor*, 15 August.

Simpson AWB (1986) *A History of the Land Law*, 2nd edn, Oxford: Oxford University Press.

Snow CP (1998/ [1959]) *The Two Cultures*, Cambridge: Cambridge University Press.

SouthCentre/CIEL (2007) 'Rwanda and Canada: Leading the Implementation of the August 2003 Decision for Import/Export of Pharmaceuticals Produced under Compulsory License', *Intellectual Property Quarterly Update*. Third Quarter, 1–9.

Stamatopoulou E (2008). 'The Right to Take Part in Cultural Life', background paper, day of General Discussion on the right to take part in cultural life (Article 15(1)(a) of the Covenant). E/C.12/40/9. 9 May.
Stanton A (2008) 'Forfeited Consent: Body Parts in Eminent Domain', in Gibson J (ed) *Patenting Lives: Life Patents, Culture and Development*, Aldershot: Ashgate.
Stiglitz J (2006) 'Give Prizes Not Patents', *New Scientist,* 16 September, 21.
Stiglitz J (2006) 'Scrooge and Intellectual Property Rights', 333 *British Medical Journal* 1279–80.
Stoneman P (2002) *The Economics of Technological Diffusion*, Oxford: Blackwell.
Stothers C (2007) *Parallel Trade in Europe*, Oxford: Hart Publishing.
Sulston J (2002) 'Heritage of Humanity', *Le Monde diplomatique*, December.
Sun H (2003) 'Reshaping the TRIPS Agreement concerning Public Health', 37 *Journal of World Trade* 163–197.
Thomas D and Richards GA (2004) 'The Importance of the Morality Exception Under the European Patent Convention: The Oncomouse Case Continues ...', 26(3)*European Intellectual Property Review* 97–104.
Throsby D (2001) *Economics and Culture*, Cambridge: Cambridge University Press.
Tobin J (2011)*The Right to Health in International Law,* Oxford: Oxford University Press.
Tsiftsoglou AS (2007) 'Biosimilars: The Impact of Their Heterogeneity on Regulatory Approval', 6(3) *Nature Reviews: Drug Discovery* C1
Vandenbogaerde A (2013) 'The Right to Development in International Human Rights Law: A Call for its Dissolution', 31(2) *Netherlands Quarterly of Human Rights* 187–209.
Watson R (1995) 'Brussels Rejects Biotechnology Directive', 310 SF*British Medical Journal,* 11 March, 619.
Wanna O (2016) 'Avastin Packs "Most Cost-Effective" Punch', www.aop.org.uk/ot/science-and-vision/research/2016/06/10/avastin-packs-most-cost-effective-punch
Weber M (1968/ [1956]) *Economy and Society: An Outline of Interpretive Sociology*, Roth G and Wittich C (eds), New York: Bedminster Press.
Weber M (1975/ [1903–6]) *Roscher and Knies: The Logical Problems of Historical Economics*, Oakes G (trans), New York: The Free Press.
Weber M (2002/ [1904–5]) *The Protestant Ethic and the Spirit of Capitalism*, Kalberg S (trans), Oxford: Blackwell.
Webster A (2007) *Health, Technology and Society: A Sociological Critique*, Basingstoke: Palgrave Macmillan.
Zon A van and Muysken J (2005) 'Health as a Principal Determinant of Economic Growth', in Lopez-Casasnovas G et al. (eds) *Health and Economic Growth: Findings and Policy Implications*, Cambridge MA: MIT Press.

Index

For Product Safety Concerns and Information please contact our EU
representative GPSR@taylorandfrancis.com
Taylor & Francis Verlag GmbH, Kaufingerstraße 24, 80331 München, Germany

www.ingramcontent.com/pod-product-compliance
Ingram Content Group UK Ltd.
Pitfield, Milton Keynes, MK11 3LW, UK
UKHW022129190926
475702UK00013B/1706
* 9 7 8 0 3 6 7 5 9 3 7 8 0 *